Avon Books are available at special quantity discounts for bulk purchases for sales promotions, premiums, fund raising or educational use. Special books, or book excerpts, can also be created to fit specific needs.

For details write or telephone the office of the Director of Special Markets, Avon Books, 959 8th Avenue, New York, New York 10019, 212-262-3361.

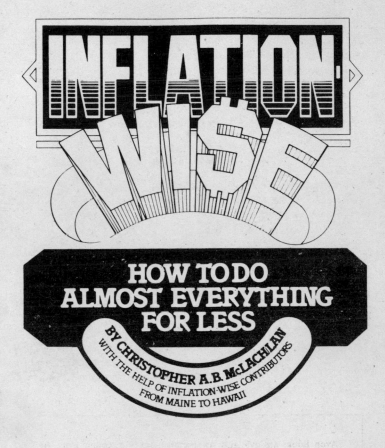

INFLATION-WISE

WISE

HOW TO DO ALMOST EVERYTHING FOR LESS

BY CHRISTOPHER A.B. McLACHLAN
WITH THE HELP OF INFLATION-WISE CONTRIBUTORS
FROM MAINE TO HAWAII

AVON
PUBLISHERS OF BARD, CAMELOT, DISCUS AND FLARE BOOKS

For
Barbara Fenhagen
(and family like that)

And for
John, James, Alexander and Kelsey McLachlan
(and friends like that)

INFLATION-WISE: HOW TO DO ALMOST EVERYTHING FOR LESS
is an original publication of Avon Books. This work has never before
appeared in book form.

AVON BOOKS
A division of
The Hearst Corporation
959 Eighth Avenue
New York, New York 10019

First Avon Printing, March, 1981

AVON TRADEMARK REG. U.S. PAT. OFF. AND IN
OTHER COUNTRIES, MARCA REGISTRADA, HECHO EN
U.S.A.

Printed in the U.S.A.

COM 10 9 8 7 6 5 4 3 2

Acknowledgments

I must first thank David Outerbridge, who relentlessly insisted that this book ought to move from my kitchen dining table into print and so took pains to make it so ... and my dearest friend, Barbara Fenhagen, who introduced me to David.

Virtually everyone I know cheered me on at one time or another during the course of this book's writing and I'm immensely grateful for that support. There were several who, at the oddest (and most necessary) moments also went out of their way to say "I like you just as is, and as was, too," among them John McLachlan, Barbara Fenhagen, Helen Felsing, Barbara Ziff, Bea Keller, Linda Sobsey, David Ziff, and Phil Fitzpatrick. For childcare which permitted me distraction-free (and, because so excellent, guilt-free) writing time at essential junctures, I'm indebted not only to John but also to Laura Grannan, Shannon Bruce, Maryann Arends, and Dana Dewees. And for the use of their typewriters for months on end without so much as a single dun, I thank David Ziff and Wendy Mitchell.

Special thanks also to those who helped by taking the time to read and comment on various parts of the manuscript—Cinda Baley, Mari Baley, Bill Howard, Phil Fitzpatrick, Laura Grannan, Mike Karpinski, Bea Keller, Maria Lago, John McLachlan, Linda Sobsey, Barbara Ziff, and David Ziff. In particular, thanks to Beth Rashbaum, my editor at Avon, who read and commented on all of it, insisting on clarity but never at the expense of my ego.

And of course I must express my gratitude to all of those who contributed to *Inflation-Wise* by completing questionnaires, responding to verbal inquiries, or raising questions that it hadn't occurred to me to ask. My thanks go to:

John and Edythe Allen
Helen Andreyewsky
Armeta Avery
Debby Bader
Judy Bailey
Cinda Baley
Heather Baley
Jim and Irene Baley
Mari L. Baley
Doris Blake

John Blake
Maureen Brennan
Lyn and Bob Bruce
Linda Bryant
Tom Byrd
Judy and Rick
  Byron Reinhard
Betye Carey
Bob Cargill
Bill Carr

Don Carter
Mary Carter
Joan Caverly
John Chapin
Kathleen Chase
Barbara Chrest
George Chrest
Peggy Clements
Marian F. Cocubinsky
L. J. Coleman

Charles and Edris Cooper
Pat Crosby
Mrs. A. C. Curtis
Bob Daughety
Bonnie Davis
Howard Debose
Charles deBruyne
Mario Deleon
Estelle Dertinger
Dana Dewees
Martha Dill
K. M. Dills
Marjorie Dix
Bob Dixon
Elaine Donaldson
Sally and Bob Douglas
Kay Drake
Forrest Dunham
Bill Duax
Virginia Eaton
Martha Edmondson
Juanita Ehman
Dennis Ellis
Susan Evans
Eddy Fahrbach
Janet Falcone
Tricia Feldman
Helen Felsing
Jan and Phil Fenty
Phil Fitzpatrick
Joan Fleck
Judy Gauldin
Jim Geheber
Nancy Gentry
June Gibson
Alice and Joe Gore
Joe Graedon
Dan Graham
Gregory Grannan
Laura Grannan
C. E. Hadfield
Shirley Harper
Boyd Harris
Ed Harris
Marie Harris
Steve Harris
Edward Harriston
Rebecca Harvey
Jim Herstein
David Hill

Joanne Hodgson
Pat Hodgson
Mr. and Mrs. R. A. Horst
Carol Howell
Mr. and Mrs. Ben Hughes
Linda Hummel
Julia Inamine
Richard Insley
B. J. Jennings
Jean Johnson
Bernadette Jones
Annette B. W. Kam
Lynn Karpinski
Bea Keller
Mike Keller
Bob Kent
George Kilby, Jr.
Pam Kilby
Grace Kissane
Jack Kissane
Ken and Karen Korach
Jim and Maryanne Lamb
Allen M. Langhans
Liz Lee
Eileen Lerch
Lou Levy
Martine Loyer
Mike Lynn
Mrs. Isadore Marcott
Mahopac, New York Office
   for the Aging
Carol Mayer
Myrna Medlin
Dottie Morse
Sandy McCain
John McLachlan
Jook McLachlan
Marge McLachlan
John Nedrud
Retha Newbold
Stanley Newbold
Mrs. John Northan
Kevin O'Donnell
Rebecca Okie
Fran and
   Bruce Oppenheimer
Jon Oravec
David Outerbridge
Lilias Outerbridge

Gerry Pettit
Boots Philyaw
Ebert Pierce
Beth Popa
Peter and Nona Provengale
Jim Reynolds
Phyllis Rigsbee
Jean Ritchey
Mary Robbins
Bonnell Robinson
A. T. Rolan
Enid Rucki
Cheryl Sandusky
Joseph Savino
Lary Savino
Ron Sechrist
Billie Sessoms
Philip Shanahan
Ruth Shanahan
Mary Siler
Jim Slate
Bob Smith
Chip Smith
Diane Smith
Linda Sobsey
Mark Sobsey
Charlene Spagnol
Melanie Spittle
L. F. Stewart
Lee Stone
Linda Stroupe
Bill Terrell
Peter Tullier
Marsha Vestal
Linda Vick
Alma Walther
Russ Walton
Bob and Sally Warner
John Warren
Paula Warren
Linda H. Washburn
Bernadette G. Watts
Ruth Wenberg
Ken Wertz
Pam Wintle
Annette Wong
Joe Woolley
Barbara Ziff
David Ziff

INTRODUCTION: The Hows and Whys and Whos

No woman is status quo at thirty-five; at least none that I know. Age thirty-five is a watershed year for women, a halfway point. It is a year in which, whether she chooses to or not, a woman feels compelled to take stock of her past and prepare to make whatever changes may be necessary in order to greet her future with pleasure. It can be depressing, even crazy-making; it can be energizing, joyous; it is seldom anything in between and often it is both.

Certainly it has been both, by turns, for me. And I think one of the things that contributed to my upheaval was the sudden realization that my parents were mortal; that what they might still have to teach me I had better learn soon.

My friend Genevieve: "When someone who has known you as a child looks at you, she sees the child as well as the adult. She remembers things—experiences, influences—that you may have already forgotten. And when she is gone, when all of the people who have known you as a child have gone, in some way the child in you will also be gone."

In fact, I think the loss, if allowed to happen, reaches even farther back. The adult you have become is inextricably bound to the childhood you experienced but in turn is bound to your parents' childhoods. The loss of that body of knowledge is unrecoverable but it isn't necessary. Circumvention is simple and enjoyable—all it takes is conversation.

So, in this, my thirty-fifth year, my year-of-the-self-evaluation, I have felt a compelling need to ferret out as much information as possible about both my own childhood and the life my mother lived in the twenty-seven years preceding our meeting. To that end we have spent many hours involved in just such conversation during this past year.

And there is more to be learned than personal history, I discovered. During the course of one of these dialogues my mother told me that in 1929 when she was twelve her father lost his business. One of the lucky ones in that he at least found a job, he began working for his brother, but the reduction in income was drastic. And yet my mother remembers those years during the Depression as full and warm and happy ones.

"When you think about it," she commented, "the Great Depression and the Terrible Inflation of today are two sides of the same coin. The effect on individual families is the same—more and more and more difficulty making ends meet."

"But how *did* your parents manage?" I wondered.

"Oh, in those days people knew all kinds of tricks to pare costs, eliminate waste, live frugally and still stay happy. I imagine a lot of them have been forgotten in the prosperous interim."

"Like what, for instance?" I asked.

"Well . . . did you know that if you have a gas range, nearly *half* the money you pay for its fuel is consumed by pilot lights alone and that you can ask your gas company to turn them off permanently and use matches instead?"

No, I didn't know that and wondered why I had never even heard it before in these conservation-minded times. In fact, to be perfectly honest, I was rather skeptical and let the conversation move on to other things.

A couple of days later, however, recalling my mother's remark, I phoned our local gas utility just to satisfy my curiosity. Yes, it *is* true, they told me. Pilot lights account—on the average—for 41% of fuel costs on surface units, 53% in the oven, and they can be turned off. I then asked them to please send whatever consumer information they had currently available on ways to save energy-money on fuel consumption. *101 Ways to Conserve Energy* arrived a few days later—in it there was no mention of pilot lights whatsoever.

Was my mother right, I wondered. Were there indeed dozens of clever ways to cut costs, eliminate wasteful spending, which were once widely known and practiced but had been lost or forgotten over the years? I decided that there probably were, that they were likely to begin resurfacing by word of mouth now that inflation had begun eating increasingly large chunks out of everyone's dollar. I also realized that, like the pilot-light tip, they might be slow to appear in the literature. So, at a friend's suggestion, I decided to collect them myself.

Enter a questionnaire, which I spent weeks writing and months handing out and mailing to hundreds of friends and relatives. My mother, naturally excited about what our conversation had set in motion, made copies for everyone she knew and called often with new tips herself. Her sister, my sisters, my father and stepmother, my mother-in-law, my sister-in-law, my husband, and many other friends contributed to the distribution cause.

In a few weeks, completed questionnaires began to trickle back, returned by inflationwise contributors from Maine to Hawaii. I wasn't surprised to find that those I was receiving from people in my mother's generation did, indeed, include many tips that didn't appear in the literature I had meanwhile been amassing. What did surprise me was that my own contemporaries had developed and adopted their own distinctly different but also previously unpublished set of cost-cutters.

The combination of those new and old ideas, as well as those I gleaned from the literature, became this book.

Inflation-Wise is not an investment guide; rather, it might be called a *pre*investment guide. Its purpose is *not* to tell the reader how to make more money with the money she or he has managed to set aside after living costs have been met; its purpose is to make possible the setting aside itself by providing the reader with a host of painless cost-cutting ideas—saving a few dollars here, many dollars there—which will cumulatively amount to a substantial sum.

Should a reader *then* wish to use that accumulated savings for investment, she will find a multitude of how-to-invest books on the market from which to choose. They are written, and properly so, by economists. I am not an economist and my understanding of the inner workings of economics and investments is so slight that it would be both presumptuous and stupid of me to pretend otherwise.

What I am is a mother of three, wife of one. My nine-year-old boy, James, who would spend his entire day sketching (if he could) has just informed me that he is out of drawing paper; I know where to get more for only 25¢ per *pound*. My seven-year-old son, Zander (Alexander), about whose protein intake I worry, refuses to drink reconstituted instant dry milk but fresh (at the rate we drink it) was costing us $60 a month; I have discovered a source he considers as tasty and as fresh but which cuts the monthly milk costs to less than $27. My three-year-old daughter, Kelsey (*alias* Max), has this month once again grown too large for her britches; a dozen more will be handed to me next week, free. My husband, John, was involved in an auto accident two months ago and we must replace the car; I know how to get the best possible deal on a new one, how to choose a good used one, and how to decide between those two options. And *I* desperately need a haircut; one of the best cuts in town will cost me nothing.

This is the sort of information I am including in *Inflation-Wise*. For this is the area of my expertise (our collective expertise, my contributors and I): finding hidden costs, locating easy savings, eliminating wasteful spending, living happily and well at bargain prices.

Of the individuals who people *Inflation-Wise,* some are single, some married, some raising children, some retired, some living in cities, some in rural areas. In all but a few permission-granted cases, names have been changed to respect privacy, and many of the people you'll meet in these pages are composites of those I know. The actual body of individual contributors, however, is substantial. I am grateful for the time they each took to both answer my questions and suggest new questions which stimulated my research. And so, I think, you will be.

Inflation-Wise is comprised of two sections. The first consists of the alphabetically listed money-savers themselves. Within some of the longer entries, like AUTOMOBILES or ENERGY, I've *attempted* an alphabetical organization, but when logic and the alphabet came in conflict, I gave in to logic. Most entries in Section 1 have been coded (with the help of my friend Edward) to indicate the estimated annual dollar and/or percentage savings possible if the idea is newly implemented by a reader. This coding should serve as an aid in weighing the value of the time a reader estimates she or he would spend against the value of the dollars she or he might expect to save.

The calculations are based on my own family's experience and may vary considerably for others depending on locale, circumstance, and, in many instances, family size. The symbols represent the following:

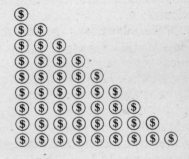

Up to one dollar	¢
Up to ten dollars	$
Up to twenty dollars	$ $
Up to thirty dollars	$ $ $
Up to forty dollars	$ $ $ $
Up to fifty dollars	$ $ $ $ $
Up to sixty dollars	$ $ $ $ $ $
Up to seventy dollars	$ $ $ $ $ $ $
Up to eighty dollars	$ $ $ $ $ $ $ $
Up to ninety dollars	$ $ $ $ $ $ $ $ $

Up to one hundred dollars	Ⓢ
Up to two hundred dollars	Ⓢ Ⓢ
Up to three hundred dollars	Ⓢ Ⓢ Ⓢ
Up to four hundred dollars	Ⓢ Ⓢ Ⓢ Ⓢ
Up to five hundred dollars	Ⓢ Ⓢ Ⓢ Ⓢ Ⓢ
Up to six hundred dollars	Ⓢ Ⓢ Ⓢ Ⓢ Ⓢ Ⓢ
Up to seven hundred dollars	Ⓢ Ⓢ Ⓢ Ⓢ Ⓢ Ⓢ Ⓢ
Up to eight hundred dollars	Ⓢ Ⓢ Ⓢ Ⓢ Ⓢ Ⓢ Ⓢ Ⓢ
Up to nine hundred dollars	Ⓢ Ⓢ Ⓢ Ⓢ Ⓢ Ⓢ Ⓢ Ⓢ Ⓢ

Up to one thousand dollars	⬤
Up to two thousand dollars	⬤ ⬤
Up to three thousand dollars	⬤ ⬤ ⬤
Up to four thousand dollars	⬤ ⬤ ⬤ ⬤
Up to five thousand dollars	⬤ ⬤ ⬤ ⬤ ⬤
Up to six thousand dollars	⬤ ⬤ ⬤ ⬤ ⬤ ⬤
Up to seven thousand dollars	⬤ ⬤ ⬤ ⬤ ⬤ ⬤ ⬤
Up to eight thousand dollars	⬤ ⬤ ⬤ ⬤ ⬤ ⬤ ⬤ ⬤
Up to nine thousand dollars	⬤ ⬤ ⬤ ⬤ ⬤ ⬤ ⬤ ⬤ ⬤

INFLATION-WISE

Up to ten percent	%
Up to twenty percent	% %
Up to thirty percent	% % %
Up to forty percent	% % % %
Up to fifty percent	% % % % %
Up to sixty percent	% % % % % %
Up to seventy percent	% % % % % % %
Up to eighty percent	% % % % % % % %
Up to ninety percent	% % % % % % % % %
Up to one hundred percent	% % % % % % % % % %

If there is no symbol it does not mean the entry is without value; only that there is no reasonable way to assign a number.

Section 2, thinner in pages but equally substantial in importance, consists of text and worksheets *re* debts and budgeting. It is the story of how one family (mine) found itself in deep financial trouble as a result of overuse and unwise use of credit, and how we managed to climb out of debt.

Finally, I would like to add that I hope readers will send me their comments, questions, and suggestions to be considered for inclusion in possible future editions of *Inflation-Wise*. Christopher McLachlan c/o Avon Books, 959 Eighth Avenue, New York, New York 10019.

Section 1

The Wisdom

Note To Reader: There is a "meet-the-contributors" portion heading some entries. Should you wish to move directly to "Go," collect your information and move on, you may easily do so by skipping past that introductory portion, which is set in italics.

AGRICULTURAL EXTENSION SERVICE
%%%%%%

Let me introduce you first to Cass. She has been my mother's best friend for as long as I can remember. They live some distance apart now, but she is the only nonblood relative I can imagine my mother going out of her way to visit. This, I think, is why: when Cass directs her smile and attention on you, she makes you feel that whatever you are saying is tremendously interesting to her, that it's important, that you are important. She really focuses, she really listens—rare and appealing qualities. Cass returned my questionnaire (very soon after my mother sent it to her) with a cover letter and several enclosures; even on paper, I could sense that smile.

Funny thing is, Cass herself is one of the most interesting people I know. I guess it figures; good listeners often are. Her curiosity is boundless and she is a perpetual student. "How's Cass, Mother?" "Oh, she's fine. She's taking a course in creative writing (or gardening or economics or . . .)" is invariably my mother's initial descriptive reply.

In Cass's cover letter, she mentioned that her current pursuit was a reupholstery workshop offered by her local Agricultural

Extension Service. She was very enthusiastic about all the courses and activities and information available through Cooperative Extension (as it is called in her locale).

This particular course, for example, meets on five consecutive Thursdays by the end of which time she will have completely reupholstered her favorite worn-out chair under the guidance of an expert, using her fabric but otherwise their materials, all for $12. The extension newsletter she enclosed with her questionnaire included articles on storing staple foods safely, weatherstripping and caulking, and fire hazards associated with woodstove installation as well as a course list and a couple of recipes. In addition to noting the reupholstering course, the newsletter also listed the other offerings that month: quilting (four classes, $10.00); weight control (six meetings, $6.00); a full day of sewing workshops (fifteen 50-minute seminars to choose from, including coordinating fabric with pattern, sewing shortcuts, detailing like a professional), free.

Cass's enthusiasm piqued my curiousity. To find out more, I looked in my phone book's white pages under our county government listings and found the number for the Agricultural Extension Service. (Extension may be harder to locate in some states, but is available nationwide to both rural and urban dwellers. If, under county government, you can't find it as above, or as Cooperative Extension, Farm Agent, or County Agent, call your County Courthouse—someone there will be able to tell you the number.)

I spoke to a County Extension Chairman, who explained that the Service is funded by the U.S. Department of Agriculture (which is funded by your tax dollars) and administered by a state's land-grant college. Its original purpose, when begun in 1914, was to disseminate to farmers the results of these colleges' research programs. Extension has now grown to include the general public in its constituency, providing free or low-cost information and education to anyone (including, through 4-H, youngsters) interested in any aspect of farming or gardening, or home economics. The offerings are invariably savings-oriented.

I asked the Chairman which services he considered most outstanding. In the agricultural sphere he named, without hesitation, soil testing. Available to anyone (free in some states,

4

nominally priced in others), the soil test determines nutrient deficiencies in your garden plot. Having this information will allow you to eliminate unnecessary fertilizer expenditures and bring you higher yields. To find out the soil-test procedure to follow (usually accomplished by mail), call your local agent.

In addition, Extension will provide information about controlling plant diseases and pests, will recommend planting times and varieties for your specific locale, and will answer any other gardening question you might have.

In the area of home economics, the Chairman suggested calling to ask that your name be added to your Service's mailing list (which I did). Their bulletins and newsletters are sent monthly and include the sort of information found in Cass's (which I described earlier). As I was writing this sentence, my letter carrier was placing my May issue in my mailbox. It includes an announcement of the dates and times when Pressure Canner Clinics will be held locally where I can have my equipment checked for safety, get answers to any freezing or canning questions I might have, and pick up the latest canning, freezing, drying, and pickling bulletins. All free.

To give you a taste of the wide range of questions the experts at your Extension office are prepared to provide answers to, a sampling of examples appears below. I gleaned these from the master list of a service being provided on a pilot project basis to North Carolinians. My friend Jane first told me about it. Called Extension Teletip, it provides toll-free phone-request information-on-tape to anyone in the state. At this writing Colorado has also initiated this service, Florida will likely follow, and something similar is available in Memphis, Tennessee, and in some counties in Wisconsin. The project has been so successful here that the possibility of Teletip being initiated in other states in the future is quite good. Watch for it in yours.

Meanwhile, you can get the same information from a live agent at any Agricultural Extension Service Office. Below is the promised more-specific category listing of their areas of expertise, including some examples. My hope is that it will serve as a reminder that the answers to many, many home and gardening questions are as close as your phone. Remember, it's your tax money. Why not benefit?

Food Buying: Of fourteen possible tapes, Jane's favorite (and mine) is "Best Food Buys—updated every two weeks," which includes exactly what it promises for meat and fruit and vegetables as well as preparation tips.

Game and Meat Cookery: including such things as "Making Sausage."

Freezing: how to go about freezing anything freezable.

Food Safety

Jams, Jellies and Preserves: detailed explanation of process and mistake-correcting.

Canning: safe processing and storage.

Pickles: how-to from choosing cucumbers to explaining "what causes soft, slippery pickles?"

Drying and Storing: including the oven method.

Flowers: how-to for specific choices.

Shrubs: how-to, including transplanting, use in landscaping, propagating, controlling disease and pests.

Lawns and Ground Covers

Fruits and Nuts

House Plants: including greenhouse considerations.

Trees: how-to including species selection and transplanting of native trees (i.e., a free source).

Forest Resources: where to find assistance *re* reforesting.

Pests in and Around the House: extermination information.

Vegetable Gardening: absolutely anything you might conceivably want to know, including diagnosis of diseased plants.

Estate Planning: what to know and do before you call a lawyer.

Family Resource Management: help with budgeting, recordkeeping, retirement, avoiding flim-flam, and more.

Consumer Tips: how to buy insurance, mortgage a home, complain, etc.

Tax Management: angles.

Energy: how-to on selection of materials and appliances, and how to save in use.

Home Repair and Maintenance

House Care—inside: as stated.

Water: how to save on, and choosing a system.

Septic Tanks: construction, avoiding and correcting problems, even recycling sludge into the garden.

Stain Removal: how to remove practically any stain or unwanted substance from practically anything.

Youth: 4-H (see EDUCATION, extracurricular for school-age children).

APPLIANCES

The final three months of work on this book saw our kitchen dining table perpetually strewn with papers and questionnaires and books; and my family, bless them each, eating their meals (when they got them at all) standing up. If that picture is clear, you can imagine the approximate state of the remainder of the house.

Now, if you will picture the precise opposite, you will have a perfect vision of Elizabeth's. And somehow she manages to keep her house both orderly and clean without ever seeming to spend time doing it. I guess the operative word is "manages." That hasn't always been true.

I have known Elizabeth nearly half our lives. When we first met I loved to visit her house because its state of chaos very nearly matched my own. I still love to visit Elizabeth, but for a different reason now—I guess because I enjoy marveling at marvelous women. Elizabeth is one of those who, once her mind is made up, never wavers. One day she simply decided that she was spending more time worrying about not cleaning than it would have taken her to clean. (She subsequently proved the premise true.) She read a few home-management books, formulated a plan for getting the job done, and has been doing it ever since, without apparent effort. She has become so well organized that at present, in addition to taking good care of her rather large house and family of four, she is working on a master's degree in philosophy.

I knew, therefore, that the questionnaire I sent Elizabeth would not be returned by the next post. I knew that it would be filed in its appropriate place in her "things to do" pile, but I also knew that it not only would be returned in due time, but returned full of tips that were well thought out, clearly written, complete. She didn't disappoint me.

"Even if an appliance purchase isn't contemplated immediately," writes Elizabeth, "whenever I have had the need to call in a repairperson to fix—for instance—my refrigerator, I ask for an opinion about brands of freezers *and* refrigerators. Then I file the information for future reference. Repairpeople are the experts in knowing which brands are trouble-free, which are lemons. And I always ask what brand *they* have bought for *their* homes; that answer is always telling and frequently surprising."

Consumer Reports
$$$$$$

Many contributors indicated that, when in the market for a new appliance, they asked friends and relatives for recommendations. When print sources were consulted, *Consumer Reports* was consistently at the top of the list.

Repairpeople, as Elizabeth suggests, have, by the nature of their work, an inside track. But suppose you do your own repair work or must purchase an appliance about which you have never questioned a repairperson? If you ask Aunt Lilly and Granny Dee and Cousin Sally and twenty other relatives and friends, you may hear about twenty-three separate brand names or find a wide variance in degree of satisfaction. So you may end up picking the brand preferred by the friend or relative you most trust. That, at least, is what I have done in the past. It is not a very scientific approach, although occasionally I have been lucky.

Consumer Reports, on the other hand, has a subscriber list topping two million. They conduct surveys of their readership's past experience with various brands of a wide range of appliances. The published result is a "Frequency of Repair Record" and this, it seems to me, constitutes a more reliable consensus than twenty-three friends and relatives no matter how well-meaning or trustworthy.

It is my guess that nearly everyone reading this book has consulted *CR* at one time or another. I took an especially close look at it, as well as other Consumers Union publications (See CONSUMERS UNION) in the course of researching *Inflation-Wise.* I expect to be using it a great deal more in the future: anyone who hasn't referred to it recently may be surprised to discover just how much information is provided.

For example, the report on clothes dryers in the most recent *Buying Guide* (which is published each December and is a

8

summary of information given in previous issues) included, among other things: operating-cost differential for gas *vs.* electric, evaluation of features such as buzzers, automatic cycles, control convenience and reliability, noise levels, accessibility of filters and drum and inner-workings (an important cost factor in repair-time expense), a section regarding gadgets now available to divert the exhaust indoors safely in winter and thus cut your heating bills, and a Frequency of Repair Record.

The dryers' ratings (including brief notes *re* advantages and disadvantages of each model tested) were listed in order of estimated overall quality, and a note explained that differences between closely ranked models were slight. One difference was not so slight: a difference of $61 between the average prices of the two top-ranked models.

Beyond *Consumer Reports*

I decided recently that it was time to replace our ten-year-old vacuum cleaner. Seeing me with the designated cash-in-hand, the children had already expropriated the old cleaner's wand pieces for use as hockey sticks, when I discovered that the model most highly recommended by *CR* was no longer available.

This happens sometimes. And model numbers matter: not infrequently, the top-rated as well as other lower-rated models are manufactured by the same company, only the model numbers differing.

Our carpet was beginning to groan under the weight of accumulated litter, but I was determined not to make a blind choice and regret it as I had done once before. So I made a note of the manufacturer's main office address and the new model number of what appeared to be a comparable machine; this information can be found printed on the appliance or can be obtained from a salesperson.

Of course I could have written, but I was impatient and called instead, asking for Customer Relations. The representative who answered quite clearly knew every word of *CR*'s article and every detail of his company's products by heart. I asked, and was told, which model in the current line was comparable to the top-rated previous model and which features had been changed. It was the top of the line of seven similar models. We discussed, in increasing detail, the differences between each of these models and finally I asked and was told which model was the best buy for the money, in his opinion, and why; surprisingly, it was not the top of the line. Within two days, specification sheets arrived in my mailbox describing the various features of the various models, which, in combination with our conversation, permitted me to make an intelligent choice. In this case I decided his was good advice.

I'm completely convinced that this call was worth the couple of dollars I spent, and many manufacturers can be called toll free (See TELEPHONE, Toll free). Unlike a written inquiry, a discussion by phone provides a much better sense of the competence of the manufacturer's representative, and makes it possible to respond to unclear answers with more specific questions immediately. I think such calls will reap great rewards in best buys whenever a substantial appliance purchase is contemplated.

If it's possible to love a vacuum cleaner, I do.

No *Consumer Reports*

When I find it necessary to purchase an appliance, or any other piece of machinery, for which no *CR* ratings are available or about which I am unable to obtain adequate information from the manufacturers, I stick to my father's advice: "Keep it simple."

He's a retired engineer and has always maintained that the fewer moving parts there are, the less likely a breakdown . . . commonsensical and, in my experience, true.

Sale Months
%%%

Cass sent me a list of traditional sale months, provided by her Cooperative Extension Service. I have reorganized the list into an easily readable chart (see SALES—Traditional Months) and have extracted some of the items for placement under specific entry headings such as this one.

The traditional sale month for appliances in department stores is January.

For specific appliances, the months usually are:

Air conditioners—January, August
Dishwashers—May, December
Dryers—March
Freezers—July
Kitchen ranges—April
Microwave ovens—May, December
Radios—January
Refrigerators—July
Stereos—January
Televisions—January, May, June
Washing machines—March

AUTOMOBILES

Basic Knowledge

The more you know about the workings of these machines the better equipped you will be to make choices among the hundreds of possible new and used models and keep your choice in good condition.

The basic components, how and why they tick, are presented in clear pictures and text in a book my family and I have found quite useful called:

The Time-Life Book of the Family Car
by the editors of Time-Life Books
Time, Inc., 1973
$15

The color-coded illustrations are simple enough for a bright seven-year-old or a novice adult to understand.

Buying, General
$ $ $ $ $

I have never heard and never expect to hear Elizabeth's husband utter the words "That's good enough to pass." Gerry is a perfectionist who carpenters the built-in cabinets for their home renovations with as much care as he prepares his law briefs. I doubt that he has ever in his life made a major purchase without really thorough research beforehand.

Gerry contributes, among others, this piece of advice: "Avoid buying any car with substantial changes in engine design during the first few years after it appears. It almost invariably takes time for the manufacturers and designers to work out the bugs." He also says: "When considering options which don't enhance the car's safety, remember that keeping it as simple as possible will keep repair costs down. Power windows and power antennas, power headlight covers, and the like, often require frequent repair—are they worth it?"

Finally, in these days of gasoline shortages and high prices, it might be well to think carefully about the mpg of the various models you are considering. Check *Consumer Reports* for actual field-tested mpg, rather than relying on Environmental Protection Agency laboratory estimates. Though the latter, available at any dealership in a booklet called *Gas Mileage Guide for New Car Buyers*, can be used for comparison between makes, actual mileage, especially in city driving, will likely be lower.

If you are concerned about gasoline consumption, your car should feature:

the lightest weight in its class
the lowest practical number of cylinders (a V-8 gets 3½ mpg less than a 6; a 6, 4½ mpg less than a 4)
manual transmission

If you haul or carry a large load only a few times a year, you might want to consider buying a small car for everyday use and renting a larger one for those few times. Check local rental fees, compare mileage costs over the long run; it might surprise you. Remember the formula:

$$\frac{\text{Cost of gas per gallon (in \$)}}{\text{Average mpg}} \times \frac{\text{miles driven}}{\text{per year}} = \frac{\text{Annual gas}}{\text{cost}}$$

Buying New
$$$$$$$$$

During the first year of our marriage, John and I lived in a small town about an hour's drive from Washington, D. C. One of our neighbors was a car dealer. We became acquainted as fellow dog owners sometimes will, chatting to keep off the chill while we allowed our respective dogs to exercise at the local park.

We were back in that town visiting friends recently and ran into our neighbor car dealer, now retired. I will call him Art. (It was during the period of this book's writing when I carried my notes everywhere and this was one time—the only one I recall—when I was glad I had.)

"Oh, Art, you are just the man I need to double-check these tips I've gathered about car buying," I ventured. I explained what I was about and he agreed to take a look.

Art is proud of the fact that, when he owned his dealership, his salesmen followed strict orders not to lie to customers. He did admit— over a drink—that although no lying was permitted, neither was certain information volunteered.

"Your book," he said afterward, "if the tips you include are actually followed by car-buyers, is going to make many a salesman swallow hard." This one, for instance. . . .

I had asked Art what would happen if I said the following to a dealer: "I see here on the order form you have written up for my new car that there is a charge of $87.50 which you tell me is for 'dealer preparation.' I read somewhere that most manufacturers of American cars (including Ford, General Motors, and Chrysler) and some European automakers reimburse dealers for the cost of performing such preparation. Why are you charging *me* as well?"

Art gulped. "If the dealer were honest, he would agree to delete the charge," he said.

Choosing a Dealer

Gerry: "After completing your research and deciding on the make and model and accessories you want in a new car, make a list of the area dealerships selling it. Begin narrowing the field by finding out from friends and relatives which dealer has the best reputation

for a *good service department.* Then, as a final check, call your Better Business Bureau or Consumer Affairs Office to ask whether any substantial number of complaints have been lodged. The dealer with the best service department may match any other price, but even if he holds out for a little more it may save in the long run to buy the car at a dealership with a good service record.

"And when you eventually go in for a test drive, try to spend a few minutes chatting with the service manager at the dealership you've chosen. Listen to the way he handles customers whose cars are presently being repaired. Ask if his shop provides transportation to and from the customer's business or home while repairs are taking place. In general, size him up. If he has no time for you before you buy, will he have time after?"

How to Get the Best Deal
💲

The basic premise under which a salesperson works, according to Art, is that *a bargain is as it is perceived.* In other words, if a buyer can be convinced that he is getting a good deal, he will feel satisfied, *regardless of discount or lack of it.* Most automobile salespeople are well trained in techniques to encourage that conviction and satisfaction while simultaneously obtaining the greatest possible dealer profit.

The buyer described in the following example is a salesperson's dream. Few, these days, would be so *completely* naive, although Art assures me they exist, are not even rare. I have conjured her up, for the sake of technique-description expediency, as one who has driven into a dealership on a whim, "just to look," totally unarmed with any prior research or knowledge. I will call her Christopher.

She is greeted, as she steps out of the car, by a salesman who begins making what appears to be smalltalk—"You live nearby? work nearby? many years?"—that sort of thing. In fact, this "smalltalk" in combination with the visual information provided by the car in which she arrived, her appearance and age, allow the salesman to size up the prospect of selling a car to this woman on this day.

When asked (finally), Christopher says she doesn't exactly know what car she wants; she thinks perhaps something small for

14

good gas mileage, imported for safety features, and, of course, with a low enough monthly payment to suit her budget. "Maybe you can help," she says. (She has just pushed this salesman's button and, if she had been watching, would have seen dollar signs—cash-register style—rrring up in his eyes.)

If she had done her homework, Christopher would have discovered that her first two assumptions were not necessarily true. Furthermore, having revealed herself as a buyer who thinks in terms of monthly payments and appears to have done little if any comparison shopping for loan terms, she is not just a salesman's dream—she's a salesman's *perfect* dream.

Concerning the low mpg of small cars: while it is true that, as a group, smaller cars *do* deliver better gas mileage than medium or large, it cannot be assumed that *every* small car will. In *Consumer Reports'* city road tests (synopsized in the April 1980 issue), averages were: small—20 mpg; medium—13.2; large—11.7. *However*, the range of each groups' test results was wide: within the small-car group a low of 13.8 mpg, a high of 29.0 mpg; medium, 9.8 mpg to 20.0 mpg; large, 10.8 mpg to 13.2 mpg. Very importantly, although *CR's* expressway road tests tended to approximate the Environmental Protection Agency's highway estimates, the gap difference between EPA city estimates—which is the figure your salesman will quote—and *CR's* actual city road tests was sometimes surprisingly large, the latter's results being lower by nearly 10 mpg in some cases.

With respect to the safety factor: In National Highway Traffic Safety Administration 35-mpg head-on crash tests of thirty 1979 models (twenty-two of them domestic), only nine protected both "driver" and front seat "passenger" from "death"—and not one of these was an import.

Concerning financing: Although a salesman's response, when asked about dealer percentage rate, may be to say, "It's comparable to other sources," the fact is that a dealer's financing terms are almost always a percentage point or more above the rate you will be able to obtain from your credit union or bank. Think about his statement—*any* two percentage points are comparable (can be compared). An actual comparison, however, may put those interest rates and thus the cost of the loan, in different ballparks, different games.

Finally, *re* the "type" of buyer: Remember the premise—a

bargain is as it is perceived. By revealing that she is a "payment buyer" (that she thinks in terms of monthly cost rather than total cost), Christopher has provided the salesman with the ammunition to sell her a car which may be priced totally beyond her reasonable means.

This is how the selling of a "payment buyer" is accomplished. Christopher has made it clear that she hasn't much more than a vague idea of what she wants and by so doing she has given control of the sale to the salesman. *He* will now steer her toward the car she will test drive and buy. Yes, buy. He will respond to questions about price with answers about filling needs. The car he chooses for her will have the highest price tag his experience and training lead him to believe he can get away with. (For Art's sake, I must add that this is only fair. An automobile dealer is in business to make a profit; the onus of getting a good deal rests on the buyer.)

Well, on with the story: the price tag on the car in this example is $6,000. As Christopher begins her test drive, the salesman points out the car's safety features, though they may or may not be relevant. At some point along the preestablished test-drive route, the salesman will suggest that they pull over and have a closer look at the car (away from the distractions of others on the lot). He will offer to answer any further questions she might have. She might ask about mpg, for instance, and will be given EPA estimates.

Meanwhile, the salesman will watch for signs that Christopher is becoming smitten with this car. He has chosen it carefully, and well. Only when those signs appear (as they will) does he respond directly to a question about price. Now, when she asks, he says, "Your monthly payment will be about $257." (This would be true for a 30-month loan of $6,000 at the dealer's 14% rate. You will notice that none of these terms are mentioned at this point.)

"Yikes!" says Christopher.

"What did you have in mind?" says the salesman.

Since she hasn't bought a car in some time, what she had in mind was the previous decade's figure—$150 per month—but she now feels foolish saying that, so she says "$175." (Are you beginning to see how it works?—he has already altered her sights upward.)

"Well," he says, "I think we might be able to get it down to $223." (This, though he doesn't mention it, of course, is for the loan of $6,000 now stretched to 36 months.)

"No, that's still too high," Christopher says, proud of her fortitude.

He begins to ask questions such as: "Do you like the car? Can I answer any other questions you have about it? Is there anything about it that bothers you?" He already knows that she will say, "Only the price."

"All right. Let's get back to the lot and I'll check with my sales manager and see what can be done."

They return, he checks, and cheerfully informs her that his manager has agreed to let the car go for $202 (a 42-month loan). Christopher again says that that is still too high but meanwhile she has moved her "acceptable" figure up another notch to $185; what's ten dollars after all, she thinks.

"Do you like the car? Do you want the car?" he says. She expects him to next say, "What's $25?" but he surprises and delights her by instead saying, "If I can work out $184 per month, will you buy it?" Of course she will, and puts her "OK," at the salesman's request, on the potential $184-per-month purchase order. (Note: He doesn't ask for a signature, which might scare her, just an "OK.")

The sales manager approves, of course, and Christopher (who came "just to look") has bought herself a new car. She will be paying $184 each and every month for 4 years (a 48-month loan) on a $6,000 car *which hasn't been discounted one penny.* In fact, the total cost of that car, including interest and loan insurance, etc., will be $8832! But she will drive it away feeling smug thinking she has saved herself $73 a month.

A bargain is as it is perceived.

Salespeople use the same technique with the other two main "types" of buyers—the "difference" buyer, who wants to know what the new car will cost with his trade-in allowance; and the "allowance" buyer, whose concern is the same but focused differently—i.e., he wants to know the actual trade-in value of his old car. The salesperson begins with much too high or much too low quotes, respectively, finally "settling" for (at worst) the figure he has known would be acceptable to his manager from the start.

Therefore, if you are going to be any buyer "type," be this type—*smart*. Here are Art's suggestions for getting the best actual (not just perceived) deal on a new car:

1. Do your homework before you drive onto the lot. You should know:
   a. As much as possible about the car(s) you are coming to test drive—i.e., the drive should be the *final* deciding factor, not the starting point. Don't hesitate to bring and/or take notes.
   b. A close approximation of wholesale (dealer's) cost. (See AUTOMOBILES—Buying New, Mark-up *re* how to find or calculate.) And, keeping in mind that dealers have overhead to cover and will expect *some* profit, decide beforehand how much *you* are willing to pay. Generally, $200 above dealer cost is about as low as they will go, but be aware that you may not be given a discount at all on extremely popular cars which are in short supply.
   c. The specific availability of financing outside the dealership. Unless you intend to pay cash from your savings, you will of course be concerned about fitting a monthly payment into your budget scheme. Perhaps it will be *necessary* for you to stretch your loan to 48 months, but *particularly* if that is true, you will want to have done some comparison-shopping for the lowest possible interest rate ahead of time in order to keep that additional cost as low as possible.
2. Make your head rule your heart. Even if it means taking a chance that a car you think suits you perfectly might be sold before you return, if the salesperson won't come close to meeting your terms (with the exception of the case in 1-b), tell him you'll think it over and come back. He may relent, if he sees that you are serious; if not, WALK OUT. Keep coming back until you are satisfied. Remember: He really wants to sell you that car. To get the best deal, just be sure you stay in the driver's seat.

(See additional AUTOMOBILE entries for tips on timing your purchase and hidden costs.)

Mark-up
💲 💲

According to Art, dealer mark-up over cost on new cars ranges from about 10% (on small-sized) to about 20% on full-sized, which means that on a $10,000 car, for example, the mark-up might be as high as $2,000.

Dealers will be delighted to make that kind of profit but what they most want to do is sell you a car, so they are not only willing to negotiate, they *expect* to.

Many dealerships, Art told me, do not actually buy their inventory outright from the manufacturer but rather receive it on something akin to a consignment basis, paying interest to the manufacturer on the car's wholesale price until it is sold. This is why it's so important to a dealer that the inventory be moved as quickly as possible; every day a car sits on his lot costs the dealer in interest charges and cuts into his profit.

This is why, Art told me, a dealer is so willing to negotiate, why he will generally, if pushed, reduce that mark-up to as low as $200 (except in the case of cars in such high demand that they are virtually presold before arrival on the lot).

But before the haggling begins, of course you must know the dealer's new-car cost. How do you find that out? The simplest way is to check at your bank or credit union where you can look up the wholesale price in one of their new-car price guides.

Or, you can figure it yourself with the help of *Consumer Reports'* April issue (the Annual Auto Round-up). The percentage of list price (called "cost-factor" by *CR*) varies from auto to auto and model to model, so to be perfectly accurate you will want to check in that issue's new-car synopses for the particular car in which you are interested.

However, you will come fairly close by using the following procedure and percentages (based on an average of 1980 *CR* cost factors): Multiply the basic list price on the sticker (without options or transportation charges) by .88 for small cars, .83 for medium cars, .79 for large cars to find out dealer cost (i.e., wholesale price is 88%, 83%, and 79% of basic list, respectively).

Now total the list prices of options you want and multiply this options only total by .83 for small cars, .79 for medium cars, .77 for large cars (again, these are averages taken from *CR*'s 1980 options cost-factors where given; this factor is not included for all

cars). Subtract from the final list price (on the sticker) the sum of these two wholesale prices and the full transportation or destination charge and you will have an estimate of your bargaining room. (Remember that the figures given here are averages and that for more exact figures you will want to check the magazine itself or a wholesale guide.)

Incidentally, each April *CR* issue, in addition to the aforementioned synopses of the current year's new foreign and domestic models (slightly more detailed for those which have been the recent subject of full reports in earlier issues) includes description and evaluation of the various options you might want to consider, frequency-of-repair records for cars built in the previous six years (based on subscriber experience), and best bets in used cars, as well as a review of the current state of safety and regulatory standards and other auto-related concerns.

Timing the Purchase
⑤ ⑤ ⑤ ⑤ ⑤
%%%

According to Art, you will be most likely to haggle the best deal possible in any given month during the last couple of days. Because salespeople are striving to meet monthly quotas (and win bonuses), they are more prone to accept a buyer's terms near the end of the month. In fact, Art says, it is not at all unusual for the number of cars sold on the thirtieth day of a month alone to match or exceed the number sold during the entire first week of a month. (See also AUTOMOBILES—Sale Months, and AUTOMOBILES—Buying New, How to Get the Best Deal.)

Buying Used
%%%%

A used car might be the best choice for you (See AUTOMOBILES—New or Used? for help in making this decision) but you must always keep in mind that when buying a used car you will be buying a piece of machinery worn by someone whose care and feeding habits you can never know precisely. For this reason it will behoove you to be as careful and precise in your choice-making as possible.

You should begin by narrowing the possibilities through

research. You are probably tired of hearing this song, but I recommend starting with *Consumer Reports*. The Frequency-of-Repair records (based on the experiences of a quarter-million subscribers) will direct you to those used cars of the past six years which are likely to give the least trouble. These can be found in the annual December issue *Buying Guide* and the April *Auto Round-up* issue. The latter also includes, listed under price ranges, *CR*'s recommendations in used cars and a list of those you will want to avoid. Consumers Union's *Guide to Used Cars* will tell you the whys behind these recommendations (see CONSUMERS UNION for where to order information or check at your library).

Another source you may want to check, particularly if you are interested in considering cars more than six years old is:

Cherries and Lemons: The Used Car Buyer's Handbook
by Joe Troise
Warner Books, Inc., 1979
$1.95

which rates models clear back to 1955.

After you have narrowed your choices to a few specific models and years, your next step is to find out what you should be paying, quite specifically, for each. The "blue book," which you can find at your credit union or bank, will tell you the current average going price of used cars, both wholesale and retail (and the amount you can expect to be loaned) for specific years and models. The most often used guide is published monthly by the National Automobile Dealers Association. There are other guides as well, some available on newsstands; "blue book" is simply the common name.

If you are interested in a car that is more than six years old, you will have to make your own estimate of fair price based on a study of classified ads.

Recommendations of where to buy vary among the experts. New-car dealers and private-owner transactions most often top the list. The former keep only those trade-ins which are, or can be easily returned to, top condition and usually only late models (the rest are wholesaled to used-car dealers or salvage companies). You can expect to pay the retail "blue book" price for such used cars but you should be able to obtain some guarantee (though generally for only a short period and usually covering less than

100% of repairs). In a private-owner transaction you will likely find that the price falls somewhere between wholesale (trade-in) and retail (dealer). There will be no guarantees given, however, so your shopping and testing should be especially thorough.

Cherries and Lemons outlines the step-by-step procedure to follow in locating and choosing a used car which will make you sing instead of swear. Troise gives information which is precise and thorough, including a breakdown of the sometimes forgotten additional costs (such as taxes, registration fees and insurance, and the tune-up, oil change, and other work you may want to have done after purchase, and explanations I have never seen elsewhere, such as how to read a classified ad, what to ask during the initial phone conversation, and other hints which will save you time, traipsing, and ultimately—money. He also provides, as do *CR*'s April issue and the *Time-Life Book of the Family Car* (see full reference under AUTOMOBILES—Basic Knowledge), a checklist for examining the car yourself, both off and on the road, and finally, if the car in question has passed all these preliminaries, a checklist for your mechanic. The mechanic's final examination and OK is considered a must by every expert.

In closing this general information section, let me pass on a couple more tips from Art: "If you are buying a used car from a dealer, ask for the name and address of the previous owner who, with nothing to lose, will provide a clearer picture of the shape the car is in. A dealer is not required to give you this information, but consider it a good sign if he will. He *is*, by law, required to *have* the information in his records. If he says he doesn't, consider it a warning; he's almost certainly lying and I would advise you to buy elsewhere.

"And—*never* buy a used car at night or in the rain, both of which can hide a multitude of defects. Believe me, if you do you'll be sorry in the morning."

New or Used?

Which is the better buy—a new car or a used one? Contributor reviews were stubbornly *insistent* and very mixed. It was on the day that my friend Fritzi called (in the market for a car) and said,

"OK, saver-lady, what's the bottom line on *that* question?" that I decided to include the cost-comparison information, which follows, in *Inflation-Wise*.

First, narrow your choices to one or two new and one or two used models by researching those you believe will fill your needs (see AUTOMOBILES—Buying New, and AUTOMOBILES—Buying Used, for recommended research sources). Then fill in the blanks in the Cost Comparison Worksheets at the end of this entry in order to compare car costs over four years of ownership. Feel free to extend it beyond the four years if it is your usual practice to keep cars longer. The major considerations, and tips for obtaining the figures required, are described below.

The *Initial Cost* of each should be an estimate based on the price you expect to pay either a dealer or a private owner. To approximate these figures, see how-to in the previously cited AUTOMOBILE entries. If paying cash, only the first-year initial-cost space will require a figure. If financing, you will be dividing these amounts over the number of years of your loan. Check with your lender for the yearly breakdown.

The *Cost of Financing* figures (if any) can also be obtained from your lender. These may vary each year depending on the method of calculation used, but the 1969 Truth-in-Lending Law requires, among other things, that a borrower be told the total dollars-and-cents finance charge. This figure must include not only interest but also any other charges on which the credit offered is contingent (such as cost of a credit report and/or any compulsory insurance). Your lender will likely break these down on a per-year basis if you ask.

Insurance figures should be calculated with the help of your agent. If the car is being purchased with financing, the lender will likely require collision to protect the investment. (See INSURANCE—Auto, for a discussion of amounts of insurance to carry.)

Gasoline is the next variable and as prices continue to rise this cost becomes more and more substantial. The average car is driven 15,000 miles per year. To calculate the dollar amounts for

the cars of your choice you must know the miles per gallon (mpg) each can be expected to provide. For current models your best bet for obtaining accurate estimates is the *Consumer Reports'* April issue. Consumers Union's *Guide to Used Cars* also contains this information for most older cars. You might also find mpg guidelines in other used-car guides, though some will be based on EPA laboratory estimates which may not be as reliable as actual road tests. For substantially older cars, you will have to rely on the previous owner's estimate and your own common sense. To figure the annual cost, use this formula:

$$\frac{\text{Cost of gasoline (in dollars) per gallon}}{\text{miles per gallon (mpg)}} \times \frac{\text{15,000 miles or miles}}{\text{you drive per year}} = \frac{\text{annual cost in dollars}}{}$$

Example: $\dfrac{\$1.60 \text{ per gallon}}{20 \text{ mpg}} \times 15{,}000 \text{ miles} = \$1{,}200.00 \text{ per year}$

$\dfrac{\$1.60 \text{ per gallon}}{10 \text{ mpg}} \times 15{,}000 \text{ miles} = \$2{,}400.00 \text{ per year}$

Cost of Maintenance and Repair	*Will average This percentage*	*of*	*Depreciated value (as percentage of original new cost)*
at one year of age	2.5%	of	70%
at two years	3.0%	of	50%
at three years	6.0%	of	35%
at four years	7.5%	of	25%
at five years	7.5%	of	15%
at six years	7.5%	of	10%
at seven years	11.0%	of	5%
at eight years	5.0%	of	2.5%
at nine years	6.5%	of	1%

The *Cost of Maintenance and Repairs* was figured by the Department of Transportation (DOT) in a study cited in *The Time-Life Book of the Family Car*. These findings allow you to figure (in conjunction with the depreciation percentages given) the average cost of this consideration in each of the four years. The DOT study's findings, as summarized on the preceding page, present these costs as a percentage of a car's value in any given age-year:

For instance, by the time a car is two years old, according to this study, it will have depreciated to 50% of its original value, and repairs and maintenance by that point in time will average about 3% of the depreciated value. Example: a car bought new for $6,000 will, by the end of its second year, be worth about $3,000; average repairs and maintenance will run 3% of $3,000 or $90.

Calculate your estimated maintenance/repair costs for each car you are considering (for each of the four years) using the DOT figures above and the formula below:

Original cost (new) X Percentage Depreciation Factor X Percentage Maintenance/Repair Factor = Given Year's Maintenance/Repair Cost

Taxes, in states where personal property taxes are levied, may be based on actual fair-market value. Check in your state to find approximations of these figures.

Resale Recovery. A car, as the depreciation table shows, is with only a handful of exceptions a lousy investment although many people seem to think of car-buying in investment terms. The depreciation is swift and stunning in the first few years; however, resale at any point will recover *some* of the outlay—the later the resale the smaller the fraction. The choice of locating this factor at the end of the fourth year was arbitrary, but was based on the fact that many experts, including Art, consider this the optimum time for trade-in (when the gap between maintenance/repair costs and market value begins to noticeably narrow). The reader may want to calculate this consideration at several different points in time according to her experience. She may, in fact, also wish to extend the Cost Comparison Worksheets provided on pages 26 and 27 for several years if her tendency is to keep a car until it dies a natural death and/or experience reveals that she regularly beats the averages.

COST COMPARISON WORKSHEETS—New or Used?

Car A—New—Make, Model, Year:

Considerations:	1st year Costs	2nd year Costs	3rd year Costs	4th year Costs
Initial Cost				
Cost of Financing				
Insurance				
Gasoline				
Cost of Maintenance and Repairs				
Taxes				
Yearly Totals				

4-year (or other) total .... $_____

Less expected cash recovered by resale at depreciated value .... −$_____

Equals total cost of 4-year (or other period*) ownership .... $_____

Car B—New—Make, Model, Year:

Considerations:	1st year Costs	2nd year Costs	3rd year Costs	4th year Costs
Initial Cost				
Cost of Financing				
Insurance				
Gasoline				
Cost of Maintenance and Repairs				
Taxes				
Yearly Totals				

4-year (or other) total .... $_____

Less expected cash recovered by resale at depreciated value .... −$_____

Equals total cost of 4-year (or other period*) ownership .... $_____

Car C—Used—Make, Model, Year:

Considerations:	1st year Costs	2nd year Costs	3rd year Costs	4th year Costs
Initial Cost				
Cost of Financing				
Insurance				
Gasoline				
Cost of Maintenance and Repairs				
Taxes				
Yearly Totals				

4-year (or other) total.. $_____

Less expected cash recovered by resale at depreci-
ated value.. −$_____

Equals total cost of 4-year (or other period*)
ownership.. $_____

Car D—Used—Make, Model, Year:

Considerations:	1st year Costs	2nd year Costs	3rd year Costs	4th year Costs
Initial Cost				
Cost of Financing				
Insurance				
Gasoline				
Cost of Maintenance and Repairs				
Taxes				
Yearly Totals				

4-year (or other) total.. $_____

Less expected cash recovered by resale at depreci-
ated value.. −$_____

Equals total cost of 4-year (or other period*)
ownership.. $_____

*Find the average yearly cost of owning any of the cars under consideration by
dividing the four-year total in each case by four. This will provide your comparison
figure. If the length of time you expect to keep a car varies (for instance, four years
if bought new, two years if bought used) divide the total cost of ownership by the
appropriate number of years in order to make comparison equitable.

Selling Old

General

⑤ ⑤
%%

Edward can remember what an artichoke was selling for seven months ago. He can tell you the cost per meal of paper napkins. His mathematics ability is so facile he can figure out a unit price in his head before I can fumble my calculator's "on" button into position. His success rate in complaint departments is legendary, his store of knowledge astounding.

In short, no one else I know knows how to squeeze value out of every penny as well as Edward. Why, you might wonder, is he not writing this book? Well, perhaps he should be, but Edward likes to talk, not write. He never quite got around to completing my questionnaire, but his verbal contributions have been abundant (as you will read) and his technical help has been invaluable.

Edward says, "Selling your old car yourself will usually net you more than trade-in. While it is unlikely that you will be able to recover money spent on repairs, cleaning it up (waxing and otherwise giving it its best appearance) will make you money. Used-car dealers don't do this with theirs just for fun."

Edward also reminds the used-car seller: "Be sure to go with the prospective buyer on her test drive. You remain liable for damage or accident as long as you own the car. And notify your insurance company as soon as you have sold it—you may be due a rebate on your premium."

Resale Value

Any bank or credit union can tell you the "blue book" (generic name for references such as *National Automobile Dealers' Association Used Car Guide*) value of any used car: Both trade-in (what a dealer will pay for it in top condition), and retail (what the dealer will resell it for) are listed as well as adjustment figures for high or low mileage and certain options. Most prospective buyers will also know these numbers; however, before setting a price to include in your ad, check the classifieds for the going rate on comparable cars. Begin with free advertising such as a sign with a phone number in your car's window, bulletin boards at work or in the community.

28

Trade-In Strategy
$ $ $ $

Even though selling your old car yourself will likely net you the highest figure—somewhere between the trade-in price a dealer will offer and the retail tag he will subsequently place on it—you may decide to avoid the hassle by trading it in. However, do not tell this to the dealer until you have negotiated a firm (written) price on the new car without trade-in, because some dealers will juggle the figures. Then, when you ask what your old car is worth, be sure you already know the wholesale value. If you feel you are not being offered enough, you may want to reconsider and sell it yourself. (See other SELLING OLD entries)

Selling Really Old
%%%%%%%%

A couple of years ago, my phone rang one afternoon as I was getting dinner started. "Hello?"

"Hello, favorite niece," said my Uncle Beeze, "I'm just calling to say that I've fallen in love."

"What!? Who is she?"

"She's a lake," said he.

My Uncle Beeze, a bachelor, was a traveling salesman at the time and about once every six months, on his swing through North Carolina, he would come wheeling into our driveway for a visit, always with his sailboat riding atop his car. Uncle Beeze lived to sail. What he was calling to announce that day, in fact, was that he was giving up selling in favor of sailing.

Indeed, within a few months he had quit his job (of twenty-odd years' duration), settled into and begun winterizing his new cottage on a South Carolina lake and commenced living on savings and the odd odd-job—a fraction of the income he had been accustomed to. I know very few, very few, who could do this and I'm certainly not one of them.

Uncle Beeze, however, has managed this enormous change in lifestyle wonderfully well because he's a scavenger of the first order with prodigious energy.

When he used to visit, invariably we would drag ourselves out of bed to find that he had been up for a couple of hours and had already repaired two broken lamps, mended the back-door screen, and finished sanding

29

the table that had been parked in the corner of the kitchen, half finished and forgotten for two months. In a single weekend, enlivened by his energy, my husband and I would accomplish six months' worth of accumulated, procrastinated home repairs and projects. I doubt that it would even occur to Uncle Beeze to call a serviceperson—for anything.

Nor would I expect him to be unable to manage most tasks without sending out for parts. If the rabbits were eating the lettuce in his garden, would he run out and buy chicken wire like anybody else? Of course not. He would walk into his nearby woods and gather dead branches and, as he walked, design a fence no rabbit could penetrate, then return home and build it.

Only trouble is, he's so busy building and sailing we hardly ever see him anymore. You can imagine the sorry state of repair our house has fallen into.

Uncle Beeze: "So you've got an old (and probably valuable to someone else) rusting but not runable car! Why not turn it into cash? Offer it as a 'spare-parts kit on wheels' (via a clever ad on the community bulletin board) to a repair-it-yourself type owner of the same model."

Servicing
$ $ $

It is a phenomenon I can't begin to explain, but nearly every family I know seems to have at least one child who is a born banker. When I was growing up, that child in my own family was my sister, Cinda.

Whenever any of us was broke, she would head directly for Cinda; first, because we knew she would lend it and second because she always had it. I think we have all matured enough now not to take such dreadful advantage of her generosity, but always in the back of my mind I know that if I am in desperate need, Cinda will not only come through but will surely be able to come through—she'll have the money to lend.

Cinda is single, and for the last several years she has chosen employment which pays next to nothing because, in the process of becoming an accomplished landscape designer, she has considered a good apprenticeship more important than a good salary. What is amazing to me is that she has been consistently managing to save an astoundingly high percentage of that low salary.

At least part of the reason she has been able to do this is that she seems to have an uncanny ability to track down the most honest and most reliable and least expensive repairpeople in any town where she has lived. And, when she has been unable to locate someone she trusts to perform a given service at a price she is willing to pay, she almost never simply accepts the inevitable (as I might do). Her tendency, instead, has been to learn to do-it-herself, so she has also developed quite a number of repair skills along the way. Cinda's basic assumption is that practically anyone can learn to do practically anything herself (if she really wants to and is willing to take the time). The point is she never assumes anything is beyond her capabilities.

Once, a few days after settling into a house in a new town, she went out to her garage to find that her car's transmission fluid had leaked out during the night. She telephoned a few auto-repair businesses listed in the Yellow Pages, described the problem as she saw it, and in each case was told that it would take two or three days before the repair could be scheduled; she was quoted prices ranging from $200 to $300.

If it had been me, without doubt the shrug and sigh and pay solution would have been employed; *later* I would find a good mechanic, *this* was an emergency. But it wasn't me, it was Cinda. She had already scheduled the following two days with dawn-to-dusk job interviews. To the idea of having to rearrange her plans, she said, "Nuts!"

She put in a call to her former mechanic, Augie, in the town from which she had just moved. She described what she was seeing under the hood and Augie talked her through the repair operation (which, it turned out, was minor). The repair cost her $8 in long distance charges and she sent a thank-you note and check for an hour's labor to Augie for the consultation.

I asked her to tell me how she located these wonderful people. "Well," she said, "first, under normal circumstances, I don't wait until something goes wrong. I normally begin asking friends for recommendations as soon as I've made a few friends in any new town. Augie was easy; his was the name mentioned ninety percent of the time. But generally a name will be repeated by three or four people, or at least repetitions will narrow the field. Then I call them each and ask a few questions about the cost of some repair I'm familiar with, and generally try to get a sense about how

each treats a potential customer. Was it with courtesy as though my business would be appreciated? Was it with the respect one would accord an intelligent being? Were my questions answered directly without hedging? Things like that; then, if I am left with a positive feeling at the end of the conversation, I usually make a point to stop by that repair shop or garage as soon as it's convenient to make a person-to-person contact with the mechanic to get a further sense of the attitudes.

"I don't know how you can quantify this for your book, Christopher," she said, "but having followed this course, my final decision is always based on instinct and I have *never* made a bad mistake. I really do believe that there *is* such a thing as an honest face (or an honest tone), and the kind of confidence a person has about his work, when he does his work well, shows in his carriage and in an absence of arrogance in the way he treats people who may not know as much about the field as he does."

Consumer Protection

Whether under warranty or not, if you have difficulty getting a fair shake from a dealer's service department, check to see if there is an AutoCAP in your area. The mediation Consumer Action Panel has been instituted in some areas by the local Automobile Dealers Association to help resolve consumer complaints. If there is no AutoCAP in your area, ask for help from your Department of Motor Vehicles or local Consumer Protection Agency.

The now-classic book about how to deal with the worst problem cars is:

> *What to Do with Your Bad Car: An Action Manual for Lemon Owners* by Ralph Nader, Lowell Dodge, and Ralf Hotchkiss Grossman, New York, 1970
> $8.95

Estimates
%%

Edward tells me that a written estimate is now required in about half the states for car repair. A Chamber of Commerce or Motor Vehicles Department can tell you if this is the case in yours.

Request a written estimate in any case; it will discourage unnecessary and unauthorized charges.

Rates
$

Christian, one of my husband John's colleagues, is an exceedingly popular fellow in our neighborhood. On any sunny Saturday morning we are apt to see him leaning under the hood of a car not necessarily, or even likely, his own. His grandfather owned a car repair business and he has been tinkering with engines since childhood.

Christian says: "Anyone who takes his or her car to a repair shop might want to know that there is a book which garages use to calculate the labor costs. It is called the *Manufacturer's Flat Rate Manual* and indicates (by make, model, and year) how long it ought to take a mechanic to complete any specific repair.

"All registered dealerships use this manual and are required to stay within the listed rates. It is a way of standardizing charges, so that if the manual indicates that a certain repair procedure is an hour-long job, you will be charged for one hour's labor (even if the mechanic is plodding and actually spends two hours); it means that you won't be charged for time spent on coffee breaks."

Some independent garages also use this *Manual* to compute charges; others merely use it as a reference tool. If you are able to locate a competent, honest mechanic (see previous entry), it is quite possible that he (or she) will charge you for actual time and that the charges will be comparable to or better than the *Manual* rates. However, if you suspect that any garage has overcharged you, asking the service manager to give you a look at the *Flat Rate Manual* should be your first recourse.

Resources

For further reading, Margaret Bresnahan Carlson (formerly a researcher at Ralph Nader's Center for Auto Study) has written a thorough and important book called *How to Get Your Car Repaired Without Getting Gypped* (Harper & Row, 1973, $5.95). She includes information to help you decide whether a repair is actually

necessary, describes common frauds, explains how to decide when it isn't worth repairing and how to decipher common trouble signs. She also counsels how to protect yourself, how to figure the proper charges, and how to get your money refunded when you have been taken.

Servicing-Them-Yourself
⑤ ⑤ ⑤ ⑤ ⑤
%%%%

Christian tells me that it is possible to obtain the repair manual for any car you own: "I don't mean the skinny little owner's manual that comes in the glove compartment. I mean the book used by garages as the reference for *their* repairwork; it provides thorough and detailed and illustrated (diagrammed) instructions which anyone who has a basic knowledge of car workings will find adequate.

"Just go to any dealer who sells your make of car and tell him you are interested in buying the *shop manual* for your car's model and year. If he doesn't have it in stock he can order it from the manufacturer. The cost is in the $10 to $15 range.

"In fact, with the interest in home-car repair on the rise, some dealers are including this shop manual among new-car options; and the newer ones are written even more clearly so that beginners should have few problems understanding them. If you have an older car you might want to supplement the shop manual with one specifically written for do-it-yourselfers such as Chilton's or Clymer's (in bookstores, costing $8 to $10)."

Sale Months (Including Parts)
⑤ ⑤

Used Cars—February, November
New cars (current year-end models)—August, September
Tires—May, August
Batteries—September
Mufflers—September

Here's more inside information from Art: "March, April, and May are the worst possible months for making the best deal on a current year's model. The winter weather is breaking and these are the most popular months for car shopping, so salesmen won't feel quite so anxious about filling quotas as they have been during the bad-weather months when business is very slow. The winter, then, is obviously going to be the optimum time to buy new, particularly right after a snowstorm.

"And although it doesn't appear on traditional sale-month lists because the selection isn't always good, if you are not too particular about color or options March is the month to shop for the previous year's models. Dealers are so anxious at this time to clear the last of the leftovers from their lots that they may be willing to mark these cars down as much as $1,500 below cost!"

BABY FOOD

Homemade
$ $
%%%%%%%

I have just returned from the supermarket and am feeling smug...and appalled. In the baby-food section, which I price-checked specifically for this entry, I found jars containing 9 cents worth of egg yolk and water selling for 46 cents!

I was appalled because when my own sons, James and Zander, now respectively nine and seven were babies I routinely fed them commercial baby food and paid equally outrageous prices. Smug because when my daughter (Max, now three) was born, my clever and very dear sister-in-law, Grace, sent a birthday present which allowed us to forego commercial baby food entirely. It was a hand-cranked baby-food grinder (available from Sears for about $6). My *very* conservative estimate is that we saved about $200 by grinding, for her, a small portion of whatever the rest of the family was being served—essentially bits of leftovers that might otherwise have ended up in the dog's scrap dish.

And this tip packs a wallop of a bonus. Only in the past two years has James begun expanding his food repertoire and been willing to experiment with new foods; Zander's list of acceptables consists of perhaps ten items (another conservative estimate). Max, on the other hand, eats virtually everything because she has been exposed from the start to such a wide variety of table food. She was never required to make the transition from a commercial baby-food recipe for tuna casserole to our own. Even more important, she will *try* anything. I figure this is saving us untold thousands in parental psychiatric treatment and pulled-hair replacement.

Homemade in Quantity

Christian's wife, Elaine, makes her baby's food in large batches by pureeing fruits or vegetables or leftovers in her blender. Then she freezes them in ice-cube trays and, when frozen, transfers the food cubes to plastic bags for storage. Individual cubes can then be thawed at mealtime in a heated baby dish or custard cup sitting in a bowl of hot water.

BACON
%%%%

Bacon is a costly source of protein, since so much of the purchase price melts off in the form of fat during cooking. To get my money's worth, I have always been careful to save that fat, keeping it in a cumulative can in the refrigerator. A couple of tablespoons of bacon fat, in place of the browning shortening called for in soups and stews, turns an ordinary meal into something really special.

Edward suggests other uses as well: "In biscuits in lieu of shortening; remelted and mixed with lemon juice as a delicious salad dressing on fresh spinach and mushrooms (the kind you pay a couple of dollars for in fancy restaurants).

"Did you know that in the old days, before there was such a

thing as bottled salad oils, salads were 'dressed' with the fat from cooking which was made less greasy by being cut with vinegar? And bread puddings, such as Yorkshire, are cooked with these fats."

BANKING
$

In our medium-sized city I count ten commercial banks, nine savings-and-loan associations, and quite a number of credit unions. Competition among them makes comparison shopping worth the effort.

When we first arrived in town we simply opened an account at the first bank suggested by a neighbor and were lucky that it happened to be a good one. Ours, for instance, provides free checking if $200 or more is kept in a savings account; usual rate for checking charges is 15¢ per check, $1 per month minimum, so we are saving at least $12 annually and also earning interest on the $200.

Instead of trusting to luck when you move to a new locale, visit several area banks and ask for their literature. Compare the services offered by each before you make a choice. Then ask colleagues and neighbors where they bank; you may thus discover that an institution offering acceptably good services has a reputation for frequent bookkeeping errors, which as it happens is true in our locale.

Christmas Clubs
%

Did you know that Christmas Clubs generally pay no interest (or *very* low interest) and that some actually charge *you* a fee for an early withdrawal? I know how holiday-cheering it is to be handed that huge chunk of money at the end of November, but if you can discipline yourself to make the same deposits in a savings account the chunk will be sufficiently larger to buy an extra gift or two.

Savings Accounts
%%

Interest-rate ceilings on savings accounts are federally regulated but banks can, and some do, pay less than the maximum. Methods of calculating and crediting that interest also differ.

On passbook savings (no minimum deposit, no time requirements), commercial banks (at this writing) may pay up to 5¼%, savings-and-loan associations up to 5½%, and credit unions up to 7%. When comparison shopping, ask the bank or credit union not only for the interest rate itself, but also for the "effective annual yield," which will take differences in compounding and days counted per year into account as well. For instance, at our commercial bank, passbook savings are compounded daily and yield $5.39 (rather than $5.25) on each $100 left untouched for a year; at a local savings and loan, the effective yield—$5.65; at our credit union, effectively $6.44. In general, look for an institution which will do as many of the following as possible:

1. Give you the highest effective annual yield
2. Pay interest from day of deposit to day of withdrawal or better (some banks have "grace" days whereby money deposited by the 10th of the month, for instance, earns interest as if it had been deposited on the 1st)
3. *Post* the interest most often (so that the interest is earning interest). Daily is best.
4. Charge no fees for withdrawal. (Ask about all charges.)

BARTER
%%%%%%%%%

Edward: "A hundred years ago, barter was common. I helped you repair your fence, you helped me split shingles was an exchange of labor; a veterinarian took payment in meat-curing, for example. We moved away from barter as the economy became more structured but the idea is still valid, I think, and it is a way of cutting a cash outlay by paying in service rather than dollars."

BATTERIES
$$$$

In addition to his less paranoid pursuits, my husband, John, is a Conspiracy Theory buff. Because his vocation is scientific research, this particular avocation stems, I suppose, from his obvious fascination with relationships. Conspiracy Theories, of course, don't require absolute hard evidence; they spring to life from perceived connections.

For Christmas, my children were given several electronic "learning" games. During the month following the holidays, as John headed out the door for replacement batteries (for the third time in as many weeks), he turned to me and said, "I think that manufacturers of household batteries are in league with manufacturers of battery-operated electronic gadgets."

We spent about $10 on batteries for such gadgets that month. When we bought our portable calculator, by chance rather than cleverness, we opted to also purchase the recharger offered with this particular model. I have just figured out that if I use the calculator nine to sixteen hours per week, recharging it for that use once a week, my operating costs will be in the range of three to four cents per year.

The point being that, given the option, purchasing a battery-operated, electrical device which is rechargable *with* recharger (typically $3 to $4), will afford you practically free use after the initial payback of only a couple of months.

BETTER BUSINESS BUREAU
%%%%%%%%

If you've read it once, I'll bet you've read it a thousand times— "Check with your Better Business Bureau." And if you are anything like me, you've thought yes of course, that makes sense, but the thought was never translated into action. Maybe, like me, you have later been sorry on occasion. That should have been the

BBB

time to register a complaint with the BBB, but I never did. Perhaps I felt a twinge of guilt for letting other consumers down this way, but I never really knew what I was missing.

What I was missing was more than a guilt-free psyche. What I was missing was the Better Business Bureau's help in settling the problem.

The Better Business Bureau, which has been in existence since 1914, in addition to providing a pre-check of a business's reputation, can help consumers recoup losses arising from doing business with disreputable (including both dishonest and simply incompetent) firms. These are the four major services provided:

1. If you call their office *before* you begin doing business with any company or organization you don't know, the BBB can pull from their massive files, and pass on to you, the following information: how long the firm has been in business, whether or not consumers have lodged complaints, the nature of the problems, and if/how they were resolved. They will not, however, make recommendations; the final decision is yours to deduce from the facts the BBB provides.

   This service applies to out-of-town businesses as well as local ones, through the BBB's nationwide network. It also includes maintaining files on organizations soliciting contributions. If a consumer call alerts them to the existence of such an organization not yet included in their files, the BBB immediately initiates an investigation.

2. Your call to the BBB *after* an unsatisfactory transaction can start you on the road to an acceptable resolution while adding to information files which will help future consumers. After hearing your complaint, the BBB will tell you whether or not it is the sort they can handle or suggest the proper place to take your problem. (The BBB does not give legal advice, test or appraise products or services, or handle complaints concerning pricing unless there is a misrepresentation involved.)

   If, however, your complaint does fall within their province, the BBB will ask that you put it in writing and will act as mediator between you and the firm in question. Additionally, if your complaint appears to be part of a pattern with any particular firm, the Bureau will follow up by sending one or more of their trained "shoppers" to investigate further.

3. The BBB regularly checks on advertising claims as well. Their experts watch for ads quoting unrealistically low prices, using misleading phrases, making deceptive or suspicious-sounding offers. When such are found, the Bureau sends its "shoppers" to investigate these potentially dishonest practices and by so doing encourages development of ethical ground rules. Businesses which continue to practice such activity will suffer the consequences of possible rejection when customers call for a beforehand check of the BBB's files.

4. The Bureau also publishes and distributes consumer information in the form of pamphlets. You can pick these up at any BBB office or, as an employee, from many member businesses. Or, send a self-addressed, stamped standard business-size (No. 10) envelope to:

Council of Better Business Bureaus, Inc.
1150 Seventeenth Street, NW
Washington, D.C. 20036

You may ask for up to five different single-copy pamphlets from the following list:

Tip Sheets

01245 Appliance Service
01206 Bait & Switch
01211 Buying by Mail
01283 Buying on Time
01292 Car Care on the Road
01248 Guarantees & Warranties
01286 Mail Order Shade Trees
01141 Home Insulation

BBB

Tip Booklets

02139   Automatic Transmissions
02247   Buying Used Cars
02230   Carpet & Rugs
02230   Drycleaning
02293   Encyclopedias
02140   Going Metric
02216   Home Fire Protection
02205   Home Improvements
02106   Home Improvements (Spanish)
02229   Home Study Schools
02219   Mail Order Profit Mirages
04113   Microwave Ovens
02239   Multi-Level Selling Plans
02111   Multi-Level Selling Plans (Spanish)
02207   Refunds and Exchanges
02107   Refunds and Exchanges (Spanish)
02244   Renting a Car
24146   Renting an Apartment
02256   Roof Coatings
02208   Sales Contracts
02108   Sales Contracts (Spanish)
02268   Slide Projectors
02236   Tires
02266   Water Conditioners
02204   Work-at-Home Schemes
02109   Work-at-Home Schemes (Spanish)
24154   Buying a Home
24153   Buying Furniture
03246   Car Repair
03201   Central Air Conditioning
03238   Health Insurance
03232   Computer Careers
03250   Hearing Aids
04135   Home Insulation
24155   Life Insurance
03227   Mobile Homes
02217   Saving Energy
03255   Selecting a Franchise

BICYCLES

Buying
$$$$$$$
%%%%%

We bought our son Zander his first very-own bike for his sixth birthday. He had contended for the previous two years with a $5 yard-sale bike handed down from his older brother, James. We had rewelded it, repainted it, and rewheeled it but no matter what we tried it still moved (even under the best of legs) like a snail. We finally gave up and decided to replace it.

I think John and I would have paid just about anything to see the look on Zander's face as he came barreling around the block toward us that first time on his birthday bike; his smile was a definition of joy.

In fact, we *had* been prepared to pay the price for a brand new bicycle—$100 at the time—and to disregard the blow to our finances. Because a child outgrows a bike in a year or two, we knew that purchasing a less-expensive used bike would have made the most fiscal sense but we were understandably wary, having been burned once at a stranger's yard sale, and knew of no other more reliable source.

John had bought, the previous summer, a bike of *his* own at a bicycles-only establishment in town and had been impressed with the shopowner's knowledgeableness and honesty. So that is where we began our search and where the search ended happily (for everyone) with the purchase of a bicycle which had been traded in, repaired (by professionals) to look and ride like new, *came with the usual guarantee*, and cost us $35.

Whether in the market for a new or used bike, shops which sell and service bikes exclusively should be your first stop. When deciding among several such shops, use the following criteria: a good one should include a tidy repair facility, should be able to answer all your questions, should ask how you expect to be using the bike (in order to sell you one which suits but doesn't exceed your needs), should accept trade-ins, assemble your new bike, provide a warranty, and give instructions concerning the bicycle's abilities and care. Department stores or stores which also sell lawn mowers and hardware may not do any of these things.

If you aren't very familiar with bicycles, it will behoove you, before beginning the search for a shop, to take a look at a book like *Bikes*, (The Chatham Press, Inc., Riverside, Connecticut 06878) by Stephen C. Henkel. This particular one, subtitled "A How-to-Do-it Guide to Selection, Care, Repair, Maintenance, Decoration, Safety, and Fun on your Bicycle," is exactly what it promises to be. It is also a nice present for a child (see next entry).

Repairs
%%%%%%%%

Edward: "The cost of having a family's worth of bikes repaired can, over the years, add up to a considerable sum. To cut down on this expenditure, I have encouraged my children to learn the basics themselves. Most bike repairs can be effected successfully at home, with relatively few and largely inexpensive tools, many of which will already be in the house. One of my boys has become so proficient at it that he is now the neighborhood consultant."

BIRTHDAY PARTIES
%%%%%%%%

If you have ever spent a small fortune on store-bought birthday-party fixings and favors, you may find that children themselves can give you ideas for low cost fun. Mine (who always begin by making their own invitations) have come up with wonderful (and inexpensive) suggestions over the years, including the two that follow. At one party, each child made and decorated a half-dozen cookies which went home as favors; at another, head-sized paper bags and plastic gallon milk jugs were collected for several weeks beforehand and during the party were cut and/or combined with construction paper to resemble *Star Wars* characters. The idea is that in lieu of playing traditional (and sometimes costly) party games, in order to win even more costly store-bought favors, the children participate in producing their own.

BOOKS

Free
$ $

%%%%%%%%

For me, life simply wouldn't be worth living without books. When I first met my friend Fritzi I quickly discovered that she felt the same way, so I was surprised the first time I visited her home. Expecting it to be wall-to-wall bookshelves, I found instead one shelf, three feet long. She uses the library extensively, almost exclusively. I have begun doing the same, though I still love a houseful of books. Now, however, when I come across a review or am told about a book that interests me, I get it first from the library. I buy it later if it is one I decide I simply *must* have under hand full-time. This has saved a lot of mistakes (and money).

Many libraries have access to other state systems and can locate and borrow nearly any book you are after, though occasionally the wait can be somewhat lengthy. I generally have requests in for several books at one time and thus never seem to be without for long.

In addition, our local library branch has given over a couple of shelves to neighborhood book traders. Patrons donate one, two, or three paperbacks they have finished and take the same number, in exchange, from these shelves. It is run on the honor system and the library is not involved except in providing the space. Ask if yours might do the same.

(See also COOPERATIVES—Libraries; LIBRARIES)

Hardcover, Reduced
%%%%%%

Our friend Lou stopped by recently to visit and brought a book he had just finished, enjoyed, and thought John would enjoy. We sat talking at the kitchen table.

"I usually wait until a book comes out in paperback before

buying it, but this was one I was too anxious to read to wait for, so I reluctantly forked over the hardcover price," said Lou.

We all, it turned out, deplored the fact that hardcover books had moved out of our range, but all liked the substantial feel of a hardback in our hand. "I keep a mental list of books I want to own and try to grab them whenever they pop up on remainder tables," I mentioned.

"Oh," Lou said, "that reminds me. I have discovered another source for hardcover at paperback prices, although the wait is just as long. When a bestseller or potential bestseller is bought in quantity by libraries, this is what happens to those books when the initial rush is over and there is no longer a need for the library to have lots of copies: the library sells them to companies like Tartan Book Sales which in turn resell them to the public. I'll get a copy of their catalog to you."

Lou is a reliable fellow; I had Tartan's catalog in my hand the next day. Get a copy yourself by sending a postcard requesting a catalog to:

Tartan Book Sales
500 Arch Street
Williamsport, Pennsylvania 17705

I quote, as follows, from the catalog Lou passed on to me:
"Tartan books are hardbound publishers' editions that have seen short-term library use. They've been protected by Plasti-Kleer Lifetime Book Jackets—and come to you that way. Our quality assurance staff inspects and approves each book before it's shipped to you.

"Titles selected are recent popular fiction and non-fiction from major publishers, including many bestsellers. They are not remainders or close-outs.

"The Tartan Book Sales Catalog is sent free-of-charge each month to libraries and individuals—for as long as you're interested. But you make no book-club style commitment, and there's never a minimum order of books. Each issue lists nearly 500 titles, with annotations describing them. Books may be re-listed as demand continues, but first-time entries are clearly indicated with an asterisk."

Lou said he had been completely satisfied with the condition of the books he had received (quite promptly, by the way) and certainly happy with the prices; for example, from the catalog he forwarded to me (January, 1980): Ted Morgan's *On Becoming American*, list—$10.95; Tartan's price—$2.98; James Jones's *Whistle*, list—$10.95, Tartan's price—$2.98.

Publishers' Overstocks
%%%%%%

"Remainders" are publishers overstocks and generally carry price tags well below original retail. According to my favorite book-store manager, Judy, it takes about a year (occasionally longer) for a hardback to reach the remainder tables after the paperback version appears. So, when I want to add such a book to my collection, I make a note of the paperback debut and begin checking about eight months later for the hardback nobody wants to pay hardback prices for anymore. Patience reaps this reward: reductions, generally, of 60% or more.

Another source of such publishers' overstocks, in addition to bookstores, offering a far wider selection is:

Publishers Central Bureau
1 Champion Avenue
Avenel, New Jersey 07131

Send them a postcard requesting that your name be added to their catalog mailing list. My friend Jane has been doing business with this company for many years and has nothing but praise for their promptness and accuracy in filling orders. Letters receive a quick response as do returns (for which refunds are prompt, no questions asked).

BOOTS
%%%%%%%%

Don't throw out those rubber boots your child tore running through the woods during the last snowfall. You can mend them with a bicycle-tube patching kit for less than a dollar.

BORROWING

The less collateral, the higher the interest rate (as a rule). In other words, money borrowed from a lending institution for an automobile loan (since a car is repossessable and easily resellable) will generally carry a lower Annual Percentage Rate (APR) than a consumer-goods loan (for such things as furniture, TVs, and the like—repossessable but not quite so easily resellable) which will generally carry a lower APR than a personal loan without collateral. But not invariably.

Many bank credit cards (like Master Charge and Visa) have APRs substantially lower on cash advances than do over-the-counter lending-institution personal loans or direct-goods purchase, although cash-advance credit lines are currently being lowered. This varies from state to state and should not be assumed, however.

And when contemplating purchase of, for instance, an appliance—even if you intend to buy it at a department store at which you have a credit account—it will behoove you, as several contributors wrote, to borrow the cash elsewhere at lower interest rates than the usual 18% charged at such stores.

In line with the collateral rule contributors suggested the following procedure for lowest interest loans: borrowing at an institution in which you have a savings account (for collateral)—called a passbook loan—can be a best buy. As one loan officer I spoke with (at a savings-and-loan association) explained: "Let's say you have a time-deposit account with us and you have decided to buy a car. Your losses on the savings account will be significant if you withdraw the money early. We will give you a loan, using your time-deposit account as collateral, at a rate substantially lower than an unsecured personal loan, *and*, you'll continue to earn interest on your savings, lowering your total interest charge even more."

Other low-interest possibilities include borrowing against stocks or bonds, or borrowing against the cash value of whole life-insurance policies (this will reduce your protection, however).

Also be aware that bank-interest rates are not absolutely fixed, they're negotiable in most cases. You will be most likely to haggle a lower rate than the usual if, in addition to collateral, you demonstrate stability of income and stability of residence. You will also find that, in general, the higher the amount loaned, the lower the interest rate.

Finally, if your debt level and credit rating make it impossible for you to borrow anywhere *except* from a finance company or auto dealership, you may be in financial trouble. See Section 2 of *Inflation-Wise* instead of taking out another loan.

(See also CREDIT UNIONS.)

Limiting Amount of Credit

My banker tells me that carrying a great deal of *unused* credit can work against you when you apply for a bank loan. Loan officers frequently count this available credit as debt; it *is*, after all, potential debt.

If you feel that it is important to have such credit available for use in case of real emergencies (such as being stuck out of town with a broken car, for instance), it still makes good sense to set upper limits on the amount.

My banker recommends that the limit be $1000 or about 20% of your yearly take-home pay—whichever is less. If you are offered credit beyond this amount, turn it down; if your limit is raised, unrequested, write and ask that it be lowered.

Limiting Credit Cards
%%%

There are a couple of good reasons to limit the number of credit cards you hold. First, on most such accounts, the interest rate drops after a certain debt level is reached (although currently this level is being raised), so you may find yourself paying 18% on ten accounts when you could be paying 12%, for a while, on one. Additionally, and importantly, it will be easier to keep track of your debt level if you are using only one or two cards and more difficult, psychologically, to wildly increase your debt (i.e., $50 on each of ten accounts doesn't *seem* nearly so much as the same $500 on one).

However, if you are finding yourself in need of employing such "tricks" more and more frequently, you might want to take a look at Section 2 in *Inflation-Wise*.

Professional Help for the Overextended

Section 2 of *Inflation-Wise* may provide you with the help you need to remedy an out-of-control debt situation. If not, you can get professional help by contacting:

The National Foundation for Consumer Credit
1819 H Street, NW
Washington, D. C. 20006

This organization will send you a list of nonprofit credit-counseling centers in your area where you can get assistance in setting up a realistic budget and formulating a plan for debt repayment (including, when necessary, intercession with your creditors).

BREAD

How-to for the Novice
$$$$$$$
%%%%%%

A decent loaf of store-bought bread (I don't mean air bread, I mean reasonably sturdy, solid, *good* bread) will cost you over a dollar (conservatively) for a 1½-pound loaf.

If you bake your own, it will cost you about 30¢ to 50¢ per loaf (1¼ to 1½ pounds), depending on ingredients—that's one-third to one-half as much (including the cost of cooking). You can judge any recipe's savings potential by assuming that every 2½ to 3 cups of flour called for will yield a loaf weighing about 1¼ pounds (20 ounces), though this may vary slightly depending on type of flour and additional ingredients used.

But perhaps you've never baked bread before, think it's extraordinarily time consuming or difficult. This entry was written for you. Please read on.

Re time—the actual work *you* will be doing (including clean-up) will take 30 to 45 minutes—less time with more practice. The rest of the work, spread over approximately three to four hours, will be done by the yeast. If a four-hour stretch of time is hard to come by in your household, you can stop the process at any point by freezing the dough, and picking up later where you stopped. The authors of *Laurel's Kitchen* (see full reference under **PROTEIN**) describe this process succinctly: "Suppose you've mixed your dough, and it's begun to rise, when suddenly you're called away. Just take the dough and divide it into loaf-sized lumps, flatten them into discs, wrap them loosely, and freeze them. If flattened, the dough will freeze (and thaw) quickly and evenly. Once it's thawed, allow it to rise and resume wherever you left off. You may leave the frozen dough in the refrigerator for weeks: the bread will be fine."

Re difficulty—baking bread is truly not as difficult as many people assume; you can make a lot of mistakes and still end up with something quite wonderful. And practice, as with most things, will quickly make perfect. Years ago a good friend who was nervous about plunging into bread-baking asked me to write out explicit directions for her. I put a lot of thought into explaining those parts of the process usually found in recipes as a single sentence, such as "Allow to rise in a warm place," i.e., telling *how* warm, *where*, etc.

The ingredients in the recipe below were provided by my friend Jane; the expanded how-to explanation is my own, telling you why whenever it's appropriate (just as I would if you were in my kitchen right now). Read the recipe through at least once before you begin—even several times, until it makes sense in every aspect. The method I've outlined, if followed reasonably closely, is reasonably foolproof. Once you've become proficient at this one, you'll be able to tackle any yeast bread recipe with confidence.

Basic White Bread Step by Step

1 scant tablespoon dry yeast (equal to one packet)
1 tablespoon sugar
2 cups of warm water (IMPORTANT: it should be between 100° and
    115° F.—"warm to the touch" books say; but skin sensitivity varies
    and the temperature at which the yeast will work—grow—and not be
    killed is crucial, so I recommend using a thermometer at first)
2/3 cup of nonfat dry milk powder
1 tablespoon salt
3 tablespoons vegetable oil
5 to 6 cups unbleached white flour

Be sure you have the following equipment at hand (the list
assumes nothing since I can't look into your cupboards):

Measuring cups
Measuring spoons
A thermometer (a candy thermometer will do if you have one but you
    may have to calculate backwards to figure out where 100° to 115°F.
    falls)
A couple of fairly large mixing bowls (one will do but you'll have to
    wash and δρω carefully between mixing and rising steps)
A wooden spoon
A wooden (cutting-type) board about 12 inches square or larger (a
    kitchen counter will also do but not as well)
2 loaf pans (8½ x 4½-inch size preferably)
A serrated-edge bread knife (optional)
A pair of clean hands (essential)

Proofing the Yeast
Combine the yeast, the sugar, and ¼ cup of the temperature-
tested water in a tall glass and give it a slight stir. Place this in your
unheated oven and on the shelf beneath place a pan of the hottest
water you can draw from the tap. Close the door and don't peek for
5 minutes. It should bubble up (double in volume) in 5 minutes
(10 at the most); if it hasn't after that time, the yeast is probably
dead. Begin again with a fresh batch or you will be wasting your
time. (For future reference—this proofing test won't be possible
in the absence of sugar.)

Mixing the Dough

Meanwhile, combine in a large bowl the milk powder, salt, and 3 cups of the flour. Add the oil, the proven yeast mixture, and another 1¾ cups temperature-tested water (use some of the water to rinse any residue of yeast out of the glass and into the bowl—you won't want to waste the least smidgen of this precious stuff).

Mix with a wooden spoon for a couple of minutes. Add 2 cups more flour and keep mixing, switching to use your hands eventually, till all 5 cups of flour have been incorporated.

Measure out the sixth cup of flour into a pie plate. You will use as little as necessary of this sixth cup to combat stickiness as you knead the dough. (The less flour you use, the lighter the loaf will be; the more proficient you become at kneading technique, the less long the dough will remain sticky.)

Kneading Is Next

I have scoured every cookbook on my shelves (that means dozens) and have been unable to find an adequate visual depiction of kneading to recommend. It's really quite a simple technique, but practically impossible to explain verbally (although I'm going to attempt it). It is best learned by watching someone do it, so my advice is to request a lesson from an accomplished friend—either a bread-baker or a potter (the "wedging" technique employed by potters is the same as kneading).

If you can't locate one or the other of these, read on: Kneading should be steady, rhythmical, and vigorous; it should be done standing with one foot slightly in front of the other, rocking back as you lift in Step No. 1 below, forward as you push and turn in Steps No. 2 and No. 3, employing your whole weight.

Sprinkle a couple of tablespoons of that flour in the pie plate onto a wooden board. Plop the dough out of the bowl onto the board and form it into a slightly flattened circle. Now:

1. Curl your fingers under the far side of the circle, lift up that edge and fold it over toward you (forming sort of a semicircle).
2. With the heels of both hands, arms now straight, press/push the dough down and away from you (i.e., toward the far side of the board).

54

3. Slide/turn the resulting disc/circle one-quarter turn (i.e., moving nine o'clock around to twelve o'clock).

Repeat and repeat and repeat steps 1 through 3 for about 8 to 12 minutes, dusting your hands and the board with flour only as much as necessary, until the dough takes on a satiny surface and is quite elastic (i.e., it should no longer be sticky and will spring back a bit if you push down on it and let go).

Once you get the hang of it you will find yourself, after the first few minutes of kneading, experiencing the sort of mellow high joggers speak of. (Baking bread regularly will strengthen your arms and calm your psyche.)

First Rise

Shape the lovely, live (it really is) dough into a ball and place it in an oiled, fairly deep mixing bowl, rolling it around to coat the surface with oil. Drape a clean dish towel over the bowl and set it in a warm place. The temperature should ideally be between 80° and 90°F. in this warm place, and it must be free of drafts. If the day and your kitchen are that warm, put the bowl in a cupboard. I have, however, found the oven method foolproof on any sort of day; as with proofing the yeast, place the bowl in an unheated oven, with, on the shelf beneath, a pan of the hottest water you can draw from the tap. Door closed.

It will take about an hour for the yeast to magically double the dough in bulk. (Actually the yeast is multiplying as it feeds on sugars in the dough, forming carbon-dioxide bubbles.) Check its readiness after an hour by sticking your fore and middle fingers into the top to about one-half inch; if doubled, the imprint will remain.

Second Rise

Punch the doubled-bulk dough, right smack in the center, with your fist. Fold the edges to the center with your fingers, breaking larger bubbles as you do so. (Some recipes will call for a second rising in the bowl at this juncture; in such a recipe, turn the dough bottom to top and proceed as in first rising.)

In this *Inflation-Wise* recipe, the second rising will take place in your loaf pans. Remove the dough from the bowl. Cut it in half (with a knife). Form each half into a loaf by rolling or pressing into

55

a rectangular shape on your wooden board, breaking any large air bubbles which appear. Then beginning at one end roll the rectangle into a tight cylinder, pinching the final seam and tucking in the ends. Place each loaf, seam down, in a well-oiled loaf pan (about 8 x 4-inch size.)

Return to unheated oven to once again double in bulk, using the same warming technique. This rising will take 45 minutes to an hour. The dough will rise almost to the top of the pans; press one finger in a corner to test for readiness. The imprint should remain.

The Baking

Remove the dough from the oven if it has been rising there. Preheat oven (a *must* in bread making, regardless of length of cooking time) to 400°F. Bake for 35 minutes.

Test the bread for doneness by turning each loaf out of its pan and rapping the bottom with your knuckles. It should sound hollow; if it doesn't, return to the oven for a few more minutes. Cool on a rack (so air can circulate) or you'll get a soggy bottom.

It's best to wait the half-hour or so until it's cool enough to slice, but the first few times you make it that may be next to impossible. A serrated-edge bread knife will make slicing hot bread easier.

And one final word about savings. This recipe will yield two 1¼-pound loaves costing 39¢ apiece (very conservatively, i.e., using *all* six cups of flour *and* 15¢ -per-packet yeast and estimating high on the cooking cost). But, don't be surprised to find that when you first begin baking bread, homemade loaves won't hang around very long. We once sat open-mouthed watching a neighbor (who had happened by as the bread came out of the oven) consume an entire loaf in a matter of minutes. But the novelty will wear off after a while and the savings will then begin to accrue.

And ah, how it will increase (and I don't mean just *inflationwise*) your standard of living.

Protein
%%%%%

You will notice, if you read store-bought bread labels, that to provide about 15 grams of usable protein (one-third, for instance, of a woman's daily requirement) would necessitate consumption of eight slices. To get the same amount of protein from only three slices, make your own favorite recipes, but substitute these protein heighteners for some of the flour:

Before filling each called-for cup measure with the recipe's recommended type of flour, spoon into the bottom
1 tablespoon soy flour
1 tablespoon dry-milk solids
1 teaspoon wheat germ

(Developed by Dr. Clive McCay at Cornell University, this is known as the Cornell Formula.)

The above idea for implementing Dr. McCay's research results was adapted from *The Joy of Cooking* (Irma S. Rombauer and Marian Rombauer Becker, The Bobbs-Merrill Company, Inc., Indianapolis, Indiana, first printing 1931, $12.95; it's also available, at slightly less than half that price, in paperback form from New American Library.) *Joy* is my basic mainstay cookbook because it includes plain (inexpensive) and fancy ways to cook almost anything imaginable as well as almost everything I've ever wanted to know about ingredients, how to "save" disasters, what to substitute when you find, halfway through a recipe, that you're out of something called for.

BUTTER

Cut It (and the Cost) but Keep the Taste
%%

My family and I think that nothing equals the taste of butter on fresh-cooked anything. Judging from quite a number of questionnaire contributors, we're not alone. We consider it one of life's necessities and have been paying the price for years.

I'm delighted to report, therefore, that during the course of my research I came across, tried, and found satisfying, a money-saving suggestion which has allowed us to continue enjoying the taste of butter but cut our cost by 25%. Here it is:

Blend equal parts of soft (not melted) butter and vegetable oil until smooth. (If you prefer salted butter, add ¼ to ½ teaspoon per cup of oil, according to taste.) Pour (yes, pour!) the mixture into a coverable container and refrigerate until it hardens, which takes about 3 hours.

This "cut" butter has the taste and creamy (rather than waxy) texture of butter but spreads as easily straight from the refrigerator as does margarine. Refrigerate as you would any butter when not being used.

If you use this technique for melted "butter," you may find that it separates out into its components, but a quick stir will remedy the problem, and you'll do right by your artichokes, popcorn, pan-fried steak or whatever.

Discount
%

I have truly racked my resources for a supplier of discount butter, but to no avail. My best advice is to watch for sales or lowered-price periods and buy as much as you can afford and have space to freeze. Butter will keep perfectly at zero degrees for six to eight months.

Margarine
%%%%%%

Even if you prefer the taste of butter that is spread or melted directly on food, you may find the difference in flavor between butter and margarine is largely obliterated by the cooking process and/or additional ingredients. This means you can substitute margarine for some or all of the butter called for in, for example, a cake recipe.

The savings can be substantial, since good margarine at usual prices is 50% less than butter, and margarine is one of those items which seems to be on sale often, discounted to half of that usual price.

CHARCOAL GRILLING
$
%%%%

My husband John is one of the best people ever born into this world. That's not just wifely partiality, it's true. You can ask anyone who knows him. He cares about people, is thoughtful toward their needs and feelings, in a way that makes the rest of us look like selfish beasts.

The thing he doesn't care about is money. I'm sure by now you've gotten the impression that he never filled out one of my questionnaires. Your impression was right. He'd have had nothing to say—for him, money is to spend (as often as possible on gifts), that's all.

I consider him a serendipitous saver. The penny-pinching he achieves is totally inadvertent, arising without a bit of forethought—out of some happenstance of life-style preference or a sudden need to jerry-rig somethingorother after the stores are closed.

And no matter how much I sweetly cajole or hatefully badger him, I'm beginning to think (after twelve years) that he'll never really change. Writing this, I realize that I hope I'm right. One penny-pincher per this household is more than enough.

Take charcoal for instance. It's a nuisance to empty out the grill after each use; John discovered that he could get two or three uses out of the same batch of briquets by closing the lid and vents right after the cooking was finished (this requires a grill with a lid obviously, but keep it in mind next time you're in the grill market). The charcoal works just fine a time or two more, cutting the usual 15-20¢ cost per grilling to 5-10¢.

And then there was the other night: We were out of starter and the nearby stores were closed. John took an empty cardboard egg carton, turned it inside out (so top and bottom then touched), and set it in the grill. He placed a briquet of charcoal in each egg place and lit the carton from the bottom; it worked perfectly, and cut starter costs from about 17¢ to 0¢.

"What a clever idea," I told him. "Perfect for *Inflation-Wise*," I told him. The next time he picked up groceries, he bought another can of charcoal starter.

But I ask you, how many men would eat those grilled hamburgers standing up, grimacing only thrice in as many

59

months? How many men would not just offer to share but actually assume all the kitchen duty while their wives typed nonstop all those months all over the kitchen table? I ask you, how many? What's money, after all? Maybe it's to spend.

CHOCOLATE
$
%%%

Cocoa and unsweetened cooking chocolate are derived from exactly the same source; the only difference between them being the cocoa butter content (lower in the former, higher in the latter).

So, you can save yourself some money by substituting for each 1 ounce (1 square in other words) of unsweetened cooking chocolate called for in your recipe, the equivalent—3 tablespoons cocoa plus 1 tablespoon fat.

A square (an ounce) of cooking chocolate at current prices is 25¢. The equivalent cocoa plus fat is:

> using margarine—16¢
> using shortening—16½¢
> using vegetable oil—17½¢
> even using butter, only—20¢.

(See COOKING—Cost of Ingredients, for more surprising price-comparison information.)

CLOTHES
%%%%%%%%

My mother likes to describe herself as a "string winder and a bag folder." In other words, she saves everything, like her father before her. Her father, an avid and accomplished gardener, died more than twenty years ago, leaving behind stacks and stacks of old gardening magazines. My sister was nine years old at the time and expected to be a ballet dancer when she grew up. In fact, she grew up to become a landscape designer and my grandfather's collection, saved all these years, now belongs to, and is used by, her.

How did my mother, who doesn't garden much herself, know that saving those gardening magazines for another twenty years was a sensible idea? She didn't, of course; "You just never can tell when this might come in handy."

Dyed-in-the-wool savers don't discriminate. I am still carting, from house to house, a box of first-grade papers my mother saved and sent me when I moved into my first apartment fourteen years ago. On the other hand, I was married in my mother's wedding veil. My third child, a girl (after two boys), came home from the hospital in the same robe and bonnet I wore home from the hospital thirty-six years ago. And my seven-year-old son Zander's favorite puzzle, a wooden jigsaw, was originally given to me on my seventh birthday.

Last month I was seized by one of my rare-as-snow-in-North Carolina housecleaning fits. Tidying the shambled bottom of my closet, I came across a pair of tall shiny brown patent-leather, really ugly, women's boots, circa 1960. They had been my mother's and I can't even remember now why she gave them to me (or why I accepted them). I wouldn't be seen in them even if they weren't too narrow to fit my feet. These are totally useless, I thought. I really should throw them out, I thought. Well, you never know, I thought without thinking, and replaced them neatly in the back corner of my now-tidy closet.

Last night, an as-rare-as-housecleaning snow began to fall on the North Carolina countryside and this afternoon it continues — ten inches predicted. The drifts are already deeper than the tops of my children's short rubber boots. My nine-year-old is outside, wearing mine. My seven-year-old, left behind, is crying. Remembering, I head for my closet. The boots, naturally, don't fit him very well, but well enough to stop the tears. You never know, I think, as I stand at the window watching the two of them making snow angels. Like my mother before me.

Mother's questionnaire came back with, among other things, a list of adages she figures were probably coined during the Depression. This was one:

"Fix it up, wear it out, make it do, do without."

Buying for Fit
%%%%%%%%

Sizes, in ready-made clothing, are not standardized; there seems to be a particularly wide variance, within any given size, in women's and children's clothes. It's maddening sometimes.

Shapes, in people, aren't standardized either. (It's delightful most times.) But a cut that looks terrific on one person may look dreadful on another even though the two might be the same weight, height, and coloring. It's something about the bones.

The point is: never, never buy clothes without first trying them on. They may look spectacular on the hanger but hang unspectacularly on you. Or they may be too small (and it's always easier to nip a seam in than to let it out). A bargain which hangs unworn in your closet is not a bargain.

Buying for Flexibility
%%%%

I was absolutely dumb-struck the first time I had a peek into Elizabeth's closet. She's one of those people who seems always to have exactly the right thing to wear for every occasion; but her closet was practically empty. (It seemed particularly so, compared to mine which, at the time, tested the laws of clothes-rack physics vs. gravity.)

Here's how she does it: "To keep my wardrobe as flexible and as useful as possible, I try to buy clothes which will span more than one season; for example, a medium-weight medium-range-color wool suit can be worn on all but the hottest of summer days, long-sleeved shirts can be worn all year (in summer, with the sleeves rolled up).

"I've found that buying tops and bottoms (skirts and shirts and pants and blazers) rather than one-piece items like dresses or jumpsuits affords me the most mixing mileage.

"I buy major items strictly in solid colors and choose only the colors I really love. That way just about everything 'goes' with everything else. But I can make the same combination look totally different by adding a striped or printed vest or scarf (within my general color scheme, of course) and keep costs down since these are less expensive items. Inexpensive jewelry is what I use to dress up an outfit."

I learned a great deal from Elizabeth that day, and am grateful (as is my clothesbar). I would add one thing more which my mother taught me: buy classic styles, and you will still be wearing them years from now.

If you always thought "classic" meant peter-pan collars and A-line skirts (as I once did), take a minute to rethink: what it really means is avoiding extremes. A skirt that's softly gathered rather than really full, pants that are gently flared or straight rather than widely so or pegged are clothes you will likely feel comfortable in year after year.

(See also FASHION for some words about hemlines and more about feeling comfortable.)

Buying for Quality

Anybody who sews will tell you that to check the quality of ready-made clothing you should begin by turning it inside out. Look for:

1. At least half-inch seams preferably sewn with 10 or more stitches to the inch. The stitches should look identical on both sides of the seam allowance or they'll soon pull out. There should be no puckers, pulls, or loose threads.
2. At least a 2-inch hem.

Then, turn it right side out again and check for:

1. Buttonholes which are reinforced at the ends. And, though even otherwise well-made clothing won't always comply— remember that buttonholes placed vertically rather than horizontally have a tendency to unbutton themselves at inopportune moments.
2. The pattern on print, striped, or plaid fabric should match where seams meet.
3. Garment should be cut on the straight of grain or true bias (diagonal) or it won't hang properly.
4. Top stitching (any stitching which actually shows on the outside) should be neat, even, and precise and not pucker the fabric anywhere. I reject more ready-made garments on this one point than any other.

Buying for Style
%%%%%%%%

Before I make any substantial ready-made purchase (assuming a garment is well made, fits my body and my budget) I ask myself five questions:

1. Will it mix well with other things in my wardrobe?
2. Does it avoid duplicating anything I already have?
3. Are the lines simple enough so that I would have felt comfortable wearing it two years ago?
4. Can I expect to wear it enough times to justify the cost?
5. Most important—is the idea of living without it unthinkable?, i.e., Do I *love* it?

A single "no" constitutes a veto. It's a system that has saved me a lot of money on potential impulse and desperation purchases.

Care
%%

Uncle Beeze: "Where do you think all that lint comes from in an automatic clothes dryer? It's the fabric slowly wearing out. To make all clothing last longer use your 'solar drier'—clothes pins, line, and outdoor sunshine.

"And while we're on the subject of fresh air, remember that wool garments require hand washing or dry cleaning less often if allowed a day to breathe in an airy space and return to shape between wearings."

Care of Handmade
%%%%%%%%

If you sew, be sure to ask for the correct permanent-care label when you buy your fabric; then sew it into the garment's waistband or seam when you're making it, so that all your money-saving effort and careful work won't be wasted the first time the garment is washed.

Drycleaning
%%%%%%

Mother: "Did you know that many laundromats also provide dry-cleaning machines? I have cut my dry-cleaning costs by two-thirds by using these coin-operated machines for those items—sweaters, etc.—which don't require special pressing or steaming."

Drycleaning *versus* Handwashing
$$$$$

Cinda: "Almost anything can be hand-washed instead of dry-cleaned. I do sometimes send very bulky coats to the cleaners, but everything else (unless the lining isn't washable—and I make a point to avoid such linings) including all my wool and silk items is washed in cold-water soap in my sink or bathtub. Even leather gloves can be washed—I simply put them on and wash as if washing my hands; then I dry them away from heat and, since drying will render them stiff, and the water will temporarily darken them, I later knead them back to their original softness and color."

Handmade
%%%%%%%

Really, when you think about it, ready-made clothes are a modern convenience. And as with any convenience—food or repair services or whatever—you pay a premium for letting someone else do the work for you.

Anyone can learn to sew and the savings can be substantial. I don't mean to imply that suddenly you will be making coats and suits and tailored shirts; it will probably take considerable practice on the basics before tackling that sort of thing. But why pay $20 for a simple wraparound skirt (no buttons, no zippers, no fancy handwork) when you can make it yourself for $4?

Inexpensive classes abound these days at technical and high-school evening sessions. Your Cooperative Extension Service is probably giving a course at this very moment. Or ask an accomplished friend to teach you. (You could tune up her car or something, in exchange.)

It would be smart to borrow some friend's machine while you are learning; don't buy one until you are sure sewing is something you will enjoy.

If you like sewing and you have children, you might want to take a tip from my neighbor Jackie, who is the very smart mother of a teenager: "I taught my daughter to sew at age seven; at age thirteen she makes most of her own clothes." Think about it.

Choosing Patterns
%%%%%%%%

The risk you take in sewing-your-own rather than picking something (usually more expensive) off the ready-made rack is that you can't try it on before you fork over your money. I think there are ways to minimize that risk by learning to see, really *see*, what you are looking at in a pattern book (and as a bonus, it's a talent you'll find useful in other pursuits as well).

The techniques involved in the sewing process itself will probably not be as difficult for most people to master as will be learning to look at a pattern sketch and *know* how the finished garment will look on you. Sewing won't be inflationwise, rather quite the opposite (in addition to maddening) if you consistently end up with clothes which neither feel nor look good on you. It's my intention, in this entry, to teach you how to avoid most such costly mistakes.

First, complete your sewing course (or read a how-to-sew book). You will then be familiar with the terms.

Set aside a bit of time for an analysis session. Remove from your closet of ready-made clothing two or three of your favorite garments and two or three of your least favorite in each of the following categories: shirts and/or blouses and/or tops; dresses; skirts; slacks or pants and shorts; suit jackets and/or blazers; vests. Be sure to include any garment made in your sewing class, whether you loathe it or love it.

Now, one category at a time, try each garment on in front of a full-length mirror. Compare and analyze the differences between those you especially like *on you* and those you don't particularly like. Make written notes of your preferences and the design "whys" behind your choices; you will end up with a list of specifics to look for (or to avoid) in future pattern-picking. Use the following (as applicable) to help guide your analysis:

Shirts or blouses or tops

Collar—is it attached directly to the neck or is there an intermediate collarband? How wide is the collar itself and how acute is the angle of the collarpoint? Is it notched or rounded or shawl?

Shoulders—dropped or vertical?

Armholes—if sleeveless, capped or extended or vertical?

Sleeves—how full? how long? how wide a wristband? Are they raglan or set-in or an extension of the bodice pieces? Puffy or tailored?

Neckline—V or round or square?

Closure—buttons on bodice piece itself or front band? Zipper front or back? Placket with or without hardware?

Cut—full (loose), semifitted, or close-fitting? And by means of darts or curved seams?

Darts—are they parallel to the bustline or at an angle beginning somewhere below or missing altogether? Are there tapering waistline darts?

Length—one of the nice things about sewing is that length is *your* choice and easily adjustable (but changes must be made before cutting, of course), so look now and note what you like.

Dresses

All of the applicable above plus:

Pockets—included or not? Opening along the seam or patch?

Skirts

Waist—how are the darts, if any, angled and where are they placed?

Style—A-line, gathered, straight, or flared?

Cut—bias or straight grain?

Closing—zippered or buttoned? Where placed?

Pockets—included? In the seam, patch or trouserlike (angled in toward waistline)?

Length—see notes under shirts.

Slacks, pants, or shorts

All of the applicable above plus:

Cut—straight, flared, or pegged? Full or fitted waist?

Jackets or blazers

Any of the applicable above plus:

Collar and lapels—notched or rounded or shawl type or collarless? Lapels wide or narrow?

Pockets—patch or welt, real or apparent?

Back or side vents; lining; shoulder pads—present or absent?

Cut—loose or semifitted or close fitting? If fitted, by means of darts or curved seams? Length?

Vests

All applicable above, particularly lining, type of closure (and whether hardware is present or absent), shape of neckline and hemline, and length.

By the end of this exercise you should have a reasonably clear idea about the sort of fit and cut and length you like and about what part various styles of necklines and collars and dartlines have played in your preferences. You will now be much better equipped for pattern-sketch analysis.

Initially, you may find it easier to choose patterns which are pictured on live models. Be sure the photographs show everything you want to know about the design specifics you have discovered above: sometimes ill-proportioned style is obscured by hands or arms or props or by photographing at odd angles.

As a beginner you will want to start with simple garments, which you will quite often find in the budget section of pattern books (a nice bonus) and which are almost invariably shown on real people in photographs. However, keep the information you've learned in the above self-examination of style in mind when making clothes from these sections.

I must add one final, personal note: my sister Cinda and I have accumulated between us about fifty-five sewing-years of practice. And both of us still occasionally make pattern-choice mistakes. But we have both found that with Butterick and Vogue patterns in particular, what you see is almost always what you get. This is a tremendous plus unless you allow wishful thinking to get in the way—e.g., if the sketch indicates boxy shoulders and you don't like boxy shoulders *on you*, don't choose that particular pattern—

your wishful thinking won't make them round, they'll come out boxy just as the sketch promised.

These two companies also include, in the pattern book and on the pattern envelope, a most thorough and precise description of the design details. Be sure to read these before you buy, as a final check—c.g., if they say loose-fitting, they really mean it.

Enjoy!

Inexpensive or Free Patterns
$$
%%%%

Watch for (and ask your fabric store about) pattern sales. It happens quite regularly in my locale that patterns go on sale for half price. I would recommend, however, doing your *choosing* at an earlier time, when the store is likely to be less crowded. Write down the numbers of the patterns you like and hang onto your list. (When the sale day arrives, you can quickly recheck your choices by looking up the number in the index in the back of the given pattern book.)

You will often find patterns in the "suits" section of pattern books which include several garments (e.g., vest and suit with slacks and skirt). These are usually slightly more expensive than single-garment patterns, so try to find one in which you like more than one of the pieces.

Our branch library has initiated a pattern-lending file. Used ones are donated; patrons borrow patterns as they do books. Libraries that do not already include such a service might be open to the suggestion from *Inflation-Wise* readers.

And consider your friends as pattern sources. Some of my favorite garments were made from patterns offered and loaned by friends, and as a bonus this is an instance where you *can* try it on before you buy. And I do the same for them when I come up with a winning pattern. Variation in fabric choices keeps us from looking like clones.

In fact, when you find a pattern you really love don't hesitate to make it in several fabrics and/or lengths. A perfect pattern can be a joy forever.

Fabrics

Just as important as choosing a pattern is suiting fabric to design. Your pattern envelope will offer fabric suggestions, but they will be fairly wide-ranging. Walk around the fabric store and freely touch; feel each fabric you are considering, bunch up a corner for a few seconds and let go to find out if it wrinkles, lift up a section and look to see how it hangs (flowingly or stiffly), hold it up to the light to see if it's opaque, check the fiber content and the cleaning-care instructions.

It is possible that this perusal will tell you everything you need to know, but an error in judgment can be an expensive way to learn. I think the best way to find out what various fabrics can and cannot do, and how to suit fabric to pattern, is to ask a knowledgeable friend to accompany you to a fabric store and teach you. Sales clerks in such stores can sometimes be helpful, too, but their time may be more limited.

After you have been sewing for a while, try looking for fabric at five-and-dimes (some of the best retail buys are there, my Aunt Rutie, the best seamstress I know, writes), but you should go into these stores knowing what you are about because the sales clerks often know nothing about sewing and the fabric-content information is not always available. Yard sales, thrift shops, and remnant tables can also offer bargains but usually under the same conditions.

Notions
%%%%%%%%

Buttons and zippers can constitute an objectionably large proportion of the cost of making a garment. Sometimes the choice of just the right notions can make such a big difference in the total final effect that you will count the button cost as worth the price. (I once made a dress for which I paid $3 for the sale fabric and sale thread and another $3 for the buttons, but any old buttons wouldn't have worked. Six dollars is still not bad for a dress!)

However, there will be many times when any old button or zipper *will* do, or when in fact you already have the perfect trimmings on an old dress—so save by using your old notions, as my friend Jackie suggests: retain the ones from clothes about to hit the ragbag or the trash, and pick up unusual ones for pennies from otherwise unusable garments found at yard sales.

Children's
%%%%%%%%%

My three-year-old daughter, Max, has such an extensive wardrobe I could do her laundry once a month and she could still wear something new every day. I say "new," but actually that's a misnomer. Only a handful of her clothes, gifts from grandmothers mainly, began their useful lives in the McLachlan household.

Ninety-nine percent are hand-me-downs from "older" friends. And because she dearly loves her older friend Katie, the dress she's wearing which was once Katie's is not "old," it's special. (Katie's mother finds it special to see Max in it, too; a memory jogger.) So everybody wins. What could be a better bargain than free? Although our family has been fortunate enough to have received hand-me-downs for all of our children through the years, as they get older and more active, the hand-me-down rate decreases as the wear-out rate increases. Eventually (if not before) clothing must be bought.

An excellent source for us has been our local thrift shop (run by the PTA here, the Junior League, and other service organizations elsewhere) where used and some new department-store remaindered clothing is tax-deductibly donated and resold to raise funds for the sponsor's work. The prices range from 5¢ for a pair of socks to 75¢ for a pair of good winter school pants—not bad.

On those rare occasions when I must buy brand new clothes for my children, I look for top quality. I don't mean high price necessarily (though extremely *low* prices often go hand in hand with cheap construction). In general, the clothes I've found to be most durable (which is the particular "quality" I am after)—well-made, of good strong fabric—have fallen in the medium-price range.

Edward: "Because we purchased quality clothing for our oldest child (of four, all boys), most of his clothing has passed through *many* lives. My boys also happen to have fourteen male first cousins, almost *all* of whom have worn the recirculating hand-me-downs."

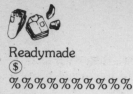

Readymade
$

%%%%%%%%

I think it's an inflation-wise practice to take your kids along when buying their clothes and shoes—and that it is important to listen and heed when they say they don't like something or that it's uncomfortable. Otherwise, you may find that your bargain buy is no bargain—it may never make its way out of the closet.

Recycling

Cinda: "I bought a beautiful, expensive (very) overcoat—wool with the warmest rabbit lining—about fourteen years ago, which I wore to bitter shreds I loved it so much. Last year, while playing in the snow, the rabbit lining fell out in the street, and though my friends pronounced it dead I couldn't give it up to the trash heap so I packed it in my cedar chest and replaced it with an equally elegant cape (made for me by a marvelous seamstress I know out of fabric left over from my old high school cheerleading uniform—many more than fourteen years old—wool).

"A few weeks ago I ran across that old coat and realized the perfect place to recycle the usable pieces of that marvelous warm rabbit lining—into the hood of my cape.

"My moral—never throw anything away; save and recycle."

Dyeing
%%%%%%%

Jane's husband, Oliver, told me that when his brother was being discharged from the Marine Corps ten years ago, he was about to discard his 100% heavyweight wool military green overcoat. Oliver asked for and was given it. He promptly took it to a dry cleaner, had them dye it black, and has been enjoying its warmth ever since.

I thought this a marvelous idea for making something new from something old. I did have some difficulty, however, locating a dry cleaner willing to take on the job. The one I finally found sends the work out (to a nearby state). Dyeing a coat, the owner said, is costly. "How much?" "About $25." "Pretty inexpensive for a new coat." "Well, I guess, if you put it that way."

Your color choice would be limited, of course, to those darker than the original. Black, he told me, gives best results. Be sure you choose a dyer who provides a satisfaction-guaranteed guarantee.

It occurred to me that home dyeing of less cumbersome items would also provide new looks. One of the cleaners I spoke to (formerly a dyer), made these suggestions for doing the job like the professionals:

1. Heat the water to at least 160°F and dissolve the dye in it. Place the garment in the pot, keeping the temperature up and stirring constantly for 10 minutes.
2. Heat clean water to 160°F and add rock salt (about ¼ cup per large pot). Immerse and stir the newly dyed garment for 8 minutes to set the color.
3. Rinse in cold water until all excess dye is gone and the water runs clear.

If You Sew
%%%%

I suspect that whoever coined the adage "waste not, want not" must have known my Aunt Rutie. She's a recycler of the first order, installing water savers in shower and sinks many years before the idea became popular, refurbishing rather than replacing her house furnishings (inherited or bought used in the first place, of course), and so on and so on. And this is the most unique, my favorite—recycling hair trimmings into pin cushions (made with fabric scraps, naturally); she says that the oil in the hair keeps pins and needles from corroding, so she never has to replace them either. Her reverence for the workings of earth and people warms me. (She was the contributor who suggested that I use the word "handmade" re clothing, rather than "homemade." You see the difference?) Makes me feel glad we're members of the same family.

"Don't discard slightly worn-out dresses," says Aunt Rutie. "There are lots of recycling possibilities. When the top wears out, remake the bottom into a skirt; when the bottom wears out, do the reverse; when the hem of a long skirt gets ragged, make it into a short one. You can get a lot of years of wear out of a single garment."

If You Don't Sew
%%%%%%%

Barrie and Marlowe returned my long questionnaire brimming enthusiastically with ideas and delightfully punctuated with sketches and verbal choreography. On one of the final pages, I had asked contributors, "How do you stay happy even when you're broke?" Barrie is a painter, Marlowe is a dancer, and their income is sporadic and unpredictable. They're probably "broke" more often than anyone else we know. But this is how they answered that question: "See previous pages." It was true.

It occurs to me as I write this that "we can't afford it" is a phrase I've never heard either of them utter. Instead they immediately propose a less expensive or free alternative—equally or more satisfying. It's a remarkable facility and one that has allowed them to structure their lives so that they make money to live, but have never lived (and never will live) to make money. We treasure their friendship immensely.

Typical of their imaginative positive approach is this from Barrie: "I've found that a few easy changes in an old dress—nipping in the waist via a belt, or removing a belt or adding or removing shoulder pads, for instance—makes it brand new and I usually get the most 'oohs and ahs' from this make-over variety. It's the patina, I think."

Sales
%%%

Traditional sale months are:
    Coats—January, April, August, October, November
    Men's and Boy's Clothing—January, April, May
    Resort Wear—January, November
    Shoes—January, July, December
    Hosiery—February, April, June

Women's Suits—February
Sportswear—February, June
Sleepwear—April
Lingerie—May, October
Handbags—May
Fabric—April, June, July, September, November
Children's Clothes—July

Winter Clearance—February, December (late in month)
Summer Clearance—August
Fall Fashions—August, October

Cass: "Because so much clothing is season- and style-dependent, I find that the very *best* buys are available during the month just following the traditional sale month. The selection isn't quite as good but is still adequate and I almost never pay more than 50% of the original price by sticking to this strategy."

COFFEE

Beans
Ⓢ

John and I consider good coffee one of life's necessities, so we're apt to spend more than others might on it. But when we're really broke, we buy the best supermarket brand and a small amount of one of the darker roasts from our local specialty shop, then mix a small amount of the latter with a majority of the former.

Keeping It Warm
$$$
%%

If you find yourself very often throwing out the overcooked coffee at the bottom of the pot you've left on the stove or coffee-maker warmer, buy a thermos and keep your coffee in that. It'll not only save money on wasted coffee but save energy money as well.

Making It
%%%%%%%

If you make coffee an equal number of times each day, your energy costs will be approximately equal (about $4 per year if made once per day), whether you use an automatic coffee-maker or pour the boiled water by hand through a filter cone.

The latter can be obtained initially at about one-third to one-tenth the average cost of the former, however. And friends have told us that their automatic coffee-maker elements have sometimes burned out after only a year or two of use.

There are expensive hand-drip systems, of course, but if you avoid the breakable variety (i.e., ceramic, glass, or lightweight plastic) and limit your choice to the high impact plastic kind (like 'Roma Cone by David Douglass) dripping the coffee into whatever container you happen to have on hand (we use the bottom part of a twelve-year-old percolator) you will have made an inexpensive purchase which should last a lifetime. Our 'Roma Cone, (manufactured by Rockline, Inc., P. O. Box 1007, Sheboygan, Wisconsin 53801) has been used two or three times a day for the past ten years and shows no sign whatsoever of burning out.

Storing It
%%

Edward: "You can often save substantial amounts by buying coffee in large quantities, but if it goes stale before it is all used the savings are not smart. This can be avoided by storing coffee, tightly covered, in the freezer in a nonporous (i.e., not paper) container."

CONSUMER PROTECTION

Published Resources

Consumer Reports and other Consumers Union publications (and doings) can go a long way toward helping you avoid purchase of merchandise and services about which you will later be sorry. (See how under CONSUMERS UNION.)

There are other good sources that do no product testing but do include well-researched consumer information *re* making intelligent choices in the marketplace, recognizing typical fraud tactics when you see them, and complaining when you don't and are victimized, in such a way that you will be sure to get your due.

The public television series "Consumer Survival Kit" was excellent; unfortunately it didn't survive. But "CSK's" weekly printed information kits, offered to viewers at the close of each show, are still available in the reference section of many libraries.

Another good resource is:

Getting What You Deserve: A Handbook for the Assertive Consumer
by Stephen Newman and Nancy Kramer
Doubleday/Dolphin, New York, 1979
$8.95

Consumer Self-Protection
%%%%%%%%

Uncle Beeze: "Save receipts! About nine months ago, I bought a pair of jeans on sale which were warranteed for a year's normal wear. A month ago the seams began to come apart and I simply went to my receipt file, located the sales slip to which I'd attached the warranty card, and returned the jeans to the store. Today I found a refund from the manufacturer in my mailbox for not the sale price but the *full* price of the jeans!—and I'd had nine months' free wear of them to boot."

CONSUMERS UNION
%%%%%%%%%

Consumer Reports is worth its weight in gold (and I mean gold at today's prices). The monthly magazine by that name, the December *Buying Guide* Issue (which includes summaries of the previous year's major product reports as well as pertinent reports, updated, from previous years), and the single subject books (such as *Guide to Consumer Services*, *Guide to Used Cars*, etc.) are all published by Consumers Union.

This nonprofit organization's purpose is to test and research products and services and provide consumers with the unbiased results, so that we can make wise purchasing choices which would otherwise be impossible. Consumers Union accomplishes this on an income derived solely from the sale of its publications; it accepts no advertising, no product samples, and, importantly, it will take measures to prevent—even prosecute—anyone attempting to capitalize commercially on its rating results. Each report provides basic general-product information, as well as safety considerations, and in addition names names and prices and rates quality. Quite often the top-rated products are not the most expensive.

CR was at the top of every comparison-shopping resource list I received, without a single exception. Our own family experience bears out this wisdom. To cite just one example, twelve years ago, newly married, John and I were in the market for a vacuum cleaner. We headed straight for the library to check *CR* and discovered that one canister model was listed as a "Best Buy"—meaning that among other highly rated models, this one was also priced very reasonably (as I recall, about 50% below the others). It has only recently begun to wear out (cost per year, about $6). Meanwhile, at the height of one of our pregnancies six years ago, John thoughtfully bought us, as a surprise, a new upright vacuum, thinking it would save me a bend or two. The thought was very dear, but the price was also dear; *CR* wasn't consulted in this case (which would have steered us to a highly rated model, comparable in price, I later discovered) and that vacuum literally fell apart three years later.

Many people would not consider buying a car before first consulting the annual *CR* car-buying issue (April's) or consider buying an appliance without first consulting the *Buying Guide*. But some of those same people may be missing great bargains and wasting many dollars by not checking *CR's* test results for less costly items: for instance, the taste and nutrition ratings of many, many food items such as breakfast cereal, spaghetti sauce, tunafish (which include cost per serving for easy comparison shopping between top-rated brands); or durability ratings for rubber gloves (of three equally top-rated brands, one may be twice as expensive as another); or folding chairs (where it might surprise them to discover how many brand names are made by a single manufacturer).

The monthly publication *Consumer Reports* ($1.25 each, January through November, at newsstands) including the enlarged December *Buying Guide* issue ($3.50 at newsstands), is available by subscription ($12 per year). For information, write to:

Consumers Union
Consumer Reports
P.O. Box 1000
Orangeburg, New York 10962

A current price list/order form for single-subject publications, which presently includes the titles previously mentioned (*Used Cars*, *Consumer Services*) as well as *Funerals: Consumers' Last Rights*, *Money-Saving Guide to Energy in the Home*, *Licit and Illicit Drugs* to name only a few, and back issues, too, can be obtained from:

Consumer Reports Books
Department B129
Orangeburg, New York 10962

Contributors to *Inflation-Wise* (including me) rate Consumers Union publications "Best Buys."

CONTAINERS

Getting the Dregs
%

My mother writes to suggest that you can get a last couple of servings from your ketchup or hand lotion bottle by propping it upside down.

My sister Heather writes to suggest that you can get a couple of extra teeth brushings by cutting off the end of your toothpaste tube when it's nearly empty.

And Elizabeth points out that make-up (such as base, mascara, and eye shadow) in cake form lasts much longer than that which comes in tubes or roll-ons or sprays. The principle is widely applicable.

Orifices
%%

My neighbor, Bart, is a pharmacist. While I was preparing my entries on toiletries and drugs, I was calling him almost daily for technical and pricing information. It turned out that he had a personal observation that he had always wanted to put into print.

The large size, he told me, isn't always a better buy than the smaller size. I replied, gently I hope, that yes, the unit price will sometimes surprise you. No, he didn't mean that. What he meant was more subtle and I believe could only have come from someone who spends the better part of his day measuring.

Larger sizes, he has noticed, quite often have larger application orifices (sometimes *much* larger) than smaller sizes. "For example," said Bart, "the application surface of the 3-ounce size of a well-known brand of stick deodorant is a full half-inch longer and quarter-inch wider than that on the 2-ounce size. A certain popular after-shave lotion sports an opening the size of a half-penny on the 4-ounce container, the size of a pencil point on the 2-ounce.

"The point is," he says, "do you measure out toothpaste by circumference of application or by the length of your toothbrush?

80

Do you measure out deodorant by precise amounts or by underarm sweeps? Do you measure out after-shave by the quarter-ounce or by number of squirts?"

When you notice this orifice-size difference on products you use, try each of the two sizes consecutively and, in each case, date your purchase, Bart suggests. That way you will be in a position to figure cost per daily use ($\frac{price}{days\ used}$), rather than cost per ounce, which might very well be deceiving. When the orifice is twice as large you may use it twice as fast.

CONVENIENCE FOODS
%%%%%%%

One of the especially nice experiences connected with the writing of Inflation-Wise *has been the opportunity of getting back in touch with people I haven't seen (or even written to) in years. Some of them, like Julia, were friends of my parents and my tendency is to remember them as they were and their children as they were.*

Cinda and I used to babysit for Julia's children; the oldest of them is now a practicing architect (difficult to believe it's been that many years, but then Cinda and I are practicing more lucrative professions than babysitting these days, too).

Julia, in her questionnaire and letter, still sounds the same as I remember her though—exuding warmth, hearth, and home. In my mind's eye she's always in an apron and a smile, in her sunny kitchen. She's teaching full-time now, so what I'm seeing must be on a Saturday or Sunday, and she's in a different kitchen. But she's still, I have no doubt, cooking from scratch.

"A neighbor," writes Julia, "calls convenience foods 'stone soup mixes.' (In the Stone Soup fable villagers complain that they have nothing with which to make soup. A visitor suggests they make stone soup. He places a kettle of water over the fire and adds stones. As it cooks he mentions that a little carrot, a little potato, a little onion, an old bone, etc., would improve the flavor. The villagers find these ingredients and a very edible stone soup is the result.) For most convenience foods you buy the mix and then *you* add all the expensive ingredients." Julia recommends the following book:

Pure and Simple
by Marion Burros
Berkley Books, 1978
$2.95 (paper)

which is mostly about cooking from scratch to avoid additives, but includes a chapter called "A Few 'Convenience' Recipes." Among them the following one (Julia's especial recommendation):

Shake It and Bake It
(enough for 6 pounds of chicken)

1   cup flour
2   teaspoons salt
1   teaspoon pepper
½   cup cracker crumbs
1   teaspoon herbs (thyme, oregano, basil or a mixture)
Milk or water

Combine dry ingredients, stirring to mix. Use half the mixture for 3 pounds of chicken. Reserve remainder in a tightly covered container. Moisten the chicken with milk or water. Shake chicken pieces with mix, a few at a time, in a paper bag. Bake in greased shallow pan at 350° F. for 45 minutes to 1 hour.

Cost (calculated by Christopher): 15¢ .
Cost of commercial product (equivalent amount): $1.00 (in both cases, *you* add milk and chicken).

My friend Jane suggested that *Inflation-Wise* readers might want to take a look at one or more of the following cookbooks as well:

Mother's in the Kitchen
edited by Roberta Johnson
La Leche League International
Franklin Park, Illinois, 1971
$4.00

which includes a good recipe for bulk "instant" Biscuit Mix, among other basics;

The Pepperidge Farm Cookbook
by Margaret Rudkin
Atheneum, 1963, $12.50

which includes a whipped topping recipe made with dry milk that her family finds quite acceptable at a fraction of the cost of purchased topping or topping made with the high-priced dairy product;

The Feingold Cookbook for Hyperactive Children and Others with Problems Associated with Food Additives and Salicylates
Helene and Ben Feingold
Random House, 1979
$10.00 (hardcover), $5.95 (paper)

for their Southern Biscuit Refrigerator Dough to make in bulk and use for a week, and more.

The point is that cooking from scratch will generally be less expensive than cooking with purchased convenience foods and that recipes such as those cited above make that scratch cooking equally convenient. There are some exceptions but these may have other drawbacks; cake mixes, for instance.

Many contributors wrote to say that they had begun (again) baking cakes from scratch in order to cut costs. Well, I was as surprised as they may be to discover that when I actually totted up the cost of fresh ingredients, I found that the price of mixes was competitive.

However, when you bake a cake from scratch you will likely use some combination of these ingredients: 100% cocoa or chocolate, flour, baking powder, salt, sugar, butter, eggs, milk, vanilla. When you bake from a mix you will probably also be including most of these ingredients: dextrose, soybean oil or palm oil or cottonseed oil, cocoa processed with alkali, propylene glycol monoesters, sodium aluminum phosphate, monocalcium phosphate, lactosterin, modified food starch, and artificial flavoring. Need I say more?

COOKBOOKS
$$
%%%%%%%%

My friend Fritzi owns very few cookbooks but her meals are always varied and delicious. She keeps a recipe file, as many cooks do, but not just to hold newspaper and magazine findings.

Fritzi, as you may remember, is my friend the library devotee. And her borrowing includes cookbooks (which never occurred to me to do before I met her). I think that's a very smart way to enlarge your recipe repertoire at no cost.

And Elizabeth suggests rechecking currently owned cookbooks for new recipes. She says, "I once read that the average person uses only four to six recipes out of each cookbook and realized that the figure was true in my case, so have made a concerted effort to make more use out of the ones I already own rather than buying new ones."

From the Bookstore and the Government
%%%%%%%%

You will find references to other cookbooks scattered throughout *Inflation-Wise*. The two cited below are good, though not necessarily better than others I've mentioned. I think they deserve special mention here, though, because they are both specifically geared toward cutting cooking costs [i.e., some cookbooks mentioned elsewhere do that incidentally by offering lower-cost vegetarian meals or plain as well as fancy (expensive) ways of cooking the same basic food].

One was written by a fellow resident of Durham:

Good Recipes for Hard Times
By Louise Newton
Houghton Mifflin Co., Boston, 1975
$6.95

This is an excellent cookbook for people on an extremely tight budget who are concerned about providing adequate nutrients on very little income. It is not strictly vegetarian, though the author does include recipes using very little meat. She is careful to balance amino acid complementaries (see PROTEIN) in her recipes to assure proper nutritive intake and includes budgets with suggested shopping lists.

The other was recommended by another North Carolina writer:

The Penny-Pinching Gourmet
By Ruth Kaswan
The Urban Alternatives Group
3475 Margarita Avenue, Oakland, California 94605
1979
$2.60

This book is a compilation of recipes collected and adapted throughout thirty years of cooking and a description of an experiment the author and her family carried out during the course of two months. In the first month, they shopped in supermarkets exclusively, though as carefully as always. During the second, they used their food co-op extensively (though still purchasing all meat and vegetables at supermarkets), and did *all* baking and soup-making from scratch.

They saved 26% during the latter month ("and ate better"). Their records show that home baking cut those costs in half, and that co-op buying saved 24% over supermarket prices (on the average).

The recipes and text are written with an eye to saving money and tasting delicious.

The government also offers several free pamphlets *re* cooking with a money-saving bias which might be of interest. Single copies of any or all of the following can be obtained by sending your request on a postcard (ask for publications by number as well as title and be sure to include your zip code) to:

Office of Governmental and Public Affairs
U. S. Department of Agriculture
Washington, D. C. 20250

- HG 43, *Money Saving Main Dishes.* Sixty-five recipes plus numerous variations on most, utilizing inexpensive nonmeat protein sources and less expensive cuts of meat. Includes some introductory pages about planning nutritious meals with economy in mind. 45 pages.

- HG 94, *Family Food Budgeting: for Good Meals and Good Nutrition.* Presents the USDA family food plans at four levels of cost. Includes guides for estimating food needs and expenditures quite specifically (updated semiannually) allowing for family size, style, and income variations. Very informative. No recipes. 14 pages.

- HC 209, *Food for the Family—a Cost-Saving Plan.* Enlarges on the low-cost food plan outlined in the publication cited immediately above. Includes sample menus (two weeks' worth each); one geared toward households with ample time to cook, one geared toward households with limited time to cook. Some recipes. 22 pages.

- HG 183, *Your Money's Worth in Foods.* Guides for budgeting, menu planning, shopping for best values.

COOKING

Gas or Electric
%%%%

Cooking with natural gas is less expensive by about 50% than cooking with electricity. Even cooking with electricity, however, is a minor expense in the energy-expenditure picture, at about $60 a year. Therefore, replacing a perfectly good electric range with a gas one in order to cut costs would not be very inflation-wise.

Still, if you are in the market for a new range/oven it's good to know that natural gas is currently the least expensive modern energy source. Be sure to look for a model with an automatic electronic ignition system instead of pilot lights, which will cut that 50% by 50%.

(And, if you already own a gas stove, see PILOT LIGHTS.)

Cost of Energy

Whether you do most of your food preparation in a frypan or a countertop broiler oven or in and on a full size gas or electric range, the cost of cooking will be a relatively minor item in your energy budget. My utility company estimates that cooking electrically costs about 16½¢ a day ($60 per year); cooking with gas runs less than half that much. So I don't think sweating over lowering the cost of cooking is worth your energy.

Still, you might painlessly shave a penny here and there by being aware of the following:

- You will make the most efficient use of your stove's surface units by matching the size of your pan to the element or burner and by keeping your reflectors and pan bottoms clean and shiny. It usually takes only five to eight minutes to preheat an oven rather than the ten minutes recipes often suggest and preheating may not be necessary at all for stews or casseroles requiring more than an hour's cooking. Use common sense.
- Coffee, left simmering on a small electric surface unit on low all day (say, twelve hours) will cost you about 7½¢ (at the current 5¢ per kwh national average); forgetting to turn your oven off after dinner and leaving it on all night (twelve hours) would cost you about ten times that much. In other words, it's overkill to use the oven to stew one stew when simmering on the surface would work just as well.
- It will cost you at least two and one-half times as much to toast your bread in your oven rather than in a toaster, or to broil your fish under your oven's broiler unit rather than in a countertop broiler oven, assuming you already own these appliances.
- Countertop appliances (like frypans, hotplates, sandwich grills) which do the work of surface units also cost about the same to run.

87

- An hour of oven baking will be approximately comparable in cost to twenty minutes of oven broiling.

Cost of Ingredients

About a month after my questionnaire was, I thought, in the hands of every inflation-wise acquaintance I knew, I discovered a gold mine of tips not ten doors down the street. Her name is Jackie (you will notice a few of her ideas already cited among the CLOTHES entries) and she was, on the night of discovery, substituting in my neighborhood bridge group.

I love playing bridge (or just engaging in conversation) with Jackie; she's a walking encyclopedia of practical facts, invariably teaches me something new, and never makes me feel stupid in the process. And she laughs a lot, at herself and the world, which I suspect is why she is such a good teacher.

She offered a number of tips that night (between hands), called the next day with more, and completed a questionnaire packed with more ideas.

Jackie is a woman who makes no assumptions. Whether deciding to make a finesse or a scratch cake, she always begins with a gathering of all the available facts.

In order to readily compare costs, Jackie told me, she maintains a regularly price-updated list of cost per measure of basic ingredients. For instance, the difference in cost between a white cake and a chocolate devil's food cake can be as much as $1.

I thought that was a clever idea and one that would prove useful to budget-conscious readers, so have included below the results of my own kitchen calculations of commonly used items. Unless prices have changed substantially, figure the total cost of your recipe by summing the appropriate "cost per measures" provided. I've also included formulas I devised to obtain my figures so that you can update the list as necessary. (An explanation of the process, including how to devise your own formulas for ingredients of your choice, follows Table A. An explanation of how to adjust for different measures than those given precedes Table B, a standard conversion chart.)

Table A—COST OF INGREDIENTS

Ingredient	Current Price of Common Sizes	Cost per Common Measure	Formula
Baking powder	at 75¢ per 10 ounces	1½¢ per teaspoon	$\dfrac{\text{Price}}{\text{ounces}} \div 5 = \underline{\quad}$ ¢ per tsp.
Baking soda	at 32¢ per 16 ounces	1¢ per tablespoon	$\dfrac{\text{Price}}{\text{ounces}} \div 2 = \underline{\quad}$ ¢ per tb.
Butter	at $1.60 per pound	80¢ per cup	$\dfrac{\text{Price}}{\text{pounds}} \div 2 = \underline{\quad}$ ¢ per cup
Chocolate, solid, unsweetened	at $2.00 per 8 ounces	25¢ per square (oz.)	$\dfrac{\text{Price}}{\text{ounces}} = \underline{\quad}$ ¢ per square (oz.)
Cocoa	at $3.20 per pound	80¢ per cup	$\dfrac{\text{Price}}{\text{pounds}} \div 4 = \underline{\quad}$ ¢ per cup
Cornstarch	at 48¢ per 16 ounces	1¢ per tablespoon	$\dfrac{\text{Price}}{\text{ounces}} \div 3 = \underline{\quad}$ ¢ per tb.
Cream of tartar	at $1.05 per 2.5 ounces	6¢ per teaspoon	$\dfrac{\text{Price}}{\text{ounces}} \div 7 = \underline{\quad}$ ¢ per tsp.
Eggs	at 72¢ per dozen	6¢ per egg	$\dfrac{\text{Price}}{12} = \underline{\quad}$ ¢ per egg

Table A—COST OF INGREDIENTS

Ingredient	Current Price of Common Sizes	Cost per Common Measure	Formula
Flour, soy	at 50¢ per pound	12½¢ per cup	$\dfrac{\text{Price}}{\text{pounds}} \div 4 = $ ____¢ per cup
Flour, wheat	at 90¢ per 5 pounds	4½¢ per cup	$\dfrac{\text{Price}}{\text{pounds}} \div 4 = $ ____¢ per cup
Margarine	at 80¢ per pound	40¢ per cup	$\dfrac{\text{Price}}{\text{pounds}} \div 2 = $ ____¢ per cup
Milk, fresh	at $2.00 per gallon	12½¢ per cup	$\dfrac{\text{Price}}{\text{gallons}} \div 16 = $ ____¢ per cup
Milk, dry reconstituted, instant	at $4.03 per 14 quarts (potential)	7¢ per cup	$\dfrac{\text{Price}}{\text{potential quarts}} \div 4 = $ ____¢ per cup
Milk, dry reconstituted, non-instant	at $1.12 per 5 quarts (potential)	5½¢ per cup	$\dfrac{\text{Price}}{\text{potential quarts}} \div 4 = $ ____¢ per cup
Milk, dry solids, instant	at $4.03 per 44.8 ounces	2¢ per tablespoon	$\dfrac{\text{Price}}{\text{ounces}} \div 4 = $ ____¢ per tb.

Milk, dry solids, non-instant	at $1.12 per 16 ounces	2¢ per tablespoon	$\frac{\text{Price}}{\text{ounces}} \div 3 =$ ____ ¢ per tb.
Mustard, dry	at 30¢ per 1.5 ounces	5¢ per tablespoon	$\frac{\text{Price}}{\text{ounces}} \div 4 =$ ____ ¢ per tb.
Oil, vegetable	at $1.60 per 32 fluid ounces	2½¢ per tablespoon	$\frac{\text{Price}}{\text{ounces}} \div 2 =$ ____ ¢ per tb.
Salt	at 26¢ per 26 ounces	2/3¢ per tablespoon	$\frac{\text{Price}}{\text{ounce}} \div 1.5 =$ ____ ¢ per tb.
Shortening	at $1.99 per 3 pounds	1½¢ per tablespoon	$\frac{\text{Price}}{\text{pounds}} \div 38 =$ ____ ¢ per tb.
Sugar, white, granulated	at $1.70 per 5 pounds	17¢ per cup	$\frac{\text{Price}}{\text{pounds}} \div 2 =$ ____ ¢ per cup
Sugar, white, XXXX	at 60¢ per pound	17¢ per cup	$\frac{\text{Price}}{\text{pounds}} \div 3.5 =$ ____ ¢ per cup
Sugar, brown	at 60¢ per pound	27¢ per cup	$\frac{\text{Price}}{\text{pounds}} \div 2.25 =$ ____ ¢ per cup
Vanilla, extract	at $1.32 per 4 fluid ounces	5½¢ per teaspoon	$\frac{\text{Price}}{\text{ounces}} \div 6 =$ ____ ¢ per tsp.

Table A — COST OF INGREDIENTS

Ingredient	Current Price of Common Sizes	Cost per Common Measure	Formula
Vanilla, imitation	at 48¢ per 8 fluid ounces	1¢ per teaspoon	$\dfrac{\text{Price}}{\text{ounces}} \div 6 = \underline{\quad}$ ¢ per tsp.
Vinegar, cider	at 32¢ per 16 fluid ounces	1¢ per tablespoon	$\dfrac{\text{Price}}{\text{ounces}} \div 2 = \underline{\quad}$ ¢ per tb.
Vinegar, wine	at 96¢ per 12 fluid ounces	4¢ per tablespoon	$\dfrac{\text{Price}}{\text{ounces}} \div 2 = \underline{\quad}$ ¢ per tb.
Wheat germ	at 72¢ per 12 ounces	2¢ per tablespoon	$\dfrac{\text{Price}}{\text{ounces}} \div 3 = \underline{\quad}$ ¢ per tb.
Yeast, dry, in 3-pack	at 45¢ per 3-pack	15¢ per individual package (1 scant tablespoon)	$\dfrac{\text{Price}}{3} = \underline{\quad}$ ¢ per package (1 scant tb.)
Yeast, dry, in bulk	at $1.92 per pound	3¢ per scant tablespoon (equivalent of 1 package)	$\dfrac{\text{Price}}{\text{pound}} \div 64 = \underline{\quad}$ ¢ per scant tb. (equivalent of 1 package)

You may want to add ingredients of your own choosing to the list in Table A. The following is an explanation of how the formulas were devised: I began by calculating cost per unit (of ounces or pounds or whatever seemed appropriate) by the ordinary unit pricing method, i.e., dividing the total price by the package net weight.

I then set about obtaining the Common Measure figures required (reflected in the final divisor in the formulas). For these I needed to know how many cups, or teaspoons or tablespoons were in a given ounce or pound; you can obtain the answers by reading package labels, or using measuring spoons and a well-calibrated scale, or checking in the excellent table of equivalents in *The Joy of Cooking* (p. 548) or in any other cookbook you have around that offers that information.

For specific example, by dividing the price of a bag of flour by the number of pounds in the bag, I came up with price per pound. Then I checked the label and found that a pound of flour contains 4 cups, so I divided price per pound by 4 to give me price per cup.

Re Table B
Should you find it necessary to further subdivide the cost per measures given—e.g., if the cost per measure given is for 1 cup but your recipe calls for 1 tablespoon—you can look at Table B to remind you that there are 16 tablespoons in a cup and that you, therefore, should divide the cost per 1 cup by 16 to obtain cost per tablespoon.

Table B—STANDARD EQUIVALENTS

Dry Ingredients
3 teaspoons = 1 tablespoon
4 tablespoons = ¼ cup
8 tablespoons = ½ cup
16 tablespoons = 1 cup
16 ounces = 1 pound

Liquid Ingredients
2 tablespoons = 1 fluid ounce
1 cup = 8 fluid ounces
2 cups = 1 pint = 16 fluid ounces
4 cups = 1 quart = 32 fluid ounces
4 quarts = 1 gallon = 128 fluid ounces

Freezing
%%%%%

Nearly half of the completed *Inflation-Wise* questionnaires I received included this tip: "We try to plan our meals so that if one dish requires oven cooking, all do. It is a more efficient use of the oven." True, though as you now know, savings fall in the penny realm. Most of those same contributors also said that they often prepared massive amounts of an oven dish and froze the excess for later use. If your freezer is full of delicious, ready-to-pop-into-the-oven meals, you will surely be less likely to opt for an expensive restaurant or costly fast or "instant" prepared foods when dinner time rolls around and energy and tempers are short.

A pamphlet prepared by the U. S. Department of Agriculture called *Freezing Combination Main Dishes* is worth having for this purpose. It includes good tips *re* what foods can and cannot be successfully frozen, on packaging, safety, and the like. Each recipe makes enough for 24 servings; each serving provides 12 grams of protein. Twenty-five recipes are included. It's free from USDA, Washington, D. C. 20250; ask for publication G 40.

Microwave Ovens
%%%%%%%

My favorite mother-in-law, Marge, and my favorite sister-in-law, Grace, are both satisfied owners of microwave ovens. If they weren't already, and if one of them called me (the "saver lady") today to ask whether buying one of these appliances was inflation-wise, I would say: It depends.

Microwave ovens are initially quite expensive (even on sale; though they are discounted so frequently that no one in the market should ever have to pay full price). They do fulfill these criteria: having a multipurpose function, low wattage (average: 1400), and extremely quick cooking time. Altogether the savings in time/energy will amount to 40% to 80% over conventional methods. *But* the energy pay-back time would be measurable only in years (and years). Still, for time-squeezed families who might otherwise eat out or purchase more expensive quick-cooking protein sources, a microwave oven might be a good buy. How's that for a hedge?

Oven Thermometers

Thermostats, particularly in aging ovens, are often miscalibrated. My own oven, for instance, consistently measures 25 degrees hotter than the dial setting. This will cost only a few pennies in energy money, but ruined food is something else again—sometimes something quite costly. I consider the couple of dollars I spent for an oven thermometer a good investment.

Pressure Cookers
$ $ $ $ $

"A pressure cooker," writes Elaine, "is a must—saving both time and energy."

She's right, a pressure-cooker *will* do the job in one-third to one-tenth the time of conventional methods, but the reduction in energy use isn't the substantial money-saver. (Dried beans, for instance, simmered for 2 hours on a large surface burner would cost you 2½¢ worth of electricity; cooking them in a pressure cooker for the maximum recommended 45 minutes would reduce that cost to slightly less than a penny. Not very exciting, as I think you would agree.)

No, it is the *time* saved by pressure cooking which has the potential to permit substantial money-saving. And I don't mean the old "time is money" saw—I mean extra cash in your hand. This is how. A number of contributors wrote that they have a job outside the home in addition to the one already held inside it. They said they found themselves tending to buy quick-cooking convenience foods or steaks and chops because they no longer had the several hours required for stewing from scratch.

The point is that a pressure cooker, or as suggested by several others, a crockpot (which, at 250 watts will cost 10¢ for eight hours' use), can make it possible to rely on less expensive sources of protein such as beans or tougher cuts of meat by shortening the time between coming in the door and getting dinner on the table. The substantial savings will be in your food budget.

COOPERATIVES

Babysitting
%%%%%%%%

In my opinion, sitters are underpaid (but then, in my opinion, so are mothers); still, on an absolute cash basis, the cost of a babysitter can sometimes double the cost of an evening out.

You can eliminate this added expense by organizing a babysitting co-op among your parenting friends and/or neighbors, exchanging time rather than money.

Word of mouth and local notices gather a group of interested parents for an initial meeting. A list is compiled noting name, address, phone number, and times available (daytime and/or evening). The master list is copied and distributed to each member along with twenty pieces of scrip, each representing one-half hour of sitting time. (Calculate and collect duplicating expenditures at delivery.)

In some co-ops it is up to each member family to locate another member-family member for any "sit." This eliminates the need for a single coordinator "secretary" (a job which in some co-ops rotates monthly among the members, is quite time-consuming, and often much dreaded). However, an honor system of keeping the balance of give and take reasonably even should be spelled out at the initial meeting for the former system to work smoothly; and it seems to work best in smaller co-ops.

Elizabeth writes that her family exchanges whole weekends, informally, with a few other close-friend families. A nice *inflation-wise* idea—hiring weekend sitters can be prohibitively costly (when you are lucky enough to find them).

Books and Magazines
$ $

From my mother: "To supplement the public library and cut down on the number of magazines we buy, a group of friends and

96

neighbors and I have begun trading from our own collections. Each of us subscribes to a couple of magazines and we're each now making a special effort, when renewal times approach, to avoid duplications within the group.

"Our book libraries are all reasonably substantial already but when someone does buy a new book she usually mentions it. The exchanges were all done informally at first, but we soon decided to devise a simple card-file system in order to avoid feelings of anger on the lender's end and guilt on the borrower's.

"At present, no time limit is imposed; we have an understanding that anybody who wants a lent book either returned or passed on, is free to call the borrower and work it out. It has been so pleasant not to have a library due date hanging over our heads that so far everyone has been careful not to abuse the privilege.

"Oh, one more thing: if you put this idea in your book, Christopher, be sure to remind readers to include more than novels in their book lendings. Some of the most expensive and most popular (and therefore hardest to get) public-library books are those on gardening and cooking and repair and other sorts of how-to. And, of course, remind them to include *your* book."

And so I have.

Car-pooling
%%%%%%%

Car-pooling is an enormous money-saver/energy-saver: with one other person, save half of your transportation costs, with two others save two-thirds, with three others save three-quarters! Working out convenient pickup and delivery times can sometimes be a hassle, but if it's at all feasible the savings are well worth it. (See also INSURANCE—Auto, for more savings *re* car-pooling.)

Food
%%%

Food co-ops flourished in the 1930s and began a resurgence in the 70s. Many such co-ops, ranging in size from five or six people (distributing out of members' kitchens) to hundreds of members (involved in store-front operations) have been formed and are forming or growing this very day throughout the country.

Members exchange their volunteered time for savings on food of up to 60% compared to supermarket prices (average savings seem to fall in the 25% range). The savings are achieved by buying at wholesale prices, in bulk divided among the membership, substituting the volunteer co-op member on a rotating basis for the paid middleperson.

It's quite likely that there is a co-op already in existence in your area; ask around. If you are unable to locate one, gather a group of interested friends with similar tastes in food, and start a co-op of your own.

It was my original intention to explain how our rather small co-op works, but I think it would provide too narrow a picture of the possibilities. Instead let me introduce you to a terrific, practical, inexpensive book on the subject:

Food Coops for Small Groups
by Tony Vellela
Workman Publishing Company
231 East 51st Street
New York, New York 10022
1975, $2.95

This book covers everything you will need to know about finding members; initial meetings; what foods are available and in what quantities; how to locate and judge wholesalers; the mechanics of buying from local (and/or mail-order) wholesalers, distributors, farmers, and others; how to handle the money, organize the work of purchase and distribution, keep records. The author concludes with flow charts and descriptions of six functioning co-ops—some large, some small. Worth every penny; I highly recommend this book.

Gardening

Suppose you are interested in growing some of your own food but have no land on which to do that. Community gardens may be the answer for you. Your Agricultural Extension Service is most likely to have available the information about locations of such community garden plots in which you can become involved.

If not (even if so) send a request to:

Gardens for All
The National Association for Gardening
180 Flynn Avenue
Burlington, Vermont 05401

for their information packet *re* community gardening. This nonprofit organization, established in 1972, is "dedicated," according to their literature, "to bringing land and people together for a greener, happier world through gardening."

They particularly promote community gardening sponsored by schools, businesses, retirement homes, residential developments, churches, service clubs, and prisons. In 1979 their Gallup-conducted poll indicated that a million families gardened in this cooperative manner.

Their *Guide to Community Gardening* (available from the address above, Department 00521, for $2 postpaid) will tell you how to find a sponsor, where to look for land and obtain the rights to use it, where to find monetary help, how to divide plots (allowing organic and chemical gardeners to hoe and harvest in separate peace), and other items of interest.

The Association also publishes a quarterly newsmagazine containing lots of good information *re* gardening *per se*. It's available for $10 per year; ask for a sample copy in your information packet request.

Skills
Ⓢ Ⓢ Ⓢ Ⓢ
%%%%%%%%

Ask your friends to join in forming a skills co-op. Each participant notes, at the top of a single page, name and phone number followed by a list of skills she or he would be willing to contribute in exchange for someone else's expertise (a special proficiency may be starred or the list may be annotated). I was surprised to find when I actually put pen to paper that my own list was quite lengthy, but even more surprised to find that many of my friends could do things I had no notion they were even interested in—things I had previously been *paying* a stranger to do. Duplicated collated "member booklets" are given each contributor at cost.

Time exchanged need not always be equal, but since needs are being fulfilled on both sides members find that trades acceptable to each are easily arranged. A skills list might include:

Appliance Repair
Assembling holiday toys (like big wheels and such)
Babysitting
Bookkeeping
Calligraphy
Carpentry
Car repair
Cooking (for parties, for instance)
Dog sitting or walking
Haircutting
Housecleaning
House-sitting (including waiting for deliveries or repairpeople
    for someone with a job outside the home)
Knitting or other needlework or teaching of same
Landscape design
Lawn-mowing
Masonry
Painting
Photography—family portraiture
Sewing
Teaching children (swimming or skiing or kitemaking or
    languages or one or another of the skills on this co-op list—or
    anything else)
Tennis lessons
Typing
Weeding
Woodsplitting

Woodworking
Wrapping holiday presents
Writing résumés or other writing (ads for instance)

Tools
$ $ $
%%%%%%%%

Edward: "The average tool-rental company computes its charge by dividing the cost of the tool by a number between 15 and 30. Therefore, if you plan to use the item only a few times a life it pays to rent."

A gas-powered chain saw, for example, which would cost close to $200 to buy new, rents in my locale for $5 per hour (3-hour minimum) or $30 per day. A lawn mower (new, $100 to $350) rents for $3 per hour (2-hour minimum) or $15 per day.

But car-repair tools such as dwell meters and timing lights aren't usually available at rental companies and it seems wasteful to own a tool which will likely be used only twice a year. Sharing, I think, may be the solution.

A tool cooperative might be set up in a manner similar to the SKILLS CO-OP (see previous entry): each of a group of neighbors providing a list of acceptably lendable tools. A few of my neighbors have organized an exchange this way and additionally have agreed to discuss contemplated large tool purchases (like table saws and such) in order to avoid duplication.

Tools generate strong emotions among their owners: a professional carpenter will rarely lend someone else his tools, for instance. A tool co-op, therefore, should perhaps be limited to those tools which are not part of one's work or craft. Responsibility for repair or replacement of tools damaged during a loan must be clearly established between co-op members at the outset.

These limitations notwithstanding, the following list demonstrates that you can save a lot of money if a group of people can establish a tool pool. How often does a person need to use a post-hole digger, for example? In the case where an owner is reluctant to lend his equipment, a variant to the co-op can be made by contributing the item plus its operation: I rototill your garden, you cut my wood for me on your bench saw. Possibilities include:

Carpentry and Do-It-Yourself

Circular saw
Drill and bits
Router and bits
Pad sander
Belt sander
Table saw
Glue gun
Planes

Clamps
Miter box and saw
Staple gun
Drill press
Vise
Plumbing tools
Snake

Auto Repair and Maintenance

Torque wrench
Socket set
Battery charger
Car ramps

Creeper
Timing light
Compression gauge
Brake tool

Lawn and Garden

Lawn mower
Weed eater
Wheel barrow
Chain saw

Maul and Wedge
Pruning tools
Rototiller
Post-hole diggers

Miscellaneous

Hand truck
Extension ladder

Step ladder
Pickup truck

COSMETICS
%%%%%%%

I spend so little—a maximum of, I would guess, $10 per year—on cosmetics that I can't get very excited about eking out savings in this category. But apparently that's unusual.

My sister Heather, who is more interested in such things (and does look quite lovely) suggests that you can find everything you need at the five and dime. She says she spends time looking very carefully at the offerings, reading and comparing labels (ingredients must be listed, by law, in order of the proportion of the whole made up by each, from most to least), ignoring brand names.

Barrie (the artist), who is perfectly beautiful without a dab of make-up, says she spends all of her mad money on cosmetics—expensive ones—because using them makes her *feel* wonderful.

Edward's wife, Joan, says that the person with the best skin she knows uses only items from the refrigerator on her face—eggs, yogurt, milk, mayonnaise—and that she read somewhere that one of the wealthiest women in America uses vegetable shortening as a moisturizer.

I occasionally give myself a free facial (they cost $15 and up in salons) by steaming my face for ten or fifteen minutes under a towel over a sinkful of hot water spiked with a pinch of herbs. Once in a while I follow this by scrubbing off the dead skin using soap, water and a bit of whole wheat flour or corn meal. It makes me feel new.

The point is that I think the way we *feel* has much more to do with whether or not we look beautiful than whatever we rub on or scrub with. But I think the cosmetics advertisers do a crackerjack job of selling us on the belief that the opposite is true.

I also suspect that people who say they spend enormous amounts on cosmetics probably buy quite a lot of things "to try" and, finding them wanting, discard them or let them accumulate in the medicine chest to astounding depths.

For instance, Grace (my sister-in-law) has lovely skin. She and I somehow slipped into a conversation about moisturizers the last time she was visiting, and she told me that she has a favorite (just as I do, just as you do). She discovered that this particular moisturizer worked best for her by trial and error—ten tries, ten errors—number eleven was just right.

I'm totally satisfied with the very inexpensive moisturizer brand I've been using for the past twenty years, but if I weren't I'd certainly try her number eleven suggestion and possibly avoid all those errors (and all that expense).

The point of *this* point is that I'll bet we could all cut our cosmetics costs (even me) simply by talking to each other more, telling each other more regularly about great cosmetic discoveries we've made *and* great mistakes, asking each other more often for suggestions, sharing, in other words, the wealth of information we've all accumulated.

CREDIT UNIONS
%

Many, many contributors to *Inflation-Wise* wrote to say that they took advantage of the lower-interest loan rates and higher-interest savings rates offered at their credit unions. There are more than 23,000 credit unions throughout the nation, operated by boards chosen from among and by their depositors (who have a common tie, usually the same employer). They are nonprofit and two-thirds are federally insured; many others are state insured. Be sure to check that one or the other, preferably the former, is true before you join.

If your place of employment does not have a credit union, you still may be eligible to join one: check with your state's Credit Union League to find out. The League's address will be obtainable by checking in the Yellow Pages under "Credit Unions," calling any one of them in your locale and asking for the information, or by writing:

Credit Union National Association
Box 431
Madison, Wisconsin 53701

DENTAL CARE

Dentists
%%%%

Several contributors wrote to suggest that if you live near a dental school, you may find that you can cut costs in half by having your dental work done there. Prospective patients are screened and not all are accepted. The work may take considerably longer but it will be excellent, accomplished under direct faculty supervision, and closely scrutinized throughout.

Also, some readers may not be aware that there is a considerable range of prices among private-practice dentists for the same piece of work. After you have collected a list of names of dentists recommended by friends, comparison shop for the least expensive by phone. Ask each the price of a one-surface amalgam (filling), a simple cleaning, and a full-mouth x-ray. You may be surprised at the variance.

Flossing
💲 💲
%%%%%%%%

This simple spool of thread, which costs $1.25 for a three-month supply, may be one of the most important preventive medical tools available.

Not everyone who doesn't floss their teeth will end up with gum disease, but current dental research indicates that proper brushing and flossing can prevent it.

The cost of periodontal (gum) surgery alone, according to my dentist, can run as high as $1,200. Additional crown work, when diseased gums have caused loosened teeth, can increase that cost. A few dollars per year on dental floss and brushes seems a small preventive price to pay.

Brushing alone cannot remove the culprit, plaque, from its lodgings under your gumline. That requires proper use of floss, every day. To quote from the American Dental Association's booklet *Cleaning Your Teeth and Gums:* "Plaque is a sticky, colorless layer of harmful bacteria that is constantly forming on your teeth. The bacteria in plaque are recognized to be a primary cause of the two most common dental diseases: (1) dental caries (tooth decay), the major cause of tooth loss in children and (2) periodontal or gum disease (pyorrhea), the major cause of tooth loss in adults.

"If you don't remove the plaque daily it will accumulate and turn into a hard deposit called calculus (tartar). Calculus can be removed only by your dentist or a dental hygienist. If calculus is not removed, more plaque can form on it, eventually leading to the destruction of teeth and gums."

Everyone should see a dentist regularly for checkups; the sooner a problem is discovered the more easily (and less expensively) it can be remedied. But I think realistically, if my family is any indication, when the budget is extremely tight the tendency is to put it off (repeatedly) till next month in lieu of cutting the grocery allotment. Penny wise and pound foolish perhaps, but even if you feel you must postpone that visit, don't postpone initiating proper cleaning technique.

The booklet mentioned earlier, *Cleaning Your Teeth and Gums*, provides clear and easily understandable instructions for these techniques, with photographs. You can ask your dentist for a free copy or for the price of a postcard request a copy from:

Bureau of Dental Health Education
American Dental Association
211 East Chicago Avenue
Chicago, Illinois 60611

It may be the highest-yielding dime investment you have ever made.

Toothpaste
%%%%%%%

Baking soda, Dennis my dentist tells me, is a perfectly good dentifrice for removing plaque and polishing teeth, and at a penny per tablespoon it's practically free. I keep it in a custard cup by the bathroom sink and throw in a few whole cloves (which doesn't do a thing for the flavor, as I had hoped, but does make it smell good).

The one thing it is lacking, however, is fluoride and we all know by heart the ads about the benefits of fluoride. The ads are true, Dennis tells me—fluoride really *has* been tested (in those toothpastes carrying the ADA seal of approval) and found to be an effective aid in preventing tooth decay. It is actually absorbed into, and strengthens, tooth enamel.

The problem is, however, that the kind of fluoride found in toothpaste loses a little of its potency each day the tube sits by your bathroom sink, so that by the time a large tube is half-used, the fluoride benefit (the only real advantage to using toothpaste rather than baking soda) is practically nil. Dennis recommends therefore, to patients who use toothpaste, that they buy it in small tubes—which of course are more costly.

There is a better way. For about $2, most dentists can provide a fluoride mouth rinse which, used daily at the recommended dosage, will last nearly two months and, importantly, *lose none of its potency during that time*, so you will really be getting your money's worth.

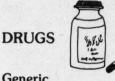

DRUGS

Generic
%%%%

If your physician prescribes, let's say, Librium, and you live in a state where your pharmacist cannot automatically fill the prescription with the least expensive equivalent of this drug (generically known as chlordiazepoxide), you could pay $17.16 for it. In its least-expensive generic form, same drug, same size, same number of tablets, same standards of manufacture, it would be $9.27.

Every newly developed drug is assigned a generic name at the birth of its testing stage. This "official" name (usually related to the drug's chemical makeup) is often long and difficult to pronounce. After it has been tested according to Food and Drug Administration standards and deemed safe and effective, the manufacturer may patent it.

The drug at this point will usually be given a brand name (a nickname essentially) which is more pronounceable than the official generic name and, the manufacturer hopes, more memorable. This brand name is the name under which the drug will be marketed and advertised for the following seventeen years, until the patent expires. At that point, other firms will be permitted to manufacture and sell the drug either under its generic name or under a different brand name. It will be the original manufacturer's goal, during the course of those seven-

107

teen years, to plant the original brand name of a patented drug so firmly in the minds of physicians that it will be the first to pop into their heads, even after the patent expires.

Generics, when they become available following the patent exclusivity period, are unadvertised and almost invariably cost less than brand-name drugs. Does the lower price also reflect lower manufacturing standards? No, according to the FDA, there is "no evidence of widespread differences between the products of large and small firms or between brand name and generic name' products." This is true because *all* drugs sold must meet the same FDA standards for safety, strength, purity, and effectiveness. *All* drug manufacturers are subject to the same FDA inspection and must follow the Administration's Current Good Manufacturing Practice Regulations, which touch on every aspect of making drugs, from building maintenance to quality control.

Still, of the two hundred most frequently prescribed drugs, about seventy are available generically but only about fifteen are prescribed that way with any frequency. It will save you a bundle to ask your physician to write your prescriptions in such a way that they can be filled by your pharmacist with the least-expensive equivalent drug available, whenever possible.

Listed below are some of the most often prescribed brand-name drugs with their generic equivalents:

Brand Name	*Generic Name*
Achromycin V®	Tetracycline HCL
Actifed®	Triprolidine HCL w/ Pseudoephrine
Aldactazide®	Spironolactone and Hydrochlorothiazide
Amcill®	Ampicillin
Amoxil®	Amoxicillin
Antivert®	Meclizine HCL
Antivert, Bonine®	Meclizine, Chewable
Apresoline®	Hydralazine
Aristocort®	Triamcinolone
Benadryl®	Diphenhydramine HCL
Bendectin®	Doxylamine Pyridoxine
Benemid®	Probenecid
Butazolidin®	Phenylbutazone
Butazolidin Alka®	Phenylbutazone Alka
Butisol Sodium®	Butabarbital Sodium

Brand Name	Generic Name
Colace®	Dioctyl Sodium Sulfosuccinate (Diocto)
Colbenemid®	Probenecid/Colchicine
Cyclopar®	Tetracycline HCL
Darvon, Dolene®	Propoxyphene HCL
Darvon, Dolene® Compound 65®	Propoxyphene w/APC
Decadron®	Dexmethasone
Dilantin Sodium®	Phenytoin
Dimetapp®	Bromaphen/Phenyle/Phenylp
Diupres®	Chlorothiazide and Reserpine
Diuril®	Chlorothiazide
Donnatal®	Belladonna/Phenobarbital
Drixoral®	Dexbrompheniramine Maleate and D-isoephedrine Sulfate
Dulcolax	Bisacodyl
Elavil®	Amitriptyline HCL
Elixophyllin®	Theophyllin
Equanil, Miltown®	Meprobamate
Erypar®	Erythromycin Stearate
Erythrocin®	Erythromycin Stearate
Feosol®	Ferrous Sulfate
Florinal®	Butalbital/APC
Gantanol®	Sulfamethoxazole
Gantrisin®	Sulfisoxazole
Hydrodiuril®	Hydrochlorothiazide
Hydropres®	Hydrochlorothiazide and Reserpine
Isordil®	Isosorbide Dinitrate
Larotid®	Amoxicillin
Librax®	Chlordiazepoxide HCL and Clidinium Bromide
Librium®	Chlordiazepoxide HCL
Lomotil®	Diphenoxylate HCL and Atropine Sulfate
Meticorten®	Prednisone
Omnipen®	Ampicillin
Orinase®	Tolbutamide
Parafon Forte®	Chlorzoxazone/Acetaminophen
Pavabid®	Papaverine HCL
Penapar VK®	Penicillin VK
Penbritin®	Ampicillin
Pentids®	Penicillin G Potassium
PEN-VEE K® V-Cillin-K®	Penicillin V Potassium
Periactin®	Cyproheptadine HCL

Brand Name	Generic Name
Peri Colace®	Casanthranol and Dioctyl Sodium Sulfosuccinate
Peritrate®	Pentaerythritol Tetranitrate (PETN)
Persantine®	Dipyridamole
Phenergan®	Promethazine HCL
Polycillin®	Ampicillin
Premarin®	Conjugated Estrogens
Principen®	Ampicillin
Pro-Banthine®	Propantheline Bromide
Quinora®	Quinidine Sulfate
Robaxin®	Methocarbamol
Robaxisal®	Methocarbamol/A.S.A.
Ser-Ap-Es®	Reserpine, Hydralazine, and Hydrochlorothiazide
Serpasil®	Reserpine
Sumox®	Amoxicillin
Sumycin®	Tetracycline HCL
Tedral®	Theophylline, Ephedrine and Phenobarbital (Azma-Aid)
Terramycin®	Oxytetracycline HCL
Tetracyn®	Tetracycline HCL
Thorazine®	Chlorpromazine HCL
Tofranil®	Imipramine HCL
Trimox®	Amoxicillin
Utimox®	Amoxicillin

Over-the-Counter
%%%%%

Cinda writes: "My biggest gripe is with ads recommending those brand-name over-the-counter drugs 'containing the pain-killer most often recommended by doctors' as though this were some mysterious magic potion. It's aspirin! Acetylsalicylic acid equals *aspirin*."

All aspirin, whether marketed as a drugstore's house brand at $1.79 per three hundred or under the brand name Bayer at $4.91 per three hundred (or under any other brand name at any other price), must be manufactured according to rigid standards of formula. Buy the least expensive, least adulterated form you can find. When you buy a brand name you're helping to pay the manufacturer's advertising bill, that's all.

Formula standards are maintained for virtually all over-the-counter drugs (as well as prescription), so always read the label and buy the active ingredients you are after at the lowest available price.

Children's Aspirin
%%%%%%%

I wonder if so-called "baby" aspirin was even available when I was a child? What I remember being given was an appropriate amount of adult aspirin crushed in a spoon and mixed with a touch of honey. If children's aspirin indeed existed thirty years ago, and respective prices were comparable, my mother was cutting her costs 75%.

At today's prices, one house-brand aspirin (see DRUGS—Over-the Counter) costs one penny (or less); the equivalent amount of "baby" aspirin costs four cents (or more).

Break a five-grain "adult" aspirin into quarters—voilà—you have four "baby" aspirins (1¼ grains each). Your pediatrician can tell you recommended dosage.

Effectiveness

If an over-the-counter preparation doesn't do the job for which it is intended, you have wasted your money. But how do you know which do and which don't? There's a terrific book:

The Medicine Show
by the editors of *Consumer Reports*
Consumers Union, 5th Edition, 1980
$5.00

which will tell you why doctors *do* recommend aspirin so often; how to treat cold symptoms, sore throats, coughs; about laxatives, sleeping aids, eye washes, health foods, vitamins and minerals, acne, itches and rashes (including athlete's foot), deodorants, sunburn preventives, and much more.

And in all cases, where the basic active ingredients are available in generic form (therefore least expensive), they will tell you what to ask your pharmacist for.

Proper Use
%%%%%%%%%

If you down your tetracycline capsule with a glass of milk, you might just as well be throwing the money you paid the pharmacist, not to mention the medical benefits, out the window. The high levels of calcium in milk products (cheese and yogurt included), green vegetables, almonds, and other such foods inhibit proper absorption of the drug; antacids have the same inhibitory effect.

And did you know that much of erythromycin's antibacterial action is destroyed if taken with acid drinks such as orange juice? Or that taking birth-control pills will deplete your blood levels of some vitamins to the extent that hefty supplements (i.e., much more than any ordinary daily supplement) will be required (therefore an added expense) if you wish to maintain adequate intake of these nutrients?

Being unaware of such drug-food or drug-drug interactions could mean wasted money. More serious interactions could cost you hospital expenses, could even cost you something more important—your life. Your doctor won't always know—or remember to tell you—what you need to know about proper use of prescription drugs.

Avoid such potential wastes and dangers by reading my sources for those noted above and many, many more:

The People's Pharmacy and *The People's Pharmacy 2*
by Joe Graedon
Avon Books, New York, 1977 and 1980 (respectively)
$4.95 and $5.95 (respectively)

In Quantity
%%%

If you expect to be taking a particular medication for an extended period of time, it will generally cost you least to buy the largest quantity you can. Be sure, however, to check with your physician or pharmacist to be sure it is a drug which will remain stable for the expected use period.

EDUCATION

Extracurricular, School-age, Children

Have you a 9- to 19-year-old who is interested in cooking? raising animals? photography? bee-keeping? electronics? sewing? or anything else which you feel you are not experienced enough to teach?

The purpose of 4-H is to make the opportunity to learn-by-doing available to any child as a supplement to school curriculum. It may have once been true, at least as I remember my childhood, that 4-H was farm-child oriented. If so, this is no longer the case.

Any interested child is free to join any existing 4-H project, led by trained adult volunteers. There are, for instance, one hundred such on going projects in our locale. To find out if an appropriate project exists which would fulfill your child's needs, call your Agricultural Extension Service (to find out how to locate their number, see AGRICULTURAL EXTENSION SERVICE in *Inflation-Wise*).

If no such project currently exists, you needn't give up. 4-H has been designed to include the kind of flexibility which allows projects to be initiated and dissolved according to community need. If you can gather the names of five or six children expressing a similar interest, and particularly (but not necessarily, only) if you can locate an adult willing to act as volunteer teacher/leader, 4-H will help get the project started.

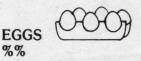

EGGS
%%

Somewhere in the recesses of my memory there was a rule about how to buy the most egg for the money. It seemed to me that the rule read something like: If the difference in price between sizes is greater than 6 cents (or was it 4 cents?), the smaller eggs are the bigger bargain.

I wanted to include the rule in this book, so to find out precisely how it read, I called my friend Rhett. Among other things, Rhett is a math whiz. "Frankly, my dear," he said (Rhett actually says things like that), "it all depends on current price levels. As prices fluctuate, the rule fluctuates. The '6-cent' rule, for instance, was applicable when large eggs were consistently about 48 cents a dozen and the usual price spread between sizes was 6 cents. It depends on percentage differences, you see?" Well, I saw, but only vaguely.

We decided that the most consistently reliable rule was the old standby, unit pricing. Egg-size standards are based on weight per dozen; the size of each egg in a weight-class carton may vary slightly. The minimum weight per dozen for the various classes are:

Jumbo	30 ounces
Extra Large	27 ounces
Large	24 ounces
Medium	21 ounces
Small	18 ounces

I include them here because although they are usually printed on the carton, this isn't always true. Note that there is a difference of 3 ounces between each weight class, so you needn't memorize the entire chart; if you simply learn that large eggs weigh 24 ounces per dozen, you can add or subtract 3 ounces as necessary. Then proceed to compare unit price (price, in this case, per ounce).

For example, if large eggs were selling for 72¢ per dozen, small for 45¢ per dozen (on sale, let's say, as they were the last time I bought eggs), small is a much better bargain (20% cheaper per ounce than large); the formula:

$$\frac{\text{price per dozen, Large}}{\text{ounces per dozen, Large}} = \frac{\$.72}{24 \text{ oz.}} = \$.03 \text{ per ounce}$$

$$\frac{\text{price per dozen, Small}}{\text{ounces per dozen, Small}} = \frac{\$.45}{18 \text{ oz.}} = \$.02\frac{1}{2} \text{ per ounce}$$

To be perfectly accurate, you should only compare eggs of the same quality (U.S. Grade AA—highest, U.S. Grade A, U.S. Grade B—lowest commercially available); *however*, although Grade AA will be the prettiest—i.e., with thick whites and firm defectless yolks and clean shells—*there is no difference in freshness or nutritive value between grades.*

ENERGY

According to recent government studies, residential energy is consumed in approximately the following percentages:

Heating and cooling..70%

Water heating..20%

Cooking and refrigeration and lighting and other...............................10%

It stands to reason, therefore, that any percentage decrease in heating or cooling functions will net larger dollar savings than the same percentage decrease in, for instance, lighting functions. This will vary, of course, across the country. As often as possible, I have included percentages saved (some averages, some locale-related), and would suggest that before you begin reading you get out your energy bills for the past year and calculate your costs so that the percentages will have some dollar meanings for you.

In this ENERGY section, I will mainly address the problem of how to cut costs in heating and cooling your home in both penny-pinching and wallet-stuffing ways. There is also some general information about figuring appliance energy costs. (See also COOKING—Cost of Energy; GASOLINE CONSUMPTION; LAUNDRY; LIGHTING; REFRIGERATORS and FREEZERS; WATER—Heating.)

Most of the information included here can be found elsewhere in the world—I have stacks of pamphlets from various government agencies and utility companies on my kitchen dining table (my family is *still* eating standing up, and *still*, remarkably, has not mutinied). Some of the pamphlets are worth sending for (I'll mention these); others have little original material; but each includes one or two unique ideas worth passing on. My intention in *Inflation-Wise* is to pass on most of them in order to save you the trouble of sending for them yourself and of finding someplace to store them (in case your family isn't as patient as mine).

There is also a good book on the market which will help you put the whole works to work in a consistent way:

The Home Energy Guide: How to Cut Your Utility Bills
by John Rothchild and Frank Tenney
Ballantine, 1978
$1.95

The authors have devised a system of auditing a household's energy-spending patterns and, based on that information, developing an energy budget. As energy costs rise at a seemingly exponential rate, I think this sort of consistent plan will become more and more crucial. The authors go on to explain how to cut costs specifically and what each cost-cutting measure will cost (lots are free). It's a very informative book, well worth the price. (I'm hoping the second edition will include an index.)

Appliances

Calculating the Cost

If you know the wattage of an appliance and the price of electricity per kilowatt hour (kwh) in your locale, you can easily figure the cost of operating that appliance.

The wattage is usually printed (stamped) on any small appliance, or you can calculate it by multiplying amps times volts, or check the chart in ENERGY—Appliances, *Comparing the Cost* to obtain an estimate.

The cost per kwh averages 5¢ nationwide at the moment but check your bill or, if it's not there, call your electric company to find out what it is where you live—it might be quite different.

Plug the numbers into the following formula and you'll know cost per hour of use:

$$\frac{\text{Watts of appliance}}{1,000} \times \text{Price per kwh} = \text{Cost per hour of operation}$$

Example:
Most clothes dryers have a wattage of about 4,850. The national average cost per kwh is 5¢, so:

$$\frac{4850}{1,000} \times .05 = 24\tfrac{1}{4}¢ \text{ per hour of use}$$

Many appliances are normally operated for only part of an hour (e.g., your washer), some for only a minute or two (e.g., your mixer), while others are thermostatically controlled and, cycling on and off to maintain temperature, are only drawing electricity during the actual time they are "on." Weigh these factors when working out costs. To calculate costs for less than one hour, plug the answer you calculated in the above equation into those below:

for 1 minute's use: $\dfrac{\text{Cost per hour}}{60}$

for 10 minutes' use: $\dfrac{\text{Cost per hour}}{6}$

for 15 minutes' use: $\dfrac{\text{Cost per hour}}{4}$

for 20 minutes' use: $\dfrac{\text{Cost per hour}}{3}$

for 30 minutes' use: $\dfrac{\text{Cost per hour}}{2}$

Example: The clothes dryer again. Usually it takes about half an hour per load, so:

$$\frac{\$.24}{2} = .12¢ \text{ per load}$$

Cheap compared to the coin-guzzling machines at a laundromat, but more costly than a clothesline, even if someone gave you the dryer as a present.

Comparing the Cost

"Remember," says Edward, "that hot is high in cost, degrees is dollars. A clothes dryer uses almost ten times the electricity of a clothes washer, a toaster ten times more than a mixer, a portable heater almost fifteen times more than a circulating fan. Reducing the use of appliances that are heat guzzlers will thus reduce your costs."

To get an idea of relative monthly costs, multiply the estimated kwh for any given appliance by your local cost per kwh referring to the chart below (courtesy of Duke Power Company). Figures have been rounded; the utilities use estimates are based on normal usage and take thermostatic control into account where applicable:

	Average Wattage	Est. kwh Used Per Month
Food Preparation		
Blender	390	1.3
Broiler	1,450	8.3
Carving Knife	95	0.7
Coffee Maker	895	8.8
Deep Fryer	1,450	6.9
Egg Cooker	500	1.2
Frypan	1,200	15.5
Hot Plate	1,250	7.5
Mixer	125	1.1
Microwave Oven	1,450	15.8
Range/Oven		
Small surface unit (low)	125	
Small surface unit (high)	1,400	
Large surface unit (low)	250	
Large surface unit (high)	2,400	
Oven broiler	3,500	
Oven baker	3,700	97.9
With self-cleaning feature	2,700	100.4
Roaster	1,300	17.1
Sandwich Grill	1,160	2.8
Toaster	1,150	3.3
Waffle Iron	1,110	1.8

	Average Wattage	Est. kwh Used Per Month
Food Preservation		
15 Cu. Ft. Freezer	340	99.6
15 Cu. Ft. Frost Free Freezer	440	146.8
12 Cu. Ft. Refrigerator	240	60.7
12 Cu. Ft. Frost Free Refrigerator	320	101.4
14 Cu. Ft. Refrigerator/Freezer	325	94.8
14 Cu. Ft. Frost Free Refrigerator/Freezer	615	152.4
Laundry		
Clothes Dryer	4,850	82.8
Hand Iron	1,000	12.0
Automatic Washing Machine	500	8.6
Non-automatic Washing Machine	290	6.3
Water Heater	4,475	400.9
Water Pump	450	18.8
Health & Beauty		
Germicidal Lamp	20	11.8
Hair Dryer	380	1.2
Infrared Heat Lamp	250	1.1
Shaver	15	0.2
Sun Lamp	280	1.3
Toothbrush	5	0.1
Vibrator	40	0.2
Heating Pad	65	0.8
Home Entertainment		
Radio	70	7.2
Radio Record Player	110	9.1
B/W Tube TV	160	29.2
B/W Solid-State TV	55	10.0
Color Tube TV	300	55.0
Color Solid-State TV	200	36.7
Housewares		
Clock	2	1.4
Floor Polisher	305	1.3
Sewing Machine	75	0.9
Vacuum Cleaner	630	3.8
Dishwasher	1,200	30.3
Trash Compactor	400	4.2
Waste Disposer	445	2.5

	Average Wattage	Est. kwh Used Per Year (in N.C.)
Seasonal Comfort Conditioning		
Air Cleaner	50	216
Electric Blanket	180	147
Dehumidifier	260	377
Attic Fan	370	291
Circulating Fan	90	43
Rollaway Fan	170	138
Window Fan	200	170
Portable Heater	1,300	176
Humidifier	180	163

(See ENERGY—Appliances, Calculating the Cost, to find out how much any appliance is costing you in dollars and cents.)

Labeling

New rules from the Federal Trade Commission have gone into effect recently (spring 1980). They will allow you to make better choices by figuring the use cost as well as the initial cost. (Energy-efficient appliances often cost more but are usually worth the extra expense in the long run—sometimes not even very long, energy costs going up as they are.) Here are the labeling specifics.

Air Conditioners (Room)

In addition to the EER (energy efficiency rating), the Energyguide label will also give highest and lowest ratings for comparable models. The higher the EER, the less electricity the unit will use to cool the same amount of air. Typical EER's range from 4 to 12; a unit rated at 4 will cost *three times as much* to run as one with an EER of 12. Below seven is considered poor. (To calculate EER for an older air conditioner, divide BTU's by watts.)

Also when you head into the marketplace, come armed with two figures: the number of hours you expect to use the unit per year and the cost per kwh in your locale. The Energyguide labels will provide the estimated yearly dollar cost according to those variables.

120

Furnaces

Furnaces will also be given an EER, but the label won't be visible. You'll have to ask for the fact sheet—available from your dealer or contractor.

Dishwashers, Clothes Washers

These will each be labeled with the estimated yearly energy cost based on national average (plus highest and lowest for comparable models). Labels will include cost for households that heat their water by gas and those that heat water by electricity. You must know your local cost per therm (100 cubic feet of gas) or kwh and the number of loads you do per week in order to make use of the charts.

Refrigerators, Freezers

Labels will include the particular model's estimated yearly energy cost (and highest and lowest comparable models) as well as a chart to figure your cost if your local price per kwh varies from the national average.

Water Heaters

Same as refrigerators—gas or oil costs shown where appropriate, of course.

The testing was done according to Department of Energy standards. Because the differences in efficiency between some like-powered appliances were so slight, they found that the cost of the labeling program (estimated price increases range from 15¢ to $5 per unit) wouldn't be worth the information. Nonlabeled appliances include color TVs, electric dryers, and microwave ovens.

Cooling

Air Conditioners
%%%%

Air conditioning is a luxury few of us remember having when we were children and most of us have grown accustomed to taking for granted now. But it may prove monetarily worth your while to reaccustom yourself to living in temperatures a few degrees higher.

According to a Department of Housing and Urban Development (HUD) study, "if you have whole-house air conditioning, you can save about 3 percent of your air conditioning bill for each degree you turn up your thermostat." Another government pamphlet says that if you raise your setting from 72° to 78°F. you should save between 12% and 47% depending on where you live.

Another potential cost saver for those who have central air conditioning is to check the location of your condenser; if it is in the sun it will have to work extra hard and will cost you extra dollars. Shade it but be careful to do so in a way that doesn't restrict air flow out and around it.

Attic Fans
%%%%%%

We live in an area of the country where summers are exceedingly hot, where air conditioning is almost a necessity. There are midsummer days when without air conditioning I would expect to get only a third of a day's work done—partly because I would have to spend so much time breaking up squabbles between the children, additionally because I myself find temperatures above 80°F. enervating.

So we are seriously considering purchasing an attic fan. John's lab assistant swears by hers; she says that she generally can forgo turning on her air conditioner entirely until late summer (when the nights are almost as hot as the days) by use of her attic fan, which lowers her electricity bills an astounding 65%.

The idea is that you keep windows and curtains closed during the day and open them and turn on the fan in the evening when the temperature outside drops below the temperature inside. The fan will pull the cool evening air into and through the house, carrying the hot inside air out through the attic.

To decide what size fan you need, estimate the cubic feet of space in your house (multiply length by width by height) then divide this (the volume) by 10 to determine the cfm (cubic feet of air moved per minute) which will be printed on the fan. (This cfm will provide complete change of air every ten minutes.)

Cooking
$$

Several contributors suggested cooking outside to cut down on kitchen-warming which the air conditioner must then overcome. If you have outdoor outlets, take your frypan out on the porch (estimated cost per frypan use, by the way, is 2 to 2½¢).

Charcoal grilling might be more expensive—10 to 15¢ for the charcoal, 17 to 20¢ for the starter, but see CHARCOAL GRILLING to find out how to make outdoor grilling an inflation-wise choice for summer cooking.

And serve more salads! Your mothers did, in the days before air conditioning.

Landscaping
%%

If you plan to do some landscaping, consider energy efficiency in your choices. Stopping the sun before it gets in through the windowpane is seven times more effective than window coverings inside.

Deciduous trees and shrubs planted on east and west sides will help cool in summer (and in winter, when the leaves fall, will allow the sun access).

Heating
⑤ ⑤

You can save up to 35% of your heating bill by using a device found in every home—your hand: turn down the thermostat. Before I get specific, however ...

CAUTION: People with circulatory problems, some children, some older citizens, those taking certain types of drugs (e.g., phenothiazines, commonly used to treat anxiety and nausea) may be vulnerable to a condition called hypothermia—a possibly fatal drop in body temperature—which can sometimes occur in temperatures below 65°F. If you have any doubts, check with your physician before you turn the thermostat down.

That said, here are the savings you can achieve (according to HUD):

If you live in:	a 5° turndown will save you:	an 8° turndown will save you:
Montana, Wyoming, North Dakota, South Dakota, Nebraska, Minnesota, Iowa, Michigan, Wisconsin, most of New York, Vermont, New Hampshire, Maine, western Massachusetts	14%	19%
Washington, Oregon, Idaho, most of Nevada, Utah, northern Arizona, northern New Mexico, Colorado, Kansas, Missouri, Illinois, Indiana, Kentucky, Ohio, West Virginia, Maryland, Pennsylvania, Delaware, New Jersey, southern tip of New York, eastern Massachusetts, Connecticut, Rhode Island	17%	24%
California, southern tip of Nevada, southern Arizona, southern New Mexico, Oklahoma, Texas, Arkansas, Louisiana, Mississippi, Tennessee, Alabama, Georgia, Virginia, North Carolina, South Carolina, Florida	25%	35%

Ah, but how to do it. A suggestion from Elizabeth:

"When we decided to lower our thermostat I knew that a sudden temperature drop would cause my family a lot of discomfort (not to mention screaming and yelling), so I took it down by ½-degree increments every couple of days and suggested an extra sweater when complaints arose. Then I held it steady for a few extra days and resumed the lowering till I reached my goal. It worked!"

And some words about how much clothes can help:

• A tip from Cinda: "Wearing a hat (wool is best) and two pair of socks indoors will keep anybody warm in a 60° house. We do this in our house and it's fun (and makes us look crazy which we enjoy)." In fact, according to a Department of Energy publication, "the body loses between half and three-quarters of its heat through the head."
• Closely woven fabrics add at least a half degree in warmth.
• Slacks are at least a degree warmer than skirts.

- A light long-sleeved sweater equals almost 2°F. in added warmth; a heavy long-sleeved sweater 3.7°. BUT two lightweight sweaters add about 5° because the layer of air between them acts as additional insulation!

The last principle above also applies to blankets. Setting the thermostat back at night to temperatures which would be unacceptable during the day can produce further savings (as shown above). BUT SEE EARLIER CAUTION. And incidentally, a thermostatically controlled electric blanket (at 180 watts) will cost you less than 4¢ per night.

If your house is unoccupied during a major portion of the day, you may be able to leave the thermostat at night temperatures until evening by planning heat-generating tasks for morning: e.g., running your dishwasher, baking bread (you've refrigerated overnight to "cool" rise), and other kitcheny things.

And a space heater (at approximately 1,320 watts) will remove early morning bathroom chill and cost about 6½¢ per hour to run.

Equipment Maintenance
$$$$
%

Properly maintained heating and cooling equipment can reduce your fuel consumption by about 10% per system (according to a HUD study). Servicing and efficiency checks should be done at the following intervals, by a serviceperson:

Oil-burning furnace—every year
Coal furnace—at the end of each heating season
Gas furnace (bottled, LP, or natural)—every three years
Electric furnace—check manufacturer's specifications (normally needs little maintenance)
Hot-water distribution system—every year
Forced hot-air distribution system—every year
Central air conditioning—every year

There are also things *you* can and should do to permit top efficiency:

Hot-water system radiators—"bleed" air from the system once or twice a year. *Carefully* (because the water is very hot) open the valve at the top of each radiator. Holding a bucket beneath, leave the valve open until water comes out.

Your boiler (in a steam-heat system)—every three weeks during the heating season, drain a bucket of water out of your boiler (ask your fuel service company to show you how the first time when they come to check your burner). Neglecting this will mean that the sediment on the bottom will act as insulator and heat which should be reaching you will go up the chimney.

Filters—every one or two months the air filters in forced air heat systems or central air systems should be taken out and vacuumed or replaced.

Furnace Damper
%%

If you are in the market for a new gas furnace, look for one which has an automatic flue damper. This will reduce heat loss when the furnace is off.

Several companies also manufacture such devices to be attached to your present furnace. Either is said to cut total fuel consumption by 20%.

You can get a list of manufacturers by writing to:

The American Gas Association
1515 Wilson Boulevard
Arlington, Virginia 22209

Heating and Cooling

Doors
$$

A friend of Cinda's is trying to train her kids to close closet and cupboard doors—what's the point in paying to heat or cool them?

Closing off unused rooms (and their vents) can accomplish

further savings. (Don't close vents if you have a heat pump; it could cause damage to the pump.)

And if you enjoy a fire once in a while, avoid some of the loss of heat (see FIREPLACES) by shutting yourselves *in* the room with it and closing that room's vents.

If your house has a vestibule without closable doors, consider curtaining it or installing doors (especially if you have children who ignore foot stamping). The tightest storm door in the world won't help if it's left open most of the time. A closed space to enter and leave from will help cut heating and cooling losses.

Insulation
%%%

Energy savings gained from insulating your home, according to government reports, can range from 5% (if you are adding to present insulation) to 30% (if you have none to begin with). The cost, however, can be quite substantial and the payback may take some years. An exception: It is generally accepted by all authorities that unless you live in a climate where cooling *and* heating costs are exceptionally low, you will get quick payback from insulating an attic *which previously was totally without insulation*—about 30%, sometimes even more.

Needs and benefits will vary enormously depending upon where you live and the design and condition of your house. I'm delighted to report that there is a booklet (more than a booklet, really—77 pages) available from the government which will allow you to precisely figure your costs vs. your savings taking all of these variables into account.

Titled *In the Bank or Up the Chimney* (include the publication No., 023-000-00411-9), it's obtainable at a cost of $1.70 postpaid from:

Superintendent of Documents
U.S. Government Printing Office
Washington, D.C. 20402

In addition to allowing you to calculate your costs and savings, it shows and tells how to do the insulating yourself wherever possible, reducing these costs by about 50% over contractors' charges.

Highly recommended. A best buy.

In the Bank or Up the Chimney recommends at least R-22* for the uninsulated attic cited above in a temperate climate; R-38* if you heat by electricity or live in a cold climate and heat by oil. The insulation options are these:

TYPE OF INSULATION

| | Batts or Blankets | | Loose Fill (Poured-In) | | |
	glass fiber	rock wool	glass fiber	rock wool	cellulosic fiber
R-11	3½″ − 4″	3″	5″	4″	3″
R-19	6″ − 6½″	5¼″	8″ − 9″	6″ − 7″	5″
R-22	6½″	6″	10″	7″ − 8″	6″
R-30	9½″ − 10½″**	9″**	13″ − 14″	10″ − 11″	8″
R-38	12″ − 13″**	10½″**	17″ − 18″	13′ − 14″	10″ − 11″

(R-values repeated at right: R-11, R-19, R-22, R-30, R-38)

**two batts or blankets*

The Government offers a free information sheet describing the various types of insulation, advantages and disadvantages, and a simple explanation of installation including safety precautions. If the unfinished, uninsulated attic will be your only project, this is the pamphlet for you. You can get it by sending a postcard request for "Insulation," No. DOE/CS-0017, to:

U.S. Department of Energy
Technical Information Center
PO Box 62
Oak Ridge, Tennessee 37830

The pamphlet also includes a weather-zone map, with R-value suggestions for attic floors, exterior walls, and ceiling over unheated crawl spaces or basement, according to locale. It is

*R-value: the number that tells you how much resistance the insulation presents to heat flowing through it; the bigger the number the better the insulation.

128

approximate but will give you some idea of whether you ought to also consider sending for *In the Bank or Up the Chimney* (cited earlier) to work out specific costs and payback for your precise location.

And a tip from Edward: "Remember that heat rises and openings to attics are often poorly insulated—or not insulated at all. Check to make sure that the door, trapdoor, or other access is insulated and weather-stripped."

Weatherstripping and Caulking
$$$$$
%

Is it worth the cost? Probably; consider this—a ¼-inch crack between the bottom of a door and its threshold, my utility company tells me, will lose as much energy as a 9-square-inch hole in the wall.

The Department of Energy estimates an annual savings of about 10% on average. Particularly if your door and window seals aren't tight (if you can slip a quarter under the door easily, you definitely need weatherstripping; if a lighted candle flame dances when held near window frames or sashes, a need for weatherstripping and/or caulking is indicated).

Caulking
It won't be *inflationwise* to scrimp on the price of caulking compounds. The differences in cost are slight compared to the differences in durability. The best (and most expensive) is the silicone-based paintable type (Sears sells one with a ten-year replace-or-refund warranty). How much will you need? HUD suggests these amounts: ½ cartridge per window or door; 4 cartridges for the foundation sill; 2 cartridges for a two-story chimney. And where? HUD again:

1. Between window drip caps (tops of windows) and siding.
2. Between door drip caps and siding.
3. At joints between window frames and siding.
4. At joints between doorframes and siding.

5. Between windowsills and siding.
6. At corners formed by siding.
7. At sills where wood structure meets the foundation.
8. Outside water faucets, or other special breaks in the outside house surface.
9. Where pipes and wires penetrate the ceiling below an unheated attic.
10. Between porches and main body of the house.
11. Where chimney or masonry meets siding.
12. Where storm windows meet the window frame, except for drain holes at windowsill.
13. And if you have a heated attic, where the wall meets the eave at the gable ends.

Weatherstripping

Rolled vinyl, with or without metal backing, is easy to install and durable, but is visible when installed. Thin spring metal is virtually invisible and very durable but somewhat difficult to install. Foam rubber with adhesive backing is inexpensive but short-lasting and not as effective as the two above (never put it where friction occurs).

There are additional alternatives where doors are concerned— interlocking metal channels, sweeps, door shoes, vinyl bulb threshold, interlocking threshold—most of which are fairly difficult to install (the last requires a skilled carpenter), but are generally quite durable and provide exceptionally good seals. Ask your hardware dealer which she would use on her doors.

Window Coverings

Inside
%%%

Even with double-pane glass, windows can lose up to nine times more heat than the same amount of insulated wall area. Keep windows covered with drapes. According to *The Home Energy*
130

Guide, drapes can cut heat loss 6% to 7% in winter, cut heat gains 33% in summer!

Window shades can sometimes be even more efficient. Optimally, the rollers should be attached on the inside of the frame (so the shade is as close to the window as possible).

According to a researcher at Cornell University, "The fairly common vinyl-coated opaque cotton shade achieved the highest percentage (31.5) of heat savings" when hung an inch from the glass. Mounted outside the frame (3½ inches from the glass), it produced only half that savings.

Translucent shades cut heat loss by 26.2% and 16.2% at 1 inch from glass and 3½ inches, respectively. All-vinyl shades cut losses 24.8% and 13.1% respectively.

You can achieve even greater savings, according to a National Bureau of Standards study, by installing shades which are sealed to the frame, when pulled down, by means of magnetic strips.

And remember that the "landscaping" principle also applies to window coverings: it is seven times more efficient to keep the sun out in the first place—consider awnings, sun shutters, trees and the like.

Outside
%%

You can save up to 15% by installing storm windows, but they can be quite an expensive investment and the payback may take years and years.

In the Bank or Up the Chimney (see ENERGY—Insulation, for full reference) recommends polyethylene plastic sheets to achieve just about equal effectiveness. This will be quite inexpensive but may have to be replaced each year. If these makeshift storm windows achieve the savings you had hoped for you might then want to consider more convenient, more permanent (more expensive) types, adding one or two of the latter with each year's savings from using the former.

ENTERTAINMENT

Free or Low-Cost Things to Do
%%%%%%%%

There are lots and lots and lots of things to do anywhere you live, for little or nothing. And before there was televison, I suspect that people did lots more of them. Barrie and Marlowe (who have no television) can come up with a dozen ideas at the snap of a thumb-twiddling finger.

Go on picnics often (even if only in your back yard); they have something precious about them.

Take a ferry ride.

Take walks. Visit a museum, or the library, or a friend.

Invite a group to make music, singing and using simple instruments—recorders, glass bottles, sand blocks, bells, and such.

Think like a tourist, i.e., call or write your own state's Chamber of Commerce and ask for their tourist packet. You'll be astounded to find out how much there is to do—mostly free or low cost—right around the corner.

When you read your Sunday paper's entertainment section, keep your calendar handy and make note of upcoming free events. Then on those "nothing to do" days, you can just check your calendar.

Play Scrabble or Monopoly or chess or checkers or bridge.

Read.

Talk!

Fun and Information
$$$$$

If you have not yet discovered National Public Radio (NPR) please permit me the pleasure of introducing you. In particular, I want to tell you about their daily news program, "All Things Considered," which I look forward to listening to each day from 5 p.m. to 6:30 p.m.

This show delivers exactly what the program title promises. It begins each of the three half-hour segments with synopses of all the day's major newsworthy events; it expands the most important of these into detailed, interview-supplemented accounts, explaining difficult points or making comments by means of short, usually humorous, "radio plays"; it follows, then, with something a little lighter.

This last might include such things as: an interview with the founder and president of a company which, for a fee, will talk you out of buying something you think you want but have misgivings about; or a report from NPR's "stringer" in Missoula, Montana about the current state of the art of mothproofing your clothes by using certain wild plants; or an on-the-air testing of the result of their staff's investigation of the Life-Saver phenomenon: if you chew Life-Savers in the dark with your mouth open, some children discovered, you'll create sparks.

The point is that what is serious in the news receives serious attention but comic relief is also essential and is provided in fair measure. The show is so wonderfully well-orchestrated that by 6:30 I almost invariably find myself feeling not only well-informed but cheerful and energized also. Meanwhile, I've simultaneously accomplished some mindless task like making dinner or washing the dishes or tidying the house. John finds the show so comprehensive that he says if he couldn't have access to a newspaper every day, "All Things Considered" would come very close to being an acceptable substitute. *And*, there are no commercials.

Your public radio station call numbers will almost invariably be located on the FM dial somewhere between 88 and 105. If you can't find it, send a self-addressed stamped envelope requesting a list of member stations to:

National Public Radio
Public Information Department
2025 M St., NW
Washington, D.C. 20036

Enjoy. (And give my regards to Susan.)

Movies
$

We share a house at the beach each summer with two other families. Each year our friend Colin brings along several films and a projector which he has borrowed from the library back home. Showing them quite perfectly (and calmly) fills the space between sunset and the children's bedtime, and allows us to forgo the expense of endless miniature golf excursions.

Films from the library make wonderful birthday party "doings" too. Or why not make it a weekly or monthly gathering of children or adults or both? Your library has many classics to lend, including excerpts from Disney, full length Bogarts, and award-winning shorts.

FASHION
%%%%%%%%

Keeping up with the whims of the fashion industry can be a costly undertaking. I'm convinced it is unnecessary, but to be served by (instead of being subservient to) this business takes some work in a couple of areas and requires an at least slightly stubborn nature. Here's how ...

The work: first, I think what we're all after is style. Does style have anything to do with standardized hemlines? I think not. Bring to mind the most stylish person you know and do an analysis. Does she (let's say) look as stylish in an old white T-shirt and army shorts as she does in the latest designer togs? I'm betting she does. I'm further betting that she's a person who views herself as a whole being (not simply a clotheshorse) and likes what she sees. In other words, I think style comes from a well-tuned psyche, not a clothes rack. It's as simple (or complicated) as this: If you feel good about yourself, you'll likely look terrific in whatever you wear, and conversely, the height of fashion will hang on you like a limp rag if you're unhappy. So the first order of business is to get your psyche in shape. I'm not saying that's necessarily easy: I'm saying that clothes, alone, don't make anybody.

Second, although you may not be aware of it, you have probably developed, over the years, a "look" you like. You will save money on future clothing buys if you will take some time to find out what that look is. Open your closet doors and scrutinize your wardrobe. You will be likely to find, as I did, that there are a few items that you absolutely love and wear a great deal, and quite a few which never find their way off their hangers. Now pull out the loved-ones, lay them out on your bed, and really *look* at them. Figure out what they have in common—a color family? a cut? a fit? a fabric? and so forth. (See also CLOTHES—Handmade, Choosing Patterns.) Once you discover exactly what it is that makes this particular group of clothes special to you, the clothing you buy in the future will be much more likely to "fit" into your present wardrobe and be *worn*.

Cinda recently recommended a book I enjoyed and from which I learned a lot about discovering and developing a personal "look"—it's *Cheap Chic* (by Caterine Milinaire and Carol Troy, beautifully designed by Bea Feitler, published by Harmony Books, New York, revised and updated 1978, $6.95). In addition to a well-written, wide-ranging and informative text, it includes copious photographs, illustrations, and interviews with everyone from Yves Saint-Laurent (of whom you've probably heard) to Ingeborg Day (of whom you've probably not heard but whose system of dividing the cost of a garment by the number of times worn to determine "cost per wear" is very revealing when applied to one's own wardrobe).

Now, finally, a word about stubbornness and how that can pay. My advice is to adopt this rule: If you don't love it, don't buy it. You will be amazed at how much this simple precept, followed faithfully, will reduce your clothing expenditures.

For instance, if the fashion industry introduces a season of design you initially find ugly or wrong for you, or just downright boring, boycott. What designers count on is the fact that people can get used to anything. They're right. But why should we? Trust your instinct. If enough consumers put their feet down instead of their money, the business of fashion will begin paying attention, will be forced to serve rather than be served. Concerned about feeling out of place in last year's clothes? Look around you. More and more people are refusing to bow, wearing what suits them physically and mentally, disregarding designers' dictates. You won't be alone.

It's easy. Just keep in mind that the fashion industry is a service industry, is handsomely well-paid for providing its service, and has no right whatsoever to intimidate any buyer into feeling even slightly anxious about the length of her skirt. May you never worry about hemlines again.

FILM

Cold Storing
$$
%%%%

Uncle Beeze wrote that he buys film which has nearly reached its expiration date at great reductions and stores it in his freezer. He suggested that it should be thawed at least twenty-four hours before being loaded into your camera. This sounded like a good cost-cutter to me but several friends were wary of taking the chance on losing a great shot to outdated film.

When I mentioned it to John, he told me that the film used in his laboratory is stored in the refrigerator. This spurred me to call an acquaintance who takes pictures for a living.

Here's what Leon pronounced: "Oh, yes. Professional photographers do that. The lowered temperatures slow down the natural oxidization process which causes film to deteriorate. You can pass the expiration date by six months and feel perfectly safe using the film if it has been stored in this manner. It will probably, in fact, be fine up to twelve months but holding it that long would be taking a bit of a chance. Be sure you wrap and seal film watertight."

Mail Order
%%%%%

Gerry buys film by calling the toll-free numbers of New York mail-order developers listed in the advertising section at the back of photo magazines. He chooses brand-name film which comes with prepaid processing and the total cost is less than half what he would pay at a retail store.

FIREPLACES
%%%%

Ordinary fireplaces deliver only about one-tenth of the wood's heating value into the room, but even that can be enough to take the chill off on those early spring or late fall days when running the furnace seems excessive. However, on days when your furnace *is* working, a fire in your fireplace (particularly at the dying-down stage) can draw a substantial amount of that expensively produced heat up the chimney in its draft.

The costs of countering the losses vary widely. The most obvious way to save, of course, is to keep the damper tightly closed and never light a fire. The cost in pleasure, however, may be as high for you as it is for me. For me, gazing into a fire on a cold winter night ranks with glimpsing a patch of violets in spring—they each represent their respective seasons in some inimitable way. Fire gazing is one of those priorities to which I can assign no price.

My friend Vicky and her husband spent about $15 to have a metal-works company (which they located through the Yellow Pages) make a tin cover to fit their fireplace opening. They used to put it in place at evening's end to seal the heat in the room (leaving the damper open for the dying fire) and held it tight with their firescreen.

I use the past tense *re* Vicky's tin cover because she most kindly gave it to us when she replaced it with tempered glass doors. (The gift allows me to take a slightly more sense-over-emotions approach to firegazing.) The cost of such glass doors can range from $40 to $600. They allow some radiant heat to pass into the room but prevent the room air from being sucked up the chimney. And they do permit a view (although it's not quite the same, somehow).

Vicky and her husband might someday want to add some sort of heat-returning grate (price range: $100 to $200) designed to push some of the heat generated by the fire back into the room—quite a lot in some cases. Used without the glass doors, such devices claim to provide about 50% return.

The next step might be a wood-burning stove, either the sort that can be installed in an existing fireplace, placed in front of it to utilize its chimney, or installed elsewhere. Cost range is exceedingly wide for these (from $300 to $1,200), many of the more expensive models being imported. Expect to pay a premium for decoration and enamel—i.e., if efficiency is your main concern you can get that and save initial costs by sticking to basics.

Wood-burning stoves can be an especially inexpensive heat source if wood is easily and cheaply available (see FIREWOOD for sources). According to the National Forest Service, one cord (which means a stack 8 feet by 4 feet by 4 feet) of air-dried hardwood will provide approximately the equivalent of 150 to 175 gallons of fuel oil or 24,000 cubic feet of natural gas, or (by my local utility company's reckoning) 7,000 kilowatts of electricity.

Working most efficiently, a woodstove won't provide any viewing pleasure, but the monetary savings might convince me to forgo that addiction. I suppose I could always get an occasional fire-gazing fix by leaving the doors open once in a while. And, too, there will always be spring violet-glimpsing to be had ... free.

(See also WOODSTOVES and WOODSTOVE SAFETY.)

FIREWOOD

Free or Cheap
$$$
%%%%%%%%%

If you live in an area near a National Forest, you can obtain a permit at your District Ranger Office which will allow you to cut any "dead or down" material, or any tree marked, in designated firewood areas of National Forests. (Your permit will specify how much you can cut—up to ten cords when supplies are adequate.)

To find out more, call your local Forest Service Office (check the phone book under U.S. Department of Agriculture) and ask for information about the "firewood program."

Uncle Beeze: "Scout your locale for new construction areas—they may provide two free sources. Lots being cleared—ask if you can cut and haul the felled trees for them in exchange for the wood. Construction sites themselves—ask building contractor for permission to pick up scrap." Check with lumberyards that do their own milling. Quite often you can pick up slab wood (the rough outside pieces left over when logs are sawed into boards) at greatly reduced prices.

Check, also, with your highway department and utility company. Either or both may permit you to haul away trees they have felled for visibility or line clearance purposes.

And from my mother: "Don't throw away any old telephone books or newspapers. The former are *very* slow burning and the latter make perfect kindling: Roll five or six sheets (not too tightly) and place them from front to back of your fireplace about six inches apart."

FLOWERS
%%%%%

Happening upon a vase of fresh flowers is always a delightful surprise (even if I put them there myself). It adds inches to my height and pounds to my energy. In winter, when weather conditions prohibit garden or pot growing but when such a lift might be most appreciated, the resort is a florist and expensive.

Elizabeth suggests that you can fill more rooms than you might think you can afford if you buy one bunch and stretch it to fill several vases by adding evergreens from yard or woods.

"Small flowering plants are great, too," she adds. I've never had much luck keeping the blossoms coming in winter myself, but even if they stop blooming, as Elizabeth points out, they often cost less initially (watch for sales) and usually do last longer than most fresh-cut flowers.

FREE INFORMATION

Government Sources
%%%%%%%

Part of your tax dollar is spent by the government in researching and writing and publishing consumer information of every sort imaginable. Since you have to pay taxes anyway, do be sure to take advantage of this service. (It's not exactly free, in other words, but if you don't use it, it *is* money wasted.)

Write for a catalog of what is currently available to:

The Consumer Information Center
Pueblo, Colorado 81009

Use a postcard and be sure to print your name and address clearly, including zip code (they will use your card as a mailing label).

A monthly government publication which I have found especially useful is *The National Consumer Buying Alert* which is also available free from the address above, Attention: Esther Peterson. It provides information about expected marketplace trends which might affect the prices of food, energy, housing and health care. Food expected to be in short or abundant supply is highlighted, for instance, so that intelligent planning can permit smart purchasing.

Published References

Want to know how much your old comic books are worth? How to build a closet? How to play the harmonica? How to avoid a nervous breakdown? You can find out, free, from pamphlets produced by consumer groups, government agencies, and businesses throughout the country. The answers are available to these questions and on nearly every other imaginable subject, for the price, most often, of a postcard. For where to write, see:

The Catalog of Free Things
Jeffrey Feinman and Mark Weiss
William Morrow and Co., Inc.
New York, 1976, $6.95

or

1001 Valuable Things You Can Get Free
Mort Weisinger
Bantam Books
New York, 1977, $1.25

GARDENS

Victory gardens are back, for the same reason they came into existence in the first place—saving money on food. But do they? Cinda, whose business and training involve her in gardening, and Edward, who has done some homesteading, both think the answer might be no.

Considering the first year's investment—shovels, trowels, fencing, hoses, possibly rental of tilling equipment—the commitment to gardening must be long-term to amortize this initial investment and make it pay.

Many new gardeners forget to add in the cost of canning or freezing equipment, the cost of fertilizer and pesticides, the cost of seeds or seedlings and of water, when figuring their actual outlay per quart. A Michigan State University Extension service study computed these costs under actual home gardening conditions in their locale and found that in 1976 a quart of home canned tomatoes from a first year garden would cost 45¢ ; a quart of green beans, 63¢ . If the commitment were in fact long term, so that capital investments were amortized over twenty years, the cost dropped to 14¢ and 32¢ respectively.

There *are* ways to economize. Edward suggests gardening organically—composting, mulching, companion planting, choosing pest-resistant crop varieties, using kitchen-made pesticides.

And Cinda suggests that gardening and preserving cooperatively, so that capital costs are shared by many, would be smart.

Of course, the first time you go out to your lovingly tended garden and pick and bite into a sun-warmed tomato, you may not count the cost. It's just smart to be aware that an individual, small, family garden may take many years to begin paying.

(See also AGRICULTURAL EXTENSION SERVICE; CO-OPERATIVES—Gardens)

Books

My favorite, without hesitation:

> *The Basic Book of Organic Gardening*
> edited by Robert Rodale, compiled by Glenn F. Johns
> Ballantine Books, 1971
> $2.25

This book will cut your gardening costs simply because so many of the organic gardening supplies and systems are inexpensive. Companion planting, homemade insecticides, free fertilizer and mulching as well as how to get the most yield for your seed money—the whens and whys and hows of planting and growing and harvest—are all here in this gem of a book.

There is also *The Encyclopedia of Organic Gardening* by the same people, the staff of *Organic Gardening and Farming Magazine*, Rodale Books, Inc., Emmaus, Pennsylvania 18049, which you might want to get after you're hooked. It is longer, covers many more specifics—even the most esoteric sort—but it is also quite a lot more expensive (the last time I checked, about $14). I recommend that you begin with *The Basic Book*.

Composting
%%%%%%%%%

Who fertilizes the lovely lush green forests you hike in? Nature, at no cost, by composting. Who fertilizes your garden? Why not you, at little or no cost, by composting?

If you garden at all and throw your kitchen wastes, your leaves, your grass clippings, your weedings into a garbage can instead of onto a compost heap, really, when you think about it, you are throwing away money.

And because compost is made from such a wide variety of plant materials which have drawn various nutrients from the soil, it will return to your garden not only major fertilizer elements but also trace elements which might not be available in commercial fertilizers.

Almost any gardening book includes instructions for making a compost heap, usually with accompanying illustrations. My personal favorite is the elegant system designed by the late Jim Crockett and included in his book *Crockett's Victory Garden* (Little, Brown and Company, 1977, $9.95, paper). His description and illustrations are clear and precise for both the bin and the composting process itself. The result is attractive enough to avoid offending even the most finicky neighbor.

Landscaping the Vegetable Garden

Ursula: "We have a great expanse of lawn in front of our suburban home and no hidden back yard area sunny enough to accommodate a vegetable garden. One of my husband's favorite summer expressions, as he watched our neighbors spending huge sums on lawn fertilizers, was 'you can't eat grass,' but we had hesitated to ruffle our neighbors' feathers by planting vegetables in front of the house. Here's the plan we finally came up with which has drawn compliments rather than complaints: We designed a garden bed with curved edges, and included marigolds (as border—and as deterrent to bean beetles and nematodes); nasturtium (planted among the cucumbers to ward off cucumber beetles); carrots (which look like border plantings above the ground); and sunflowers (along the back border, as both decoration and food crop, for us as well as the birds we feed in winter). The long kidney-shaped garden was placed at a pleasant angle along a corner of the yard and one neighbor actually asked if we had hired a landscape designer!"

Mulching
$$$$

Cass: "The first year I planted a vegetable garden our water use nearly doubled. Then a friend suggested mulching, and by doing this I not only cut the need for watering back to manageable levels but provided my plants with free fertilizer and saved myself the enormous amounts of time I'd spent on weeding the previous year. I used grass clippings—my own and my neighbors'—and have since read that, if you happen to live in farm country, many farmers are delighted to have you haul off their slightly rotted hay. Any vegetable matter which rots will do, and enriches the soil more and more each year."

Free Sources of Fertilizer, Compost Material, Mulch . . .
%%%%%%%%

- —Local egg farms, stables, feed lots for manure
- —Worm farmers for discarded worm-worked soil
- —Tobacco farmers for plant stems (compost—potassium, nitrogen)
- —Farmers for spoiled hay (mulch)
- —Barbers for hair clippings (compost—nitrogen)
- —Grocers for spoiled fruit and vegetables (compost)
- —Wineries for solid matter left after juice is fermented
- —Breweries for spent hops (compost)
- —Sawmills for sawdust (mulch)
- —Neighbors for grass clippings and leaves (mulch and compost)
- —Incinerators for ash (phosphorus, potassium)
- —Your fireplace for wood ashes (potassium)
- —The woods for pine needles (mulch)
- —Fisheries for scraps (phosphorus, nitrogen, potassium)
- —Chicken hatcheries for eggshells (lime, nitrogen)
- —Sewage treatment plants for dried activated sludge (nitrogen, phosphorus)
- —Your garden for plant refuse, including weeds (compost)
- —The ocean for seaweed (potassium, nitrogen)

—Your kitchen for eggshelis, vegetable, fruit and fish scraps, coffee grounds, pressure-cooked bones, nut shells, etc., etc. (compost)

Pesticides, Cheap (and Safe)

Cinda says to cut down on gardening expenses (and avoid the many commercial pesticides which kill bees and other natural aids to productivity) you can make a pest spray right in the kitchen.

Liquefy, in a blender:

1 garlic clove
1 quart water
2 tablespoons cayenne pepper
4 medium onions

Stir in: 1 tablespoon soap flakes.

Seeds
$
%%%%

A few years ago, when Cinda was completing her horticulture studies, she happened to mention that I could save a bit of gardening money by not assuming that my seeds weren't viable past the date on the packet. I had not taken special care of them (as recommended below), but you know me by now, I *had* saved *all* my half-used packets from the couple of previous years.

She explained how to test them by placing a few from each packet between paper towels kept moistened for a few days (length: germination time on packet) to see if any sprouted. Most did, and so I *did* save on seeds that year and now, knowing how to store them, I save every year.

Organic Gardening and Farming Magazine (Rodale Press, 33 East Minor Street, Emmaus, Pennsylvania 18049, $6.85 per year) included the following information in their January 1976 issue (article by Jeff Cox).

To store, reseal the seed packets with freezer tape, place them in a freezer container, and seal the container with freezer tape as well, being sure to mark and date it. Place in freezer.

Approximate viability periods for some vegetables:

One to two years—hybrid tomatoes, leeks, onions, parsnips, spinach, corn

Three years—beans, carrots, peas

Four years—chard, fennel, mustard, pumpkin, beet, pepper, rutabaga, standard tomatoes

Five years—brussels sprouts, broccoli, cabbage, cauliflower, cantaloupe, celeriac, celery, Chinese cabbage, collards, cress, cucumbers, endive, kale, kohlrabi, lettuce, melons, radishes, squash, turnips

You can also save seed produced by your plants, as gardeners did (I bet my grandfather did) years ago as a hedge against gardening costs. Only standard varieties, however, will produce vigorous plants; hybrids won't. The seed should be washed with plain water, naturally dried, and stored as above.

And if as quite often happens you find that you don't use all the seeds in the packet, then next time you buy seed, why not check first with friends to see if any want to share the cost and contents of a packet or ten.

GASOLINE CONSUMPTION

Driving Style
%%

Smooth and steady wins the jackpot. Jack-rabbit starts and unnecessary accelerating and braking can cost you plenty. Jumpy starts and fast getaways, according to Department of Transportation tests, can burn over 50% more gasoline than normal acceleration.

Robert Sikorsky, author of *How to Get More Miles per Gallon* (St. Martin's Press, 1978, $2.95), suggests imagining an apple sitting on your hood. The idea is to accelerate so smoothly that the apple wouldn't fall off.

He also points out that it takes up to six times more gas to get a car moving from a dead stop than from even a few miles per hour. By anticipating traffic flow and traffic lights, avoiding such full stops and brake-slamming whenever possible by slowing down sooner, you can improve gas mileage 10% to 25%.

These techniques really work, really save gas. My own implementation of the smooth and steady methods described in this book (those above and others) increased my mpg 10% in the first week.

And the book includes many, many more—282 tips *re* parking, upkeep, buying, gadgets, etc.—which really will reduce gas consumption if implemented.

Idling
$$$$$$$$$

According to the most recent U.S. Department of Energy literature on the subject, the rule governing idling is this: *if you expect to be at a standstill for more than 30 seconds, shutting off your engine and restarting will use less gas than idling.*

When idling, your mpg is zero. Studies indicate that each fifteen minutes of idling wastes one quart of gas, a gallon an hour. Seems as though you would have to do a lot of idling to tote up that hour, doesn't it?

But look at it this way: If you let your car idle just ten minutes a day (say, five minutes in the morning while you wait for your child to run back into the house for the lunchbox she forgot and five minutes in the evening while you chat with a colleague in the parking lot before heading for home), in one month (thirty days) you will have spent *five hours* idling. At $1.50 per gallon, idling thus will cost you $7.50 per month, *$90 per year.*

Oil Choice

The Department of Energy recommends using "good quality SE multi-grade oils like 10W-30 and 10W-40 to reduce internal engine friction and get better gas mileage." Even lower viscosities are recommended during winter months in cold climates.

Planning Ahead
$ $ $

As often as possible, combine trips. To provide real incentive, figure your per trip cost and then calculate what you'll save per year by eliminating one or two or three of your usual trips per week.

For instance, we live about twelve miles from the nearest town, our car gets 15 mpg, gas costs $1.20 per gallon at this writing. So... $1.20 ÷ 15 = $.08 per mile; thus, each round trip I eliminate will save me nearly $2.

Now suppose I plan ahead and combine what might potentially be four trips into one—keep a dental appointment, then attend a class, then visit a friend, then pick up the groceries—I'll save $6. If I combine four trips into one every week, I'll save about $300 a year!

Also consider joint trips—I don't mean just car-pooling to places of employment—I mean car-pooling to the grocery store as some of my neighbors do. Cinda always calls a couple of neighbors whenever she's heading out to shop to ask if she can pick up anything for them; they do the same.

And if you live in an area where mass transit is available, making use of it can save much gas.

Speed
% %

The most efficient range is between 35 and 45 miles per hour, and exceeding 55 can really begin to cost you. At 50 mph, for instance, you'll get 18% better gas mileage than at 65 (and 20% better mpg at 55 than at 70).

And as a bonus savings, you'll avoid the expense of speeding tickets (or worse).

Tires
%

Save 5% on gas by regularly checking and maintaining tires inflated to the manufacturer's highest recommendations.

Save 3% to 10% by tiring your car with radials. (They also last longer than conventional ones.)

Tune-up
%

Keep your car tuned according to recommendations in your owner's manual (available from the manufacturer if you don't have one), or about once every 6,000 to 12,000 miles, and save up to 12% on gasoline bills.

If you haven't a manual to guide you, be on the lookout for the telltale signs of a car in need of tune-up—hard starting, hesitation, sputtering, rough idle. In addition to cleaning and adjusting plugs and points, checking timing, replacing air and fuel elements, the U.S. Department of Energy suggests:

- Removing foreign matter from the exhaust gas recirculatory valve and hoses, and checking the controls following the manufacturer's specifications.
- Checking for leaks in the fuel system
- Checking, cleaning, or, if necessary, replacing the positive crankcase ventilating valve (PCV)
- Checking all electrical ignition wiring and connections for voltage drop and resistance—cleaning, tightening, and replacing as necessary
- Inspecting the choke for proper operation
- Setting idle speed to manufacturer's specifications

All will help keep your mpg at its highest.

GIFTS

Handmade
%%%%%%

"When you think about it," writes Cinda, "the original idea behind gift-giving was to say 'I love you' to the recipient." In the days before the mad-holiday-department-store-scramble, people sent that message by giving each other loaves of bread or hand-knit mittens.

Any gift, whether store-bought or handmade (and in any price range) can be special as long as it says that the giver cared enough to spend that precious commodity—time—in the choosing or the making. And gifts made by the giver are almost invariably less expensive than store-bought presents.

I hear people saying they don't know how. But I agree with Cinda's earlier statement—practically anybody can learn to do practically anything herself (or himself). Here's what I suggest: Learn a new craft a year and practice till perfect by employing your new-found skill making holiday presents. It can be learned at home, from a book, or a friend; and courses are inexpensive at craft shops, evening schools, and through your Agricultural Extension Service. (See also GIFTS—Handmade, *Recommended Books*.)

My sisters and I were taught by our mother—at her knee, as the saying goes. She had more than talent, she also had a plan. Each and every autumn, from the year we turned six to the year we finished high school, she taught us some new craft so that we could make Christmas presents for about fifteen relatives and friends.

I can remember embroidering initials on the corner of fifteen handkerchiefs at about age eight, knitting fifteen simple scarves at age nine, designing and executing fifteen picture calendars at age ten, filling fifteen tins with homemade candy at age eleven, and hand-lettering (with ruffles and flourishes) fifteen copies of my favorite poem at age twelve.

Her plan worked wonderfully well: After you've done something fifteen times in succession, you will truly have *learned* that skill.

And if I were the betting kind, I'd bet my last dollar that my Uncle Beeze still remembers (maybe even still *has*) that 15¢ handkerchief with the slightly off-center initials on the corner. And further, I'd take my two-dollar winnings and bet that if I spent 25¢ on a similar handkerchief this autumn and embroidered his initials on *it*, he would be equally touched by my "I love you."

Planning Ahead
%%%%

When a friend or relative mentions a craving or gift wish, my mother makes a written note of it. She keeps the list in her wallet

150

and can often pick up gifts perfectly suited to the recipient whenever she spots them on sale, thereby allowing her to buy gifts she wouldn't be able to afford during the full-price holiday season.

Once your kids reach school age, you will find that they will be invited to a birthday party or two nearly every month. Running out before each one to pay $3 to $5 per present quickly adds up. Instead, I keep a treasure chest of toys and books accumulated in multiples when I find them on sale and my children can choose appropriate gifts for their friends from this box.

Recommended Books
%%%%

Elizabeth, a perfectionist craftswoman who makes few recommendations without at least some reservation or another, writes: "A really fine book for making things for yourself or others is:

Decorations for Holidays and Celebrations
by Barbara B. Stephan
Crown Publishers, Inc., New York, 1978
$8.95

Worth the price! This," she says, "is my all-time favorite craft book, very comprehensive—beautiful things."

I was intrigued by her enthusiasm and took a look at the book myself. It's now on my bookshelf, too. The title is misleading in a way because although the designs described in the examples are geared toward holiday celebrations, the techniques could be used for making gifts for any occasion. It *is* a wonderful book—lavishly illustrated, the text clear, thorough, and precise. Fine for beginners, and old hands will find new inspirations.

It includes several chapters *re* crafts based on natural things collected from the fields; crafts using eggs, fabric, paper, metal, and glass; and kitchen crafts.

I am always on the lookout for some new craft to try. (The urge tends to be especially strong around September.) Jann Johnson's *Discovery Book of Crafts* (Reader's Digest Press, New York, 1975, $14.95) is a book I've enjoyed borrowing from our library several times because it includes among its sixty-five projects something or other to interest every dabbler.

The photographs are seductive, the variety of crafts rather astounding—aluminum foilwork, antiquing photos, applique, basketmaking, batik, bookbinding, bread sculpture, cake decorating, claywork, cooking, crochet, decoupage, embossing, embroidery, flower-drying, glass etching, glass-painting, knitting, macramé, mosaic, needlepoint, papier mâché, plasticwork, printmaking, quilting, rhinestone-studding, rug-hooking, sewing, shellwork, silverwork, stained glass, stenciling, soapmaking, tie-dying, waxwork, weaving, and woodworking.

The directions in some cases make assumptions about the reader's background knowledge and I would suspect that beginners might sometimes find such gaps frustrating, but anyone who has done a fair amount of craftwork will enjoy this book.

Talent and Time
%%%%%%%%

You will find that giving your time and/or talent is much appreciated. But it's nice to give a package that can be opened, too, so make these offerings in the form of a "coupon" book. Below are some examples of what I mean, the kinds of "books" John and I have presented to friends and relations over the years. (We've found that a brainstorming session to come up with coupon ideas which suit the recipient's current circumstances works best.)

—To the parents of a new baby, a coupon book containing five "tickets" each reading: "This coupon good for 4-hour relief. Redeemable at any mutually agreed upon time for an evening of babysitting (when absence will make the heart grow fonder)."

—To a recent college graduate beginning her first office job, a coupon book containing tickets for a free car wash, free haircut, or whatever, and one reading: "This coupon good for making you distinguished. Redeemable for monogramming on any article of clothing. Limited to 3-letter words (or initials)."

—To a friend redecorating (or opening) an office, a coupon book offering help with moving or painting or cleaning or the like and including something like the following: "This coupon good for ruffles and flourishes. Redeemable for a calligraphic rendering of a poem or proverb of your choice, suitable for framing."

—To your mother, who complains that you never write, twelve "tickets" reading: "This coupon good for updates. Redeemable at a rate no oftener than one per month, for a three-page chatty family newsletter. Guaranteed to be paid within one week of receipt."

The idea is to match your talents to the recipient's needs or desires. If she's admired your bread-baking or cooking, give her lesson coupons; if he travels a lot and you stay around town, give him dog-sitting or lawn-mowing coupons. Make the coupon book itself as elaborate as you like; you can perforate the pages for easy tear-off by running them under a threadless sewing-machine needle.

We've found this to be a never-fail gift, and as much fun for us to think up as for the recipient to cash in.

GIFTWRAPPING
$$
%%%%%%%

Whenever I run across closeout sales on ribbons or lace at my fabric store I buy it in bulk and use it instead of commercial wrapping ribbon. Yard for yard it is much cheaper, and look for look much more elegant.

And Elizabeth suggests cutting leftover fabric into strips with pinking shears for use as ribbon.

Children's Gifts
$$
%%%%%%%%

Sunday comic pages make terrific wrapping paper for children's gifts. My children also like to decorate plain old printed newspaper with magic marker pictures appropriate to the season or receiver.

HAIR CARE

Hot Oil Treatment
$

I made a few calls to local beauty salons and discovered that for $8 to $12, they would give my hair a hot oil treatment to remoisturize and condition it.

Or, I could do it myself for 5¢, the way my mother used to when I was a child, this way: Warm a tablespoon of olive or vegetable oil, massage it into your scalp, wrap with an as-hot-as-you-can-stand-it moist towel, wrap the towel in plastic wrap, leave it on for 20 minutes, then wash hair.

Rinse
%%%%%%%

Cinda: "Getting all the soap out (after shampooing) with a lemon juice and water rinse has become an expensive practice as the price of lemons rises. White vinegar (mixed 1:4 with water) does the same trick at about a quarter of the cost."

HAIRCUTS

At Home
$ $ $ $ $ $ $ $
%%%%%%%%

Professional haircuts every four to six weeks, as recommended by professionals, can total quite a hefty sum over the course of a year—up to about $200 *per family member*.

There are ways to cut down on this cost (see HAIRCUTS—Professional) and there is a way to eliminate this cost entirely—by

154

learning to do it yourself. Many contributors made this suggestion and it is not as difficult a skill to learn as you might think.

Several books are available. One of them, *How to Cut Your Own or Anybody Else's Hair* (by Bob Bent, Simon and Schuster, New York, 1977, $4.95) is large, so the illustrations can be easily seen and referred to mid-cut, and spiral bound, so that the book can be laid open flat—two important assets.

I have been cutting the hair on my own family's heads as long as I've known them, and according to this book (which is right) I have been doing it wrong for twelve years. Nevertheless I give quite good haircuts. All it takes is practice.

The very nicest thing about learning this skill is that you *can't* do irreparable damage. Hair grows back! Keeping that in mind will do wonders for your nerves when you first begin to learn.

Here are a few hints:

1. A good pair of barber shears are essential. Don't skimp on the price of these. They will cost you less than a professional cut and thus pay for themselves the first time you use them.
2. Begin gingerly, calmly, when you and your subject are both in good moods. Cut just a little, 1/4 inch or so, the first few times; you will have to give haircuts more often, of course, but that will just give you more practice, so it's a plus.
3. You may want to alternate home cuts with professional cuts for the first six months or so while you build your skill and confidence. If so, go along, and *watch* carefully as the haircut is given—you will learn a great deal and improve your technique each time.

Professional
%%%%

If you have your hair cut professionally and get the whole works—shampoo, cut, blow dry—about 50% of the cost will be for the cut itself. Save the other half by shampooing before you go to the salon and blowing your own hair after you get back home.

I have also found that if you have the work done at a barber shop rather than a beauty salon the whole works will be at least 25% less expensive; in my locale barbers throw in the blow-drying free.

But don't just walk in any old where off the street—a bad haircut is not just a waste of money, it can make you miserable for weeks. Though I cut my own hair now, the style I wear was carefully chosen to suit my face shape and hair texture by a professional. And I found her by asking everyone I knew whose haircut looked as though it "belonged" to her who had done the cutting. The same name was repeatedly mentioned, and I, too, found happiness in a perfect hairstyle.

HANGERS
%%%%%%%%%

If you're running short of clothes hangers, ask your dry cleaners if they have any bent ones to give away—I have more than once received a whole bag for the asking.

Small clothing stores are another possible source.

HEALTH CARE

Cinda: "My advice on how to save money on health care: eat foods that are good for you, not junk; find a sport, anything which forces you to exercise; get enough sleep; *and*, don't be a hypochondriac—find less expensive ways to get attention."

THE Book
$ $
%%%%%%%%

The quickest payback we have ever had on any book we have ever bought was on this one:

Take Care of Yourself: A Consumer's Guide to Medical Care
by Donald M. Vickery, M.D., and James F. Fries, M.D.
Addison-Wesley Publishing Company, 1976
$5.95

156

We saved a $20 visit to our pediatrician in the first week it was on our shelves, and countless sums of money—and moments of anxiety—since.

The book is divided into two sections. The first, "Skills for the Medical Consumer," includes these chapters: Your Habits and Your Health, The Annual Checkup and Other Myths, Finding the Right Medical Facility, Reducing Your Medication Costs, The Home Pharmacy, and Avoiding Medical Fraud.

The second section, "The Patient and the Common Complaint," is the one you will turn to most often and comprises three-quarters of the book. It consists of flow charts coupled with written text for seventy common medical problems. As I write this sentence, looking for a simple example to include here, my copy falls open of its own accord to "Problem No. 8: Head Injury" (little wonder, with three gymnastic children and a house surrounded by trees). The right-hand page looks something like this:

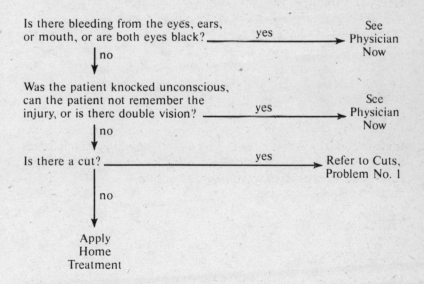

Across from this flow chart, on the left-hand page, many details and fine points are outlined. Home treatment is described for every "Problem" as well as "What to Expect at the Doctor's Office."

This is a book I would place in the invaluable category; I don't just recommend it without reservation, I recommend it with enthusiasm.

Apparently Blue Cross/Blue Shield agrees (which makes good sense since its use should cut down on unnecessary hospital and doctor visits). In my locale Blue Cross/Blue Shield offers their reprint of this book for only $2.50. The cost may be slightly higher or lower in other areas. If you're interested, give your Blue Cross/Blue Shield Public Relations office a call.

(See also HEALTH CARE—Literature.)

Literature

Blue Cross/Blue Shield offices in many locales offer free or low-cost pamphlets and books on a variety of health concerns, including alcoholism, drug problems, nutrition, prenatal care, new baby care, physical fitness, and the like. To find out what is available from your local office (the list varies from locale to locale), call their Public Relations Department.

The U.S. government also offers a wide range of health-care information; over forty publications are listed under "Health" in the current Consumer Information Catalog. Most are free. Write for your catalog (use a postcard) to:

Consumer Information Center
Pueblo, Colorado 81009

Surgery
Ⓢ Ⓢ Ⓢ
%%%%%%%%

If nonemergency surgery has been recommended to you—particularly a hysterectomy, hemorrhoidectomy or tonsillectomy (those operations which are most often performed unnecessarily)—get a second opinion. You may save both money and trauma.

Don't get it from your physician's partner; don't even ask for a referral from him. Ask among your friends or neighbors or call the Department of Health, Education and Welfare's toll-free number: 800-325-6400. They will provide the name of a specialist near you.

Medicare pays for the second opinion at its usual rates. In some

158

states Medicaid and Blue Cross/Blue Shield or other private insurance will also pay—check with them.

On the same sort of note, recent television exposés of unscrupulous gynecologists performing fake abortions on women who were not, in fact, pregnant, indicates that it would be wise, if you are considering an abortion, to have the pregnancy test performed at some place that doesn't have a stake in the matter—a women's health-counseling clinic, for example.

And when you do have any surgery performed (elective or otherwise) ask if it can be done on an outpatient basis, and/or whether any necessary presurgical tests can be done *before* you enter the hospital to shorten your length of stay and thus cut costs (unless insurance coverage would then be jeopardized).

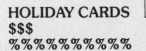

HOLIDAY CARDS
$$$
%%%%%%%%

My Grandmother Deedee (mother of my mother and my Uncle Beeze and my Aunt Rutie among others) used to cut the message page from the Christmas cards she received and send the front part as her own card the following year, writing her note on the back. Often, she would tell who had sent *her* the card, how they were, etc., creating a round-robin sense among a large group of friends.

Barrie and Marlowe assign the designing of their card to their now six-year-old daughter, then have it duplicated on cardweight paper (to be folded with the design and message inside so that it is its own envelope). It's fun for recipients to see her artistic progression through the years, and the cost is about $5 per hundred.

HOUSECLEANING
$$$
%%%%

You have heard the phrase, "If you need something done, ask a busy woman." Jane is one of those women who gets asked . . . often. She

159

mothers full-time, writes and teaches (often as a volunteer) part-time, serves as a board member for several local organizations, has organized several local organizations, and, when her friends are in need, Jane always seems to find the time to make them dinner (from scratch of course) or care for their children. On top of all that, she keeps a spotless house.

Jane: "I use two rather unusual cleaning agents which are inexpensive (particularly when purchased in giant sizes, which is the way I buy them) and work well. The first is white vinegar mixed at the rate of 1/2 cup to 1/2 gallon water which I use to damp-mop my no-wax floor between scrubbings; it shines beautifully because it cuts the soap. Straight vinegar is also the best nonstreaking cleaner available for windows. The second is 70% isopropyl alcohol which I pour on a washcloth or rag and use to clean and shine my bathroom each day—it not only shines, it disinfects too."

Cinda "Don't buy fancy brand-name cleaners. Use ammonia and water for windows, floors, and woodwork—they're the working ingredients most often found in these products. I use household bleach for sink and toilet and tub.

Also from Cinda: "Empty out vacuum-cleaner bags instead of throwing them away. I also wash vacuum-cleaner and air-conditioner filters and hang them on the line to dry rather than replacing them with new ones."

Cinda and Julia both wrote that they are happy to report savings in vacuum-cleaner bags, sponges, cleaning products, and energy (personal and public) by *not*, as Cinda puts it, "cleaning so frenetically." (I'll bet *I've* saved a small fortune.)

Ovens
$
%%%%

My friend Fritzi has just bought a new range/oven that cleans itself as it cooks at normal temperatures. A good money-saving choice, all other prices being equal.

A self-cleaning oven which requires those exceedingly high temperatures (averaging 1,000°F) to do the job isn't so cost-efficient. The cleaning-feature element, entirely independent

160

from the baking and broiling elements, draws 2,700 watts an hour for two hours (1½ hours if the process is begun with an already heated oven, note), so it could cost you as much as 27¢ per cleaning (at 5¢ per kwh). (However, do remember that these ovens are *much* better insulated than conventionally cleanable ones, so will save on cooking energy costs.)

My friend Jane suggests elbow grease, steel wool, and soap and water, messy and time-consuming perhaps, but certainly inexpensive. And to help cut down on those last two factors, she suggests rubbing a thin layer of vegetable oil on your clean oven to make removing spills easier.

HUMIDIFIERS

Free
$$$
%%%%%%%%

Edward's wife Joan: "If you have radiators, why waste money on still another appliance? Turn your heat-makers into humidifiers as well by placing pans of water atop them. If you put in pebbles and plants (which will thrive) you'll add color and oxygen as well. As a bonus, since moist heat is more comfortable than dry, you may be able to turn down your thermostat a couple of degrees and really add on savings."

And, from Cinda's friend Matthew: "Get a bonus from your bathwater. Don't drain the tub till the water has completely cooled—it'll add humidity to the air, too."

INSURANCE
Ⓢ Ⓢ
%%

The scope of *Inflation-Wise* is not wide enough to cover all of the ins and outs of choosing the appropriate insurance coverage and company for you. Whole books have been written on that subject: one I found especially useful, particulary for learning the terminology, is:

Your Insurance Adviser
by Saul Sokol
Barnes and Noble Books, 1977
$3.50

This is a readable, concise "guide to evaluating and buying Life, Health, Auto, Property and Liability insurance."

It does not rate companies, however. The comparison shopping, once you know what kind of policy you are after, is up to you. Yes, you do hear the strains of my old song wafting in—*Consumer Reports* is what you'll want to check for both rate comparisons and service data. (Incidentally, both choosing coverage in general and comparing life insurance companies in particular are given quite thorough play in a long, in-depth report in the February and March 1980 issues. Check for them at your library or write to Consumers Union for these back issues. Their address is noted under CONSUMERS UNION.)

The point I want to make here is that premiums vary *widely* between companies, that insurance is something you will likely be paying for, in one form or another, virtually every year of your life, that its prepurchase research deserves as much devotion as you'd give to any other large expenditure.

Many contributors said they were at a loss to offer suggestions in response to my question *re* methods of reducing insurance costs. I could not imagine that there weren't a number of possibilities, though, so I called my own insurance company and, with surprisingly few "let-me-transfer-yous," was connected with a wizard, thoroughly knowledgeable and generous with his time.

The majority of the tips on the following pages are his suggestions. His basic overall advice was this: Keep your insurance company up to date *re* changes in your life. If you retire, a child heads off for college, you move, you begin car-pooling, whatever—keep them advised. It could save you money.

Be aware that the following percentage discounts may not apply cumulatively—i.e., the insurance company won't reduce your premium to zero dollars if you implement five 20% discount tips—but it is likely to make *some* premium-decreasing adjustment for each.

Auto

Car-pooling or Van-pooling
%

If you drive back and forth to work only one or two days each week, you will qualify for a lower insurance rate—pleasure use. So car-pooling or van-pooling or bus-pooling can save both gasoline *and* insurance costs.

Commuting
%

If you should change jobs or residences and find that this means you are less than three miles (one way) from work, you will qualify for the less expensive pleasure rate. Be sure to let your insurance company know.

Comprehensive
%

You can reduce the comprehensive portion of your premium by installing an antitheft device. If it is the "active" sort (i.e., the kind which must be set by the driver before leaving the car), the discount is 5%. If it is the passive sort (i.e., automatic, always set), the discount is 15%.

Comprehensive and Collision
$$$$$

These sections of your insurance premiums which cover repairing or replacing the car itself will be reduced according to how much of the risk of coverage you decide you are willing and able to handle. The higher the deductible (the initial amount for which you agree to be liable) the lower the premium.

For example, for an average price car which is two years old (insured through my company):

On Comprehensive

If I agree to cover any loss up to:	My premium will be:
$0	$28 per year
$50	$22 per year
$100	$19 per year

On Collision

$50	$132 per year
$100	$106 per year
$150	$101 per year
$250	$89 per year

Keep track of the actual market value of your car (which, as noted elsewhere, is all you will be paid for a total loss). Some companies require a deductible on all policies written, and when the actual value less the deductible less the insurance premium begins to approach zero, you will want to consider dropping comprehensive and collision coverages altogether. Also, remember that collision damage costs are tax deductible.

Defensive Driver Discount
%

Any principal operator (i.e., one who drives a particular insured car more than anyone else in the family) can receive up to a 10% discount on premiums for having completed the Defensive Driving Course sponsored by the National Safety Council. In a few states—Texas, New York, and some others soon—this discount is mandatory.

Ask for the "Defensive Driver Course Discount."

Illegal Driving
$ $ $ $ $

Presumably everyone is aware that driving safely is the best way to keep insurance costs down. But by definition an accident is unintentional, so insurance increases resulting from accidents would fall into the category of the unavoidable.

Driving illegally, however, is something you can avoid, and it can increase your premium, in some instances by surprisingly substantial amounts.

For instance, if you are convicted in North Carolina of driving with blood-alcohol level greater than 0.10% (a 100-pound person drinking 3 beers in 40 minutes will raise his blood level to 0.11%), it will raise your insurance premium to 450% of your previous rate—i.e., for each $100 you paid before the conviction, you will subsequently pay $450.

Maybe you are careful, for both safety and saving's sake, to avoid driving when you have been drinking. But what about last Saturday, when one of the baby's shoes was misplaced and by the time you found it you were fifteen minutes late starting off to cousin Susie's wedding, and all you did was speed a little?

If you had been ticketed and convicted for exceeding the 55 mph speed limit, each $100 of premium you had been paying would subsequently cost you $140; if you had been exceeding 75 mph, conviction would have doubled your premium.

Medical
%%%%

In no-fault states where personal injury protection is mandatory, if you already have other medical coverage you should ask your insurance company about a "Coordination of Benefits" plan so that you are not paying for duplicate coverage.

Safety Devices
%

Although you will receive no discount for active safety devices (like seat belts you must fasten yourself), you can get a 15%

discount for having such passive safety devices as air bags or seat belts which automatically strap you in when you get in your car and shut the door.

Youth (College Discount)
%%%%

You may save as much as 50% on a young person's premium when he begins college. To qualify, he must go to college without taking the car and the college must be more than one hundred miles away.

Youth (Driver Education Discount)
%%

The "Driver Education Discount," available up to age 20, can reduce your premium as much as 20%. Credit is given for satisfactory completion of an approved (usually by the State Board of Education) Driver's Ed course, generally given at high schools.

Youth (Good Student Discount)
%%

Up to 20% discount on premiums of young people carrying a B average or better, or on Dean's List/Honor Roll, or in the upper 20 percentile of their class is available from the beginning of high school through the end of college.

Called the "Good Student Discount," it requires proof. Your insurance company can provide a form which must be signed by a school official. When it's difficult to obtain this proof, (e.g., in mid-summer), most companies will accept an official grade sheet.

Homeowners

Burglar Alarm
%

Installing a burglar-alarm system may get you a 3% to 5% discount. Be sure to check with your insurance company *re* which are acceptable.

New House
%

If you buy a house which is less than five years old you should get a 10% discount each year up to the fifth year of its life.

Smoke Alarm
%

Install a smoke alarm and reduce your premiums 3% to 5%.

Life

Jogger's Discount
%%

If you jog or swim or bicycle regularly (at least three times a week for twenty minutes each for a year) you may qualify for a "Jogger's Discount" (all other aspects of your life style being healthy.) It could be as much as 20%. In addition to submitting a signed statement you will be required to pass a physical indicating that your actual physical condition reflects your exercise program—low pulse rate, low blood pressure, optimum weight.

Nonsmoker's Discount
%

Quite a number of companies offer reduced premiums to nonsmokers as preferred risks. The usual discount is .5% and requires a signed statement that 5 ' have been smoke-free for a certain period of time.

INVESTMENT BOOKS

As I've mentioned, I know practically nothing about the area of investments, but I have read a book that made sense and some other contributors have offered suggestions. Those mentioned most often are noted below.

The book I read and liked was:

The Only Investment Guide You'll Ever Need
by Andrew Tobias
Bantam Books, 1979
$2.50 (tax deductible)

It was recommended by my friend Tam specifically because of the second chapter, "A Penny Saved Is Two Pennies Earned," which is an explanation of how, because our system of taxation is graduated, you pay the largest percentage in taxes on the last few dollars—the "margin," Tobias calls it. The point he makes in this chapter is that one of the best ways to make more spendable income, therefore, is *not* by earning more (which, as margin, will be heavily taxed—i.e., in the 50% bracket you'll obviously have to earn twice as much as the amount you need since the government will take half of your earnings) but *by spending less*. The chapter concludes with a mini-*Inflation-Wise*—three pages of the sort of tips this whole book is about. Here's what it means, as he shows it, in dollars and cents:

Saving this much annually by shopping, driving, phoning, flying, financing, etc., more efficiently:	$ 250	$ 500	$ 750	$ 1,000	$ 1,500
is as good as having this much earning 5½ percent taxable interest for you in a savings account: (given your current tax bracket)					
10%	$ 5,051	$10,101	$15,152	$20,202	$30,303
20%	$ 5,682	$11,364	$17,046	$22,728	$34,092
30%	$ 6,493	$12,987	$19,480	$25,973	$38,961
40%	$ 7,576	$15,152	$22,727	$30,303	$45,454
50%	$ 9,091	$18,182	$27,273	$36,364	$54,545
60%	$11,363	$22,727	$34,091	$45,454	$68,182

This book goes on in subsequent chapters to explain just what the possibilities are for investing—which are minimum-risk bets, which are high-risk bets, how and why to make your choices.

It's a very nice book to give you background knowledge. The

writing style is readable, understandable, fun. I actually enjoyed it immensely and learned a great deal in the process.

Other books recommended by other contributors are:

How to Buy Stocks
by Louis Engel in collaboration with Peter Wycoff
Bantam, 1977
$2.50

How to Beat the Salary Trap
by Richard K. Rifenbark with David H. Johnson
Avon Books,
$2.50

LAUNDRY

Energy-Saving Drying
%

When you are in the market for a new dryer, look for one with an automatic sensor feature which will shut the dryer off when the clothes are dry. You'll save a lot of extra minutes of unnecessary overdrying.

I haven't been able to locate a percent-saved figure for this one, but I *know* my dryer takes longer to do the job when the lint filter isn't cleaned between loads. Unremoved lint impedes the air flow so your machine must work harder and will use more energy. (See also CLOTHES—Care, for a comment about that lint.)

A solar dryer (as it's now popularly referred to), i.e., a clothesline, will pay for itself rather quickly if used exclusively. Even if you only hang sheets on a line, you can cut dryer use time by 10% to 15%.

Energy-Saving Washing
%

If you are in the market for a new machine, consider looking for one which includes a suds-saver feature—allowing you to use one tubful of hot water for a couple of loads.

169

Particularly if your water is heated electrically (which means it is one of the major energy consumers in your home), it will behoove you to wash your clothes whenever possible in cold water. Washing full loads (unless your machine has a water level adjustment feature) and presoaking badly soiled items (which might otherwise require double washing) will also help.

LIBRARIES
%%%%%%%%

Libraries lend more than books, offer more than lending. They shouldn't be taken for granted, they should be taken advantage of.

You can call a library and ask for the reference desk and find out just about anything you might want to know.

At most libraries you can borrow cassette players and tapes, puzzles, games, sewing patterns, art prints, records, films, record players, and projectors.

At some libraries you can take classes, join discussion groups, treat your children to a free afternoon of storytelling, treat yourself to a free evening of movie classics.

If you haven't visited your library lately you might be missing something.

LIGHTING

Indoor

If you have read ENERGY—Appliances, Calculating the Cost, you will immediately be aware that it will take quite a lot of forgetting to turn off lights to add up to a substantial expenditure—the wattage is so very low. For instance, it will cost you 5¢ to burn a 100-watt bulb for ten hours. Still, there are some things worth knowing about lighting, because those pennies can add up unnecessarily, *and the cost of bulbs can be substantial.*

Incandescents should be turned off whenever they are not being used, but fluorescents are a different matter. My industry source tells me that because the switching on and off is the costly part of burning fluorescents, you shouldn't turn these off unless you expect to be out of the room for 5 to 10 minutes or more.

In addition, fluorescent lighting is three to five times more efficient than incandescent. For example, you can get twice the light of a 100-watt standard incandescent with one 40-watt fluorescent tube. The point is, if you are installing new lighting fixtures fluorescents are a better energy buy and nowadays that harsh glare usually associated with them is no longer necessary to endure; they now come in bulbs which approximate the look of natural light.

Outdoor
$$$$$

According to government figures, turning off one outdoor gas lamp (the decorative variety) might save from $40 to $50 a year in natural gas costs.

Eight such gas lamps burning year-round use as much natural gas as it takes to heat an average-size home for a winter heating season.

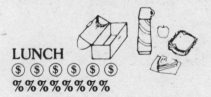

LUNCH
$ $ $ $ $ $
%%%%%%

If you carry your lunch to work instead of going out or sending out, think for a minute how much you'll save...

Let's say you spend, in restaurants, $3 per day. Now suppose you packed and carried some variation on this theme:

Two thick egg salad sandwiches on homemade bread	34¢
One large lovely crisp apple	9¢
One juicy carrot	3¢
A 2-cup thermos of coffee	14¢
	60¢

That's a savings of $12 per week—$624 a year!

MAPS
%%%%%%%%

Once upon a time, gas stations gave out road maps free for the asking; nowadays their maps will cost you as much as 75¢ apiece. But there are still free sources.

My Uncle Beeze makes it a point to stop at the Welcome Centers of any state he is passing through (these are located on major highways, and usually near a border) where he gets not only free maps but other information as well about the state's tourist attractions (including many ideas for low- or no-cost entertainment, the location of points of sightseeing interest, restaurants, and sometimes the whereabouts of some of the state's factory outlet stores where low overhead can provide enormous bargains).

This same information (including free maps) can be obtained by writing any state's Chamber of Commerce in its state capital, according to my stepmother, who has worked as a travel agent.

MILK
$ $ $ $
%%%%

When was the last time you paid less than a dollar for a gallon of milk? We pay, at the *most*, 88¢ per gallon! My family of five drinks a gallon a day; fresh milk in our locale sells for $2 per gallon, so in one year we will save more than $400!

I must thank Ursula and Ruth, two women in my food co-op, for this wonderful windfall. They introduced me to *non*-instant dry milk, which is what dairy-product factories use in making ice cream and the like (listed on labels as "milk solids").

Non-instant dry milk is comparable in price to the instant kind on your supermarket shelf. Many people find instant dry milk unpalatable but have discovered, as a lot of contributors suggested to me, that mixing it 1:1 with fresh milk and chilling it well renders it practically undistinguishable from fresh. This method will cut milk costs by 25%.

Using *non*-instant dry milk, however, will reduce milk expenditures by 50%; it need not be mixed with fresh. Because it is processed at much lower temperatures than instant, reconstituted non-instant tastes exactly like fresh milk—even at room temperature.

I know what you are thinking; I was skeptical, too. My seven-year-old, Zander, has taste buds so refined, so particular, that when on occasion I have bought bread with sesame seeds atop and surreptitiously removed them ("they're yucky"), this child can taste the traces. He calls instant dry milk "dog milk" because it is what we once fed to some sick puppies, and no matter how well-chilled it is, he can recognize it. If reconstituted non-instant can pass *his* scrutiny, I thought, we're rich.

Ruth kindly gave me a half-pound to test. I mixed it up, poured a glass straight from the blender, and took it to Zander. "What's this, Mom?" he said, after a taste. "It's milk," I said. "Oh," Zander said, "it's warm." Note: not "yucky," "warm." He doesn't much care for warm fresh milk either; the point is he *tasted* no difference. My family has been drinking it, and saving more than half on milk expenditures, ever since.

Non-instant dry milk powder has another advantage for households that consume substantially less milk than ours but find the instant variety unpalatable. In such households a gallon of fresh milk may sour before it is consumed, necessitating buying it in smaller, and more costly, amounts. Non-instant should be stored in a watertight bag or other container in a cool dry place (a freezer is ideal) and can be mixed a quart at a time as needed.

It is sold by the pound (one pound makes five quarts) and can be obtained from various sources. Cost varies widely; in general, the larger the quantity purchased, the greater the savings. The most expensive I found was by the single pound at a health-food store for $1.96 (including 4% tax), which makes it, reconstituted, $1.57 per gallon.

The least expensive source was a wholesale dairy-products store (which I located under "Dairies" in the Yellow Pages)—25 kilos (55 pounds) for $53 (including tax), which is 96¢ per pound or 77¢ per gallon. This is quite a large quantity, if storage is a problem, but might be divided among several friends. Not all dairies will sell to the general public, however, but in my experience assertive matter-of-factness will get you everywhere.

I generally buy it through our food co-op, in quantities somewhere in between (12 to 25 pounds, depending on my current storage space) and pay $1.10 per pound (including tax and inventory charges)—88¢ per gallon.

Reconstitution of non-instant, by the foolproof method described below, takes no more time than reconstitution of instant—about 2 minutes per quart, start to finish. Which means that I can mix up a gallon each evening in less than half the time it would take me to run out to the convenience store (when, as often happened, I would suddenly discover at 10:30 p.m. that there was no milk left for breakfast the next day). And think of all the gas I'm saving!

This method was contributed by Ursula, the kind of woman who, given any problem, will always figure out the best solution:

1. Measure out and set aside approximately ¾ cup of dry milk.
2. Place 2 cups (16 ounces) of *water only* in your blender and turn it on (low speed).
3. Spoon the milk powder into the center of the churning water and continue blending for a few seconds.
4. Pour the result into a coverable container, *add two more cups of water* to it, and swish.
5. Store as you would fresh.

This makes one quart. The blending causes it to foam, so a gallon container will comfortably hold only two quarts initially; the foam will subside in about 15 minutes. Since I'm the impatient sort, I simply use two one-gallon containers to hold two quarts each.

A nutritional note: non-instant skim is what we use (the whole is too difficult to keep). In the process of skimming the fat off, the fat-soluble vitamins also get removed. Some of them, vitamins A and D, are routinely replaced in fresh and instant dry milk; if this is of concern to you (i.e., if you feel that other sources don't suffice), you should verify that the non-instant you are buying has indeed had those vitamins put back in.

NATURAL FOODS
%%%%

You can pay quite a premium for additive-free food at some health-food stores. Joining a natural-foods co-op is one way to cut down costs if additives concern you. Here is another:

The Supermarket Handbook: Access to Whole Foods
by Nikki and David Goldbeck
Signet, 1976
$2.25, paper

This book names the brand names of chemical-free products from beans to nuts which can be found on supermarket shelves across the country as of 1976. Although plant-derived protein and vitamin sources are emphasized, chapters on choosing meat and fish are also included.

In every case, the Goldbecks tell why a particular chemical or additive should be avoided. For example, they recommend against buying any product containing cottonseed oil (which is sometimes found in margarines, prepared salad dressings, canned fish, and "pure" vegetable oils). They say, "We do not feel cottonseed oil is suitable for human consumption! Cotton is not generally regarded as an edible crop, thus it is treated with heavy doses of chemical sprays. The residue of this spray may be transmitted to the oil."

Lots of good general nutrition information is included as well as many, many recipes and hints for preparation and storage.

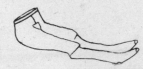

PANTYHOSE
$$

From Julia: "If you always buy the same brand and color of pantyhose, when one leg runs you can cut it off and wear it together with another half-pair to which the same thing has happened. I don't know why but the 'new pair' seems to last an especially long time."

PAPER

Drawing
%%%%%% -

Particularly in the case of my oldest son, James (for whom life without drawing wouldn't be worth living), keeping my children supplied with paper was becoming an expensive proposition until my friend Helen suggested that I check at our local newspaper office.

There I discovered that they would sell me end rolls of unprinted newsprint paper for 25¢ per pound. For purposes of comparison—notebook paper: at $2.50 for 300 sheets, you are paying about $1.00 per pound; low-grade typing paper at $1.20 for 100 sheets is costing you $1.37 per pound. So newspaper end rolls are an excellent buy—nice for murals and body tracings, too. Some newspapers also sell unprinted paper already cut.

PAPER PRODUCTS
$

An enormous proportion of the contributors who mentioned that they had lived through the Depression told me that they wouldn't have *considered* using a paper towel only once. Paper towels were hung to dry and reused again and again until they actually became soiled, and even then they weren't thrown away but instead were taken to the garage or workshop where they were used till they fell apart.

I personally find the idea of pinching pennies *that* carefully rather depressing but I think the notion of being more thoughtful about our levels of consumption is worthy of consideration. And it will save a few dollars a year.

If, for instance, you keep a bag of rags in the kitchen, as Elizabeth suggests, these can be used for most kitchen towel jobs with the possible exceptions (John's) of draining bacon (for which

176

you can use brown paper grocery bags) or cleaning up broken eggs. Or, as Uncle Beeze writes, "Keep your paper towels in a drawer to make getting to them just difficult enough to provoke thoughtfulness about wasting trees unnecessarily."

Cinda and Aunt Rutie and Edward (among many others) point out that cloth napkins not only save money and trees, but contribute elegance.

And finally, a word about toilet paper. If you squash the roll flat before loading it into the dispenser (and my mother suggests loading it so that it unrolls from the back), cats and toddlers will be less likely to present you with a mountain of paper on the floor and it will serve as a reminder that the earth's resources aren't unlimited and that we ought to be careful to use only what we really need.

PENS
¢

Most felt-tip pens have a removable cap on the bottom end. You can get a bit of extra mileage out of them when they begin to dry up by removing that cap and drizzling a couple of drops of water into the end.

PET FOOD
%%%

Did you know that canned dog food is about 70% *water* and only about 10% digestible protein? According to my vets, dogs need about 16% to 20% digestible protein, which can be best found least expensively (isn't it nice!) in any dry dog food manufactured by a reputable firm. Check with your own veterinarian for a brand recommendation, or write to the company and ask what the "Total Digestible Protein Percentage" is.

Dogs fed such dry food as a regular diet, my vets say, maintain better teeth, better weight, have less likelihood of developing diarrhea, and require veterinary care less often. Super-high protein types, they add, aren't necessary except for dogs that really work hard—e.g., run, really run, ten miles a day or so.

They said that the *worst* choice is the soft moist types because of the high level of preservatives they contain.

So, happily, this is one of those rare cases where least expensive turns out to be best!

PETS
%%%

Edward: "We kept meaning to have our female cat neutered, but never remembered until she again reminded us she was in heat. It pays to remember because you will be charged more if the vet does the operation while she is in heat."

PILOT LIGHTS

Burners
$
%%%%

This is the inflation-wise tip which sparked the book you now hold in your hands. It came from my mother, and though it is included in the introduction, I reiterate it below and add further information from Edward.

"Almost *half* (41% in the oven, 53% on the surface) of the money you pay for the cooking portion of your gas bill can be attributed to pilot lights alone. You can ask your gas company to turn them off permanently and use matches instead."

According to Edward you can turn off your pilot lights yourself. *DON'T BLOW THEM OUT;* gas will continue to escape, creating a dangerous situation. Follow the method Edward suggests: "If you

178

lift the stove cover, as if you were going to clean around the burners, you can easily trace the gas line back from the pilot light to its connection with an on-off valve. This will be a small screw. If you turn it clockwise until it stops you will see the pilot light lower and then go out. The gas to your pilot light is now off. You can test this by holding a lighted match over the opening. If you have more than one pilot light, trace and turn off each in the same way. For those who may not have been pilot-lightless before, when lighting the burner the match should be lit and held close by the burner *before* the gas is gradually turned on till the burner catches."

And, further, should you be in the market for a new gas range, look for one with an automatic (electric) ignition system instead of pilot lights which will afford the same savings.

Furnace
$
%%%%%%%%

If you heat by natural gas and your furnace is turned off in summer, remember the pilot light—it is burning worthlessly and costing you money. Ask that the pilot flame be turned off and ask the serviceman to show you how to relight it when the heating season approaches.

PLANTS

Collecting
$$$

Contributors from every generation offered this suggestion: Build your house-plant collection least expensively by giving and receiving cuttings. Prepotted ones (started soon enough beforehand to be sure they will live) make much-appreciated inflationwise gifts, special because homemade but quick and easy for the maker.

Fertilizing
%%%%%%%%%

Cinda suggests: "The water you've boiled your eggs in, when cooled to room temperature, makes a nutritious drink for your house plants.

"Or, crush and freeze eggshells and store in the freezer; spread them on a cookie sheet and stick whatever amount you have collected into the oven whenever you bake. They'll disintegrate and can be added to house-plant soil (or compost)."

POSTAGE

Postcards
¢

Uncle Beeze frequently sends postcards rather than letters, saving himself a nickel each time. He suggests: "If you buy plain postcards, then you can use both sides for your message, allowing half of one side for the stamp and address (as on a picture postcard)."

Four-by-six file cards make nice postcards, I've discovered, and give you that much more space. (Don't go much larger, though; those superlarge picture postcards cost the same as sending a letter.)

Or, get free postcards from the post office; prestamped, they will charge only for the postage, not the card.

PROTEIN

...is a dietary essential for building and maintaining body tissues, making enzymes and insulin, forming antibodies, regulating water and acid/base balance, and much more. Proportionately larger amounts are necessary when a body is growing new tissue rapidly—during pregnancy, lactation, childhood and adolescence, or following surgery or injury.

But on the average, according to the U. S. Department of Health, Education and Welfare, "most [Americans] eat more protein than [their] bodies need. This excess protein consumption ... is economically wasteful. ... Some protein is needed regularly in the diet because the body has little protein reserve, but if more protein is eaten than is required for the nitrogen needs of the body, the extra protein is used for calories or is converted to body fat." Other calorie sources are cheaper. And few of us are in need of extra calories, anyway.

Furthermore, most Americans think of protein in terms of meat, poultry, and seafood. Protein from these sources (especially when consumed in excessive amounts) can constitute a high proportion of the average food budget. There are other, often less costly sources—dairy products, eggs, legumes (beans and peas—including peanuts) grains/cereals, nuts, and seeds.

Protein is not a single substance; rather it is made up of over twenty amino acids. About half of these can be synthesized by the body, half must be ingested and are termed "essential" amino acids. "The essential amino acids are required in different amounts by the human body. Food proteins providing all of the essential amino acids in the proportions needed by humans are called 'complete' or high quality." These include virtually all animal-derived protein—i.e., diary products, eggs, seafood, poultry, and meat.

A protein low in an essential amino acid is said to have a "limiting" amino acid; it proportionately limits the usability of the other amino acids present in that food. Most vegetable sources are low in one or another of these essential amino acids and therefore, if eaten regularly as a single protein source, will not provide adequate protein.

Fortunately, however, it's quite easy to provide high-quality protein from vegetable sources by including a variety of them in the diet. Particular sources are known to complement each other. For example, the limiting amino acid in legumes is abundant in grains, and the limiting amino acid in grains is abundant in legumes—so they fit together like two jigsaw puzzle pieces forming complete protein which is higher in quality than either alone.

181

The optimum all-vegetable protein couplings are combinations of cereals (rice, wheat, oats, corn, etc.) with legumes (beans, peas, lentils, peanuts, etc.) and some seeds and nuts with legumes. Vegetable sources of complete protein, according to *Laurel's Kitchen* (referenced below) are: wheat germ, soybean products (soy milk, tofu—soybean curd, and tempeh—fermented soybeans), and black walnuts.

Adding even small amounts of animal-derived protein such as milk or eggs heightens the utilizability of vegetable-source protein.

A more thorough scientific explanation of protein complementarity, taking the latest nutrition research findings into account, can be found in:

Laurel's Kitchen: A Handbook for Vegetarian Cookery and Nutrition
by Laurel Robertson, Carol Flinders, and Bronwen Godfrey
Bantam Books, Inc., New York, 1978
$3.95, paper

This 641-page book is precisely what the subtitle suggests—half cookbook, half nutritional guide for those who are cooking vegetarian meals more often or planning to. It's well written (readable and enjoyable), thoroughly and well researched, and extraordinarily comprehensive—covering all aspects of providing high-quality nutrition relying on vegetables, fruits, grains, legumes, seeds, nuts, and with or without milk and eggs. If you plan to buy any vegetarian cookbooks in your quest for food budget cutting, I would suggest that you consider this one first.

There are other vegetarian cookbooks, of course. I've listed some of them below:

Diet for a Small Planet
by Frances Moore Lappe
Ballantine, revised 1975
$2.50

This is the now-classic book which introduced the principle of protein complementarity to the general public in 1971. Includes recipes.

Recipes for a Small Planet
by Ellen Buchman Ewald
Ballantine, 1973
$2.50

This is the companion volume to the above, based on the same principles. Less scientific explanation; more recipes.

The Vegetarian Epicure
by Anna Thomas
Random House, 1972
$5.95, paper

Cheerful.

The Vegetarian Feast
by Martha Rose Shulman
Harper and Row, 1979
$12.95

A vegetarian friend recommended this book in which many of the recipes are adapted from non-American cuisine. Reading the introduction reminded me again that long before nutrition became a research discipline, peoples all over the world were eating delicious, inexpensive meals and practicing protein complementarity.

In other words, look for cookbooks presenting the cuisine of the Middle East, Africa, Mexico, India, and the Orient and you will be likely to find good-tasting possibilities, nutritious and at low cost.

(See also PROTEIN—Cost Comparisons.)

Cost Comparisons

The following table will permit you to compare the costs of equal amounts of protein from various sources. You will notice that these costs are not figured per serving (though per serving costs can easily be figured from the information given). The amount compared, 15 grams, in conjunction with the Recommended Daily Allowance chart, will give you an idea of the actual amount of protein now being consumed in your home, i.e., whether in excessive (costly) or optimal amounts, and will allow you to figure how changes might reduce those costs.

PROTEIN COST COMPARISON TABLE

Amount Providing Approx. 15 grams	Source	Formula		Current Average Cost per 15 grams
	Little or no bone			
	Boned lean steak		___¢ =	$1.00
	Boned lean roast		___¢ =	80¢
1/5 pound, as purchased	Hamburger	$\dfrac{\text{Price}}{\text{Pounds}} \div 5$	___¢ =	40¢
	Liver		___¢ =	50¢
	Fish fillet		___¢ =	50¢
	Canned boned meat		___¢ =	50¢
	Canned boned poultry		___¢ =	50¢
	Other _____		___¢ =	50¢
	Medium bone			
	Steak		___¢ =	$1.00
	Chops		___¢ =	50¢
1/4 pound, as purchased	Roast	$\dfrac{\text{Price}}{\text{Pounds}} \div 4$	___¢ =	75¢
	Poultry		___¢ =	28¢
	Dressed fish		___¢ =	50¢
	Other _____		___¢ =	
	Much bone, gristle or fat			
	Brisket		___¢ =	$1.00
	Spareribs		___¢ =	75¢
1/2 pound, as purchased	Short ribs	$\dfrac{\text{Price}}{\text{Pounds}} \div 2$	___¢ =	1.00
	Pork sausage		___¢ =	75¢
	Other _____		___¢ =	

Food	Amount	Formula		Cost
Frankfurters	4 oz. (about 2)	$\dfrac{\text{Price}}{\text{Pounds}} \div 4$	= ____¢	38¢
Bologna	4 oz. (about 4 slices)	$\dfrac{\text{Price}}{\text{Pounds}} \div 4$	= ____¢	38¢
Bacon	1/2 pound (8 slices, medium thick)	$\dfrac{\text{Price}}{\text{Pounds}} \div 2$	= ____¢	75¢
Eggs	2½ (large)	$\dfrac{\text{Price/Dozen}}{12} \times 2.5$	= ____¢	17¢
Milk—fluid	2 cups			
Whole		$\dfrac{\text{Price per gallon}}{8}$	= ____¢	25¢
Skim		$\dfrac{\text{Price per half-gallon}}{4}$	= ____¢	30¢
Buttermilk		$\dfrac{\text{Price per quart}}{2}$	= ____¢	35¢
Milk—nonfat dry	2/3 cup (dry)	$\dfrac{\text{Price}}{\text{Pounds}} \div 8$	= ____¢	13¢

PROTEIN COST COMPARISON TABLE

Amount Providing Approx. 15 grams	Source	Formula	Current Average Cost per 15 grams
2 cups	Yogurt		
	Commercial	Price per 8 oz. cup X 2 = _____¢	80¢
	Home-made	Same as 2 cups of whatever milk used = _____¢	25¢
	Cheese		
2 oz.	Swiss, American	$\dfrac{\text{Price}}{\text{Pounds}} \div 8$ = _____¢	31¢
1/2 cup	Cottage	$\dfrac{\text{Price}}{\text{Pounds}} \div 4$ = _____¢	25¢
*4 tablespoons	Peanut Butter	$\dfrac{\text{Price}}{\text{Pounds}} \div 7$ = _____¢	11¢
*1 cup (raw)	Rice	$\dfrac{\text{Price}}{\text{Pounds}} \div 2$ = _____¢	25¢

*1/3 cup (dry)	Dry beans, peas			
	Check package label: if 1 2/3 dry cups = 1 pound	$\dfrac{\text{Price}}{\text{Pounds}} \div 5$	= _____¢	9¢
	if 2 dry cups = 1 pound	$\dfrac{\text{Price}}{\text{Pounds}} \div 6$	= _____¢	7½¢
	if 2 1/3 dry cups = 1 pound	$\dfrac{\text{Price}}{\text{Pounds}} \div 7$	= _____¢	6½¢
	if 2 2/3 dry cups = 1 pound	$\dfrac{\text{Price}}{\text{Pounds}} \div 8$	= _____¢	5½¢
	Beans, cooked, canned	$\dfrac{\text{Price}}{\text{Pounds}} \div 2$	= _____¢	15¢
*8 slices	Bread (store-bought)	$\dfrac{\text{Price per loaf}}{\text{Servings per loaf (check the label)}} \times 4$	= _____¢	40¢
*1 cup of 4 oz. dry	Macaroni	$\dfrac{\text{Price}}{\text{Pounds}} \div 4$	= _____¢	20¢

*See PROTEIN

From the National Academy of Sciences, Food and Nutrition Board (1979):

RDA's OF CALORIES AND PROTEIN

	Age (yrs.)	Wt. (lbs.)	Ht. (in.)	Calories	Protein (gr.)
Infants	0-½	13 (6 kg)	24	95-145	kg x 2.2
	½-1	20 (9 kg)	28	80-135	kg x 2
Children	1-3	29	35	1300	23
	4-6	44	44	1700	30
	7-10	62	52	2400	34
Males	11-14	99	62	2700	45
	15-18	145	69	2800	56
	19-22	154	70	2900	56
	23-50	154	70	2700	56
	51+	154	70	2400	56
Females	11-14	101	62	2200	46
	15-18	120	64	2100	46
	19-22	120	64	2100	44
	23-50	120	64	2000	44
	51+	120	64	1800	44
Pregnant				+300	+30
Nursing				+500	+20

RECREATION

Camping

National parks offer some of the most beautiful and inexpensive campgrounds in America. Individual entrance fees, at those National Park Service facilities which charge them, range from 50¢ per person to $3 per car. If you expect to take advantage of these facilities often, you can save by purchasing a Golden Eagle Passport ($10) which permits holder and family or carload one year's entrance to parks, monuments, and recreation areas administered by the Federal Government which charge entrance fees (not all do).

188

The pass can be bought by mail from:

National Park Service Headquarters
U. S. Department of the Interior
Room 1013
18th and C Streets, N. W.
Washington, D. C. 20240

Canoes

As recreational vehicles go, canoes, it seems to me, can be a good buy, providing hours of pleasure at relatively low cost. But to find out if it's the sort of pleasure which pleases *you*, begin by renting one. Rental prices in my locale currently (spring, 1980) are: $7.50 per day for a weekday; $15 per day for a Saturday or Sunday.

You can find local canoe liveries under "Boats" or "Canoes" in the Yellow Pages, or if your intention is to travel and rent a canoe at your destination, send a postcard to:

Grumman Boats
Marathon, New York 13803

and ask for their free *Rent-A-Canoe Directory, No. 896.* This booklet lists more than 900 sources of rental canoes in the United States and Canada.

While you are at it, ask Grumman for their other free literature: *Learn-To-Canoe, No. 892,* which lists 250 locations from which to learn, and *Group Camping by Canoe, No. 897,* which gives hints, tips, what to take and how-to information.

If you decide that a canoe is for you, take some advice from our friend Colin, who looks like a lumberjack and thinks like a philosopher, but is in fact an English Literature teacher at a nearby college who spends every minute he can spare roughing it. He's an accomplished woodsman and, in particular, an expert canoeist. I asked him to provide some marketplace pointers.

The first thing you must decide, he told me, is what sort of canoeing you are interested in doing—white water or/and smooth water. Advantages and disadvantages of the various types are listed below, in order of current price:

Built of	Uses	Advantages	Disadvantages
Aluminum	Lakes, smooth rivers; mild white water	Least expensive Fairly lightweight	Too rigid for serious white water—rock damage more likely to be irreparable
Fiberglass	Any water—white or smooth	Very lightweight Versatile Less rigid, so less easily damaged	Medium price currently but tied to oil price hikes, so . . .
Wood	Lakes Rockless rivers	Most beautiful (Colin's opinion, and mine) Smoothest riding	Most expensive Heaviest Least versatile

A used canoe will run between $150 and $500 depending on type and condition. Colin says that purchase from a private owner will usually afford the lowest price, but that good prices on canoes bought from rental facilities can be had sometimes, particularly during late October and early November. (It's a good idea to begin looking at the end of the summer, though.)

Check a used canoe carefully for holes, see that all rivets are tight, that any dents are creaseless (so that when you pound them out they won't weaken the structure).

Most canoe shops (particularly canoes-only shops) have knowledgeable personnel and can answer any question you might have. New canoes range in price from $300 to $800 currently and in timing a purchase you'll want to know that price increases usually take place in January and February. Comparison-shop as widely as possible—discounting takes place in the spring as competition warrants.

My friend Fritzi, who has just bought a new canoe, recommends an informative book she found at her library which includes both an explanation of kinds of canoes for various uses and a section listing canoes available by brand name:

190

Canoes and Kayaks: A Complete Buyer's Guide
Contemporary Books, Inc., 1979
$9.95 (Hardback) $5.95 (Paperback)

REFRIGERATOR

Anti-Sweat Devices
%%

Most refrigerators have heating elements in their walls or door to
prevent "sweating" on the outside. This can amount to 16% of
your refrigerator energy costs. If you are in the market for a new
unit, look for one which has a power-saver switch to turn this
heating element off when it is not needed.

Gaskets
%%%%

Slip a dollar bill between the door and the body of the refrigerator,
and close the door. If you can pull it out easily, you probably need a
new gasket. According to *The Home Energy Guide* (see full
reference in ENERGY—Where the Money Goes), a bad gasket
can double or triple the cost of running the appliance.

Thermometers

Controls that are set too cold waste energy and too warm can waste
food. Use a thermometer to periodically check temperatures. A
refrigerator should maintain 34° to 40°, a freezer 0° to 5°.

REFRIGERATOR/FREEZER

Efficiency
$

Defrost a freezer whenever the frost becomes ¼" thick; frost acts as an insulator which makes your freezer work harder to maintain the proper temperature.

REPAIRS
Ⓢ Ⓢ
%%%%%%%

Julia contributed this variation on the old theme: "A friend's mother advised her: marry a rich man or one who is handy around the house. One is as good as the other." (I trust she would have given parallel advice to her son.)

The point is well taken and *Inflation-Wise* contributors including Elizabeth and Gerry, Jackie and her husband, Mark, Julia and her husband, and of course Cinda (among many others) indicated that learning to do their own repairs was a major source of cost-cutting in their households.

They learned by reading (see REPAIRS—*THE* Book), by logical thinking, by asking people who know. Occasionally, even in these homes, a repairperson must be called. Contributors suggest getting your money's worth from these expensive house visits by observing the work and asking lots of questions. Cinda says you needn't feel shy about picking their brains: "Most people who enjoy their work are so delighted to find someone interested in learning about it that they'll tell you most anything you want to know."

Mark goes one step further. (He is already quite accomplished at home and appliance repairs, so he is familiar with the terms.) Mark has found that it's often possible, by using an assertive but respectful tone, to call repairpeople and get answers to most questions over the phone—even parts' inventory numbers which he then orders himself.

THE Book
%%%%%%%

The one book invariably recommended by do-it-themselves repairers is: Reader's Digest's *Fix-It-Yourself Manual* (The Reader's Digest Association, Inc., Pleasantville, New York, 1977), which really lives up to its subtitle, "How to repair, clean, and maintain anything and everything in and around your home." Table of contents includes these chapter headings: "Around the Home" (such things as bookbinding, repairing china, plumbing, stain removal and so on), "Furniture Repair and Refinishing," "Reupholstering," "Electrical Appliances/Repair Fundamentals," "Small Appliances," "Large Appliances," "Audio and Visual," "The Automobile," "Lawn, Basement, Garage and Garden," "Sports and Camping." The cost is just about the same as what you will pay a repairperson to drive to your home, look at your broken thing, tell you what you already knew—that it is broken—and make an appointment to *come back* to fix it. Even if you eventually do call a repairperson, the book will familiarize you with terms, which will save the repairer's time and your money.

RESTAURANTS
%%%

If an occasional restaurant meal is a priority for you (as it is for us) there are still ways to keep the costs down. For instance, from Barrie: "We eat a bit of something like cheese before heading out. It takes the edge off our appetites and keeps us from overordering due to starvation eyes (being bigger than stomachs)."

From Jackie: "We always have our before-dinner drink before leaving the house. Restaurant liquor prices are exorbitantly inflated."

From Marlowe: "Sometimes, when we've gone to try a new restaurant and found the prices for complete dinners too high, we make a meal of the interesting appetizers."

From us: When John and I lived in D.C. we did our new-restaurant testing at noon. Most restaurant lunch menus are exactly (or nearly) the same as their dinner menus, except that lunch prices are 50% less.

From Julia: "When we realized that we could no longer afford restaurant meals, my family decided that getting dressed up and being waited upon were among the main reasons we like to go out in the first place. So, once every fortnight we cook a special meal together, set the table with candles and flowers, put on our most elegant togs, and take biweekly turns 'waiting on' the rest of the family."

And from Edward: "I once lost a bet in which a dinner out at a restaurant of the winner's choice was my penalty. Since I love to cook and am good at it, the winner agreed to my spending the equivalent amount on groceries and cooking the meal at home. The hardest part of the task was managing to spend *enough* money to equal the cost of a restaurant meal! Now, before going out, I consider how many filet mignons the price of a restaurant meal would allow me to buy and cook myself."

SALES

Traditional Months
%%%

If you can time your purchases to coincide with traditional sale months, you may be able to acquire, at less than full price, practically anything you might need. Cass's Agricultural Extension Service provided a list of these traditional sale months, which I have rearranged alphabetically, in chart form, below.

You might use it this way: If, for instance, you decide in November that it is time to replace your bed, check the *Inflation-Wise* chart to see if it is likely that bedding will be discounted within the next few months. Then make a telephone survey of area stores to find out which ones will be following tradition—in the case of bedding, discounting in January. If you can postpone your purchase for a few months you will be sleeping in January on a new bed which might have cost you 20% or 30% more in November. Doesn't that sound comfortable?

	Jan	Feb	Mar	Apr	May	Jun	Jul	Aug	Sep	Oct	Nov	Dec
Air conditioners	⊗	X	X	X	X	X	X	⊗	X	X	X	X
Appliances	⊗	X	X	X	X	X	X	X	X	X	X	X
Automobiles—current year	X	X	X	X	X	X	X	⊗	⊗	X	X	X
—used	X	⊗	X	X	X	X	X	X	X	X	⊗	X
Baby clothes and furniture	X	X	X	X	X	X	X	X	X	X	X	⊗
Batteries (car)	X	X	X	X	X	X	X	X	⊗	X	X	X
Bedding	⊗	X	X	X	X	X	⊗	⊗	X	X	X	X
Bicycles	X	⊗	X	X	X	X	X	X	X	X	X	X
Blankets	X	X	X	X	X	X	X	X	X	X	⊗	X
Boyswear	⊗	X	X	⊗	⊗	X	X	X	X	X	X	X
Camping gear	X	X	X	X	X	X	X	⊗	X	X	X	X
Campwear	X	X	X	X	X	⊗	X	X	X	X	X	X
Children's Wear	X	X	X	X	X	X	⊗	X	⊗	X	X	X
China	X	X	⊗	X	X	X	X	X	X	⊗	X	X
Cleaning supplies	X	X	X	⊗	⊗	X	X	X	X	X	X	X
Clothing (general)	X	⊗	X	X	X	X	X	X	⊗	X	⊗	X	⊗
Coats	⊗	X	X	⊗	X	X	X	X	⊗	X	⊗	⊗	X
Curtains	X	X	X	X	X	X	⊗	X	X	X	X	X
Dishwashers	X	X	X	X	⊗	X	X	X	X	X	X	⊗
Dryers	X	X	⊗	X	X	X	X	X	X	X	X	X
Fabric	X	X	X	⊗	X	⊗	⊗	X	⊗	X	⊗	X
Freezers	X	X	X	X	X	X	⊗	X	X	X	X	X
Fuel Oil	X	X	X	X	X	X	⊗	X	X	X	X	X
Furniture	⊗	⊗	X	X	X	X	⊗	⊗	X	X	X	X

	January	February	March	April	May	June	July	August	September	October	November	December
Garden equipment and supplies	X	X	⊗	⊗	X	X	⊗	⊗	X	X	X	X
Gifts	⊗	X	X	X	X	X	X	X	X	X	X	X
Glassware	X	X	⊗	X	X	X	X	X	X	X	X	X
Handbags	X	X	X	X	⊗	X	X	X	X	X	X	X
Hardware	X	X	X	X	X	X	X	⊗	⊗	X	X	X
Holiday cards and wrappings	⊗	X	X	X	X	X	X	X	X	X	X	X
Homebuilding materials	X	X	X	X	X	⊗	X	X	X	X	X	X
Hosiery	X	⊗	X	⊗	X	⊗	X	X	X	X	X	X
Housewares	X	⊗	X	X	X	X	X	X	⊗	X	X	X
Jewelry	X	⊗	X	⊗	X	X	X	X	X	X	X	X
Linens—"white sales"	⊗	X	X	X	⊗	X	X	⊗	X	X	X	X
Lingerie	X	X	X	X	⊗	X	X	X	X	⊗	X	X
Luggage	X	X	⊗	X	⊗	X	X	X	X	X	X	X
Menswear	⊗	X	X	⊗	⊗	X	X	X	X	X	X	X
Microwave ovens	X	X	X	X	⊗	X	X	X	X	X	X	⊗
Mufflers	X	X	X	X	X	X	X	X	⊗	X	X	X
Outdoor furniture	X	X	X	X	X	X	⊗	X	X	X	X	X
Paint	X	X	X	⊗	X	X	X	⊗	⊗	X	X	X
Radios	⊗	X	X	X	X	X	X	X	X	X	X	X
Ranges, kitchen	X	X	X	⊗	X	X	X	X	X	X	X	X
Refrigerators	X	X	X	X	X	X	⊗	X	X	X	X	X
Resortwear	⊗	X	X	X	X	X	X	X	X	X	⊗	X
Rugs	⊗	X	X	X	X	X	⊗	⊗	X	X	X	X
Sewing notions	X	⊗	X	X	X	X	X	X	X	X	X	X
Shoes	⊗	X	X	X	X	X	⊗	X	X	X	X	X
Silver	X	X	⊗	X	X	X	X	X	X	X	⊗	X
Ski equipment	X	X	⊗	X	X	X	X	X	X	X	X	X
Sleepwear	X	X	X	⊗	X	X	X	X	X	X	X	X

	January	February	March	April	May	June	July	August	September	October	November	December
Sporting goods	X	X	X	X	X	X	X	X	⊗	X	X	X
Sportswear	X	⊗	X	X	X	⊗	X	X	X	X	X	X
Stereos	⊗	X	X	X	X	X	X	X	X	X	X	X
Storm windows	X	X	X	X	X	⊗	X	⊗	X	X	X	X
Stoves	X	X	X	⊗	X	X	X	X	X	X	X	X
Table linens	X	X	X	X	X	X	X	X	X	X	⊗	X
Televisions	⊗	X	X	X	⊗	⊗	X	X	X	X	X	X
Tires	X	X	X	X	⊗	X	X	⊗	X	X	X	X
Toiletries	⊗	X	X	X	X	X	X	X	X	X	X	X
Tools	X	X	X	X	X	X	X	X	⊗	X	X	X
Toys	⊗	X	X	X	X	X	X	X	X	X	X	X
Typewriters	X	X	X	X	X	⊗	X	X	X	X	X	X
Washing machines	X	X	⊗	X	X	X	X	X	X	X	X	X
Women's Wear	X	⊗	X	X	X	X	X	X	X	X	X	X

In addition, nearly every month boasts at least one day of traditional storewide specials. These are listed below, by month:

January—Post-holiday sales (early in month)
February—Lincoln's Birthday sales and Washington's Birthday sales
March/April—Post-Easter sales
May—Memorial Day sales
July—July 4th sales (continuing throughout the month)
August/September—Back-to-school specials
October—Columbus Day sales
November—Veterans' Day sales
      Thanksgiving Weekend sales
      Preholiday specials
December—Postholiday sales (late in the month)

Unadvertised
%%%

My mother writes: "Some small grocery stores will give you a reduced price on packages of bacon on which the cellophane is slightly torn or cartons of eggs in which one is broken—if you simply ask."

I've found this to be true not only at small independent grocers but also at large chains. If the stockclerk has carelessly slashed into the cereal boxes when opening the delivery carton, if the dishsoap bottle has leaked a bit because it was accidentally shipped upside-down—ask the manager for a reduction. It will usually amount to about 20% to 30%. In fact, I've come to keep an eye out for such potential bargains.

The same principle applies to clothing. If you find a ready-made garment in need of minor repair (a loosening hem, button, or seam) stores will often quite substantially discount the item if you ask.

SHOES
%%%%

Shoe-outlet stores are marvels, are cropping up all over the country, and can save you an enormous amount of money—often half or more of retail prices. I haunt our local one, where new shipments arrive frequently. When I find a shoe that is classic (simple) and comfortable I often buy it in a couple of colors.

Be sure, as always, to check the store's return policy.

SMOKING
$ $ $ $

If you smoke, take a few minutes right now to figure out how much you spend per year. It may astound you; it did me—nearly $450—and I live in one of those low-cigarette-tax states!

198

Well, I've decided to quit—not primarily because of the savings but it certainly sweetens the prospect.

I've discovered that there's lots of help available. Some programs are costly (though for me the payback on the costliest of these would be exactly one year). However, free or minimal-fee help can be obtained from the American Cancer Society (group meetings twice weekly for 4 weeks, each lasting approximately 2 hours) or the American Lung Association (group meetings lasting 1½ hours each, twice a month indefinitely). Both programs utilize the volunteer assistance of physicians, psychiatrists, therapists, and ex-smokers. Positive reinforcement and group interaction are stressed. Participants number 8 to 18.

There's lots of quitting information available in print, too. The best I've seen is a pamphlet called *Calling It Quits* (HEW Publication No. NIH 79-1824)—the hints are specific and practical. You can get a free copy by writing or calling:

Office of Cancer Communications
National Cancer Institute
National Institute of Health
Bethesda, Maryland 20014

(800) 638-6694 or Maryland residents: (800) 492-6600

I've a hint to add—chewing sugarless bubble gum as a substitute gives you something to blow. It helps.

SNACKS

Drinks
¢

Colas contain carbonated water, sugar, caramel color, phosphoric acid, natural flavorings, and caffeine. A glass of cola will cost you between 11¢ and 17¢ depending on how you buy it (in returnable bottles is least expensive, by the way).

Orange juice contains the juice of oranges (including vitamin

C). A glass of orange juice will cost you about 11½¢ . If you cut it (or any other juice) with seltzer or club soda, you further reduce the cost *and* get the carbonation of cola.

Movies
$$
%%%%%%%

When you treat yourself to a movie, is it a movie if you don't buy popcorn? Take your own. You can spice it a bit with tarragon or chili powder, even parsley. Alternatively take raisins or grapes for a change of pace.

I know someone who also brings her own drinks.

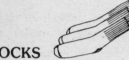

SOCKS

Even the very best housekeepers among my friends complain that the washing machine seems to "eat" socks. We have a shopping bag full of socks without mates—I can hope, can't I?

Here's a better idea from Edward: "You'll replace socks less often if each family member chooses (and you stock) a single solid color. You'll then always have a match and they'll be easier for the owner to locate when the laundry folding has fallen behind."

SPROUTS
%%%%%%%

Cinda: "Sprouting seeds and beans seems to be a favorite kitchen job for children. And it's a perfect way for city or apartment dwellers to grow fresh vegetables without land. Sprouted seeds and beans are outstanding sources of vitamins B and C, protein, and minerals—better by far than unsprouted. For instance, soybeans increase in vitamin C 553% in sprouting, oats increase B_2 1,350% (in five days), mung beans increase in niacin 400%. Possible sproutables include alfalfa seeds, any grain, garbanzos and other beans, mung beans, clover, lentils, soybeans. And they're extremely inexpensive if you sprout them yourself.

"To sprout, soak beans or seeds overnight in water; next morning drain and rinse. I use a sieve or colander depending on seed size, but a quart-size mason jar with a piece of cheesecloth stretched over the mouth and secured by the screwed-on ring or a rubber-band is most commonly used (anything which allows good air circulation and easy rinsing/draining). Set the seed-containing vessel in a cupboard or any dark place, rinse by filling the jar with fresh water and draining it well through the cheesecloth whenever you think of it but at least two times per day for four or five days until the sprouts are about an inch long (but before leaves appear). Some people like to green them up by exposure to light on the last day. Store in a plastic bag in the fridge.

"Most kids I know like to eat them plain, as a snack. I also add them to stir-fry dishes or use them on sandwiches (in lieu of lettuce) or in salads (in lieu of celery) or in soups (added at the last moment, for prolonged exposure to heat will destroy the nutritive value sprouting has accomplished)."

STEREO EQUIPMENT
$$$$$

Gerry (of Elizabeth and Gerry) tells me that although this is not a good way to buy speakers, he has found that receivers and turntables can be bought by mail, including shipping, at $40 to $50 less than at discount stores.

He says, "Do your comparison shopping locally, make your choices, and then check the mail-order price from companies listed in *HiFi Magazine* and/or the New York *Times*."

STORAGE

Furniture
Ⓢ Ⓢ Ⓢ
%%%%%%%%

Cinda: "If you have to store your furniture for any extended period, ask each of your friends to take a few pieces (keep a careful list and give each individual a list so she doesn't accidentally include your things in a yard sale). Choose friends you trust, of course."

TAXES

General Information

If you compute your own income taxes to save the cost of a preparer's services (such help is tax-deductible by the way), be aware that the information booklet provided by the IRS with your tax forms does not list all the possible deductions within a category—only a sampling of the most common ones. However, you can obtain more detailed information from the IRS without cost.

You don't even have to pay postage on your request. Their toll-free number is listed in the white pages under U.S. Government, Internal Revenue Service, Federal Tax Information & Forms. Call in December (pamphlets are revised in November) and ask for Publication 17, *Your Federal Income Tax*, and Publication 900, *Catalog and Quick Index to Taxpayer Information*; the first is a much more thorough guide to filling out your tax forms, the second, self-explanatory.

Staff at the same toll-free number will answer any specific tax questions you might have (but be advised that though they make every effort to provide you with correct answers, you will still be responsible for payment of the correct tax and any interest should they make a mistake). I have found that the early-morning and late-afternoon hours are best times for getting through and, naturally, the closer to the filing deadline the more difficulty you will have finding a free line.

There are also income-tax guides for sale at bookstores. But be wary: Government publications are considered "in the public domain" and can be reprinted by anyone without even crediting the source; don't pay three or four dollars for someone else's reprint of the IRS's Publication 17. If you open a tax-saver book and it looks pretty much like your IRS Tax Forms booklet, save your money.

Energy Conservation Credits
$

You can receive quite substantial tax credits for energy-conserving improvements made in your home. To find out what is currently eligible and to obtain all of the specifics about qualifying, write:

National Energy Act Information Kit
Department of Energy
Technical Information Center
PO Box 62
Oak Ridge, Tennessee 37830

Refunds
$

If you claim fewer than the allowable exemptions on your W4 form so that the IRS sends a refund at tax time, the government is earning (and you are losing) interest on *your* money. If the reason you do this—like me—is that you love having that huge chunk of money arrive each spring, change the form to include all exemptions to which you are entitled and deposit (or ask your employer to deposit, if that's possible) the difference in a savings account. Then, if you like, you can refund yourself at tax time— with interest!

Saving Sales Receipts

The IRS will allow deduction of state sales taxes according to their tables *or your records*. If you think you pay more than their tables indicate, keep *all* receipts for everything on which you pay such tax and tote them up at year's end. Naturally, the IRS tables bear average figures, so, particularly in those years when you've made lots of big-dollar purchases (sales tax paid on cars or boats or mobile homes is an add-on to the table already), you may very well find receipt-saving worthwhile (and hang on to them; if your deduction is questioned, the IRS will ask for proof).

TELEPHONE

Beating the System
%%%

Most people, when making a long-distance call from the house of a friend, make it collect or charge it to their home phone or ask for time and charges—all of which involve an operator's help in making the connection or monitoring the call and so increase the cost over the least expensive dial-direct rates. And then there's my Uncle Beeze ... who, during his last visit, did none of these (although he *did* get an operator's assistance), paid me accurately on the spot, and saved one-third.

His system: call the operator *before* placing your call and ask him to tell you the *per-minute rate* (this *precall* operator assistance costs nothing). Then dial direct and time your call, execute the math, and pay your hostess. Remember, it's a 30% savings.

Buying Your Own

Now that you can buy your own phone, if you do so at a Bell Telephone store be aware that you will continue to pay rent on it each month—you own only the casing, Bell still owns the insides.

Furthermore, if you move into an area which is not served by Bell, you must return (and I don't mean sell back) those insides (they don't work in a non-Bell system anyway).

Discount Hours
%%%%%

Many contributors indicated that they made their long-distance calls during discount hours, but seemed in some cases to have a rather vague idea of exactly when those hours were.

Not only *when* you place a call but *how* you place it can make a surprising difference in the cost. For instance, if I were to make an 11-minute call from Durham, North Carolina, to Dallas, Texas, dialing it myself (excluding tax) I would pay:

$4.12 (if I placed it at 4 p.m. on a Friday)
$2.73 (if I placed it at 5. p.m. on Friday)
$1.70 (if I waited until Saturday—and placed it anytime that day)

An operator-assisted call (of equal length) between these two cities could run as high as:

$6.45! (at person-to-person, weekday rates)

Clearly, substantial savings will accrue if, whenever possible, calls are made during discount-rate periods, listed below:

Out of State

Full rate applies weekdays (8 a.m. to 4:59 p.m.)
35% discount applies Sunday through Friday (5 p.m. to 10:59 p.m.) and on these holidays (8 a.m. to 10:59 p.m.): New Year's Day, July 4th, Labor Day, Thanksgiving, Christmas (unless the holiday falls on Saturday or Sunday, in which case the 60% discount would apply)
60% discount applies every night (11 p.m. to 7:59 a.m.) and between 11 p.m. Friday and 4:59 p.m. Sunday)

Within State

25% and 50%, respectively, at the above times

Discounts apply to *all minutes* of all calls *dialed direct* but operator-assisted calls (which include person-to-person, coin, collect, credit card, billed to a third number, hotel guest, and time-and-charges requests) are only discounted after the initial three minutes.

Furthermore, when you dial direct and talk for one minute you will be charged for one minute; if an operator assists, you will be charged (at higher rates) for a minimum of three minutes, even if you only talk for one.

Noonday Rate
%%

Here's a money-saver you may not have discovered—many states are now instituting a noonday rate which provides customers with a 25% discount on in-state calls made between 12 noon and 1 p.m. Check with your phone company.

Small-Town Rate
%%%%

We live in a small town surrounded by other small towns, each with its own separate and distinct phone system so that calls made between towns are long distance and the charges, though not much per call, quickly add up to a hefty sum. My phone company has recently offered a set per-month rate which will be less expensive by half for me. If your location is similar, it will pay you to ask your phone company if such a service is available to you.

Suspending Service
%%%%

Uncle Beeze: "If you are planning an absence from home lasting more than one but less than three months, call your phone company and ask about 'suspended' or 'vacation' service. You'll be charged only half the local service rate and be assured of retaining your phone number.

'If you expect to be away more than three months, it will likely cost less to have the phone company disconnect your phone when you leave and reconnect it on your return. The Bell System, on request, will not reassign your number for up to a year but some smaller systems, because their number bank is not so large, cannot guarantee the same number—so be sure to ask (if a change in your number matters to you)."

Toll-free Numbers
%%%%%%%%

Thousands of businesses, hotel chains and the like now have toll-free numbers. Whenever you must make a call to such as these, check with the information operator (800-555-1212) to find out if such a number exists for the business you wish to reach. The phone company hasn't published the list to date, but it is available for $3.49 (postpaid) from Dial 800 Publishing Company, Box 995, Radio City Station, New York, New York 10019. It's called *Dial Free: Dial 800* and is arranged alphabetically by subject.

Wrong Numbers
%%%%%%%%

If you dial a wrong number long distance, shrugging your shoulders and trying again will cost you money. Call the operator immediately and request credit for the misdialing. The same applies if you make a bad connection and must replace the call in order to hear; even if it happens in the middle of your conversation, before you redial, call the operator and ask that credit be applied to the portion during which you were unable to hear or be heard clearly.

It is also a good idea to keep a running list of long-distance calls by the phone with dates and times and approximate minutes. Check it against your bill to be sure you've been credited properly for difficulties such as the above and in general for mistakes— phone companies do make them and you might be surprised at how often.

TENNIS BALLS

A suggestion from Julia's daughter's gym teacher: you don't have to replace your tennis balls so often. Revitalize the old deadish ones by washing them in your washing machine and drying them in your dryer. It puts back the bounce.

TOILETRIES

Baby and Bath Powder
%%%%

Cornstarch, rather than baby powder, is what most of my mother's generation used to make babies' bottoms feel silky smooth.

And if you have a favorite (perhaps costly) bath powder for your own use, you can extend that use (and still enjoy the fragrance) by mixing it half-and-half with cornstarch—which will make *your* skin feel silky smooth, too. (Cornstarch costs about a penny per tablespoon or 3¢ per ounce.)

Deodorants/Antiperspirants
$$
%%%%%%%

Several contributors from my mother's generation reminded me that, before drugstore shelves were loaded with commercial products designed to keep the public smelling sweet, people used a combination of baking soda and cornstarch.

It sounded worth a try. I found that it really *does* work—mixed half-and-half, applied with a cottonball. It has a pleasant, fresh smell, and when I figured the cost I discovered that it was even more worthy—a penny per tablespoon.

This homemade deodorant won't keep you dry, however. If that is a concern, check your drugstore shelves for aluminum chloride

208

(25% solution). You can get 4 ounces of this for $1.29 which should last at least six months; it's the active ingredient in many commercial antiperspirants costing $3 for 2 ounces. Apply with a cotton ball.

Mouthwash

Cinda: "Don't send the parsley back to the kitchen. Eat it. It makes the best breath freshener after a garlicky meal—much better than mouthwash."

Pumice Stone
%%%%%%%

Ten years ago, Cinda noticed that my feet (which I keep bare as much as possible) were very callused. She gave me the pumice stone sitting by her bathtub, which is what people used for rubbing off calluses on hands and feet before the cosmetics industry came up with a chemical preparation for such prettying.

The industry beauty aids currently cost about $2 for 2 ounces (about ten applications or less). Pumice stones are still available in drugstores at a cost of about $1 apiece (about one million applications or more).

Shampoo
%%%%

Whenever my shampoo bottle got down to the last remnants, I found I could add some water and get several extra shampoos, so I began to cut down the amount I used from the beginning, am using about a sixth of the amount I once did and finding it does the job just fine and rinses out more easily too.

Cinda buys her shampoo (from the hairdresser) in the concentrate form, mixing it up with more water than officially called for. This cuts her shampoo costs in half.

Beauty shop supply houses are also cropping up everywhere, are now open to the public, and sell at wholesale prices.

TOYS

Best Buys
%%%%%%%%

Remember the story about the baby who was given an expensive new toy, played with it for only a few minutes, and quickly returned to playing with the pots and pans in the kitchen? Elizabeth's rule is this: "There are so many things available at high prices which make a fantastic first impression but aren't much fun beyond that, that before I buy any toy I try to imagine the kids playing with it for an extended period of time and if I can't, I don't buy it."

Brands most often recommended by parents with some toy-buying experience are Fisher-Price and Lego. They are colorful and remarkably durable and are designed so that the child does the exciting imaginative thing, not the toy.

My mother saved the Fisher-Price toys I played with thirty years ago and now has passed them down to my own children. A saver myself, I've no doubt they'll be passed on to a third generation, as will the Lego (to a second, and eventually a third). If you don't possess such family heirlooms, you may be able to acquire them: A friend of mine has completely furnished her child's toy supply with Fisher-Price from nonsavers' yard sales. Even new they're a smart buy.

And be sure to take a look at the Appendices in Fitzhugh Dodson's *How to Parent* (Signet, 1971) where you will find a thorough coverage of good toys and books and records for children. Dr. Dodson tells *why* certain toys are appropriate for particular ages and includes (Appendix B) an A to Z of toys parents can make, free or very inexpensively.

Felt-tip Markers
$

"Kids always love felt-tip markers for presents," writes Marlowe. Certainly they pass Elizabeth's test, affording hours and hours of

210

pleasure; in addition they are relatively inexpensive to begin with so that the cost per use is quite low.

The one problem is that the caps are generally small and cylindrical and tend to roll off tables, under couches—to remain unfound until the marker has dried up. Thus, if you must replace them often, it won't be long before they move into the category of an expensive toy.

There is a solution. Several years ago, my friend Fritzi introduced me to a twelve-color felt-tip marker set which has eliminated the lost-cap problem. Called, appropriately, Cappers, these markers fit into *caps which are attached together* so that to lose one is to lose all (much more difficult), and of course they don't roll. They are initially more expensive (about $5) but my children are still using the set we bought more than a year ago, and the quality of the marker itself is also excellent. About four months after we bought them, our baby Max (at just about age two) found the set and proceeded to remove half the markers and squirrel away the capped remainder in one of her secret places. I didn't locate the cap section for an entire week and the markers left uncapped for that period were still writing as well as ever.

I noticed recently that a less-expensive imitation had come on the market and bought a set to test. I returned them the next day— eight of the twelve had already begun to dry out because of improper fit. This is clearly a case where paying a little more for quality initially really saves in the long run.

Playdough
%%%%%%

I received several recipes for homemade playdough and appreciate these suggestions. My friend Jane, however, warned me that some of them had been tested by a number of nursery-school mothers and found to give unreliable results. The recipe I myself use has been well-tested and found consistent (I once made ten batches to provide thirty kindergarten children with party favors).

The recipe was given to me years ago by a friend I will here thank again by calling it *"Joey's Playdough."*

Mix together and set aside:

1½ cups flour
¾ cup salt
1 tablespoon cream of tartar

Mix together and set aside:
1½ cups water
1½ tablespoons cooking oil
Food coloring (optional)

Then, in a saucepan, mix together wet and dry ingredients and heat over low heat till it gets stiff and makes a ball. Remove from heat, knead slightly. Store in plastic bag in refrigerator.

Yield: more than 1½ pounds. Cost: less than 40¢ . (Commercial playdough: 1½ pounds—$1.60.)

TRAVEL

Bargain Trips
$
%%%%

When Elaine discovered that she was pregnant the first time, she and Christian decided to have one last travel fling before becoming parents. They found a terrific bargain which is still available called Unlimited Mileage Fare (by Eastern or Delta) and Liberty Fare (by U. S. Air).

The idea is that for a fixed amount (at this writing $425, $369, and $249 respectively, before taxes), and under certain time conditions, you can fly to any number of cities on the chosen airline's route (with some exceptions, but not what could be called burdensome exceptions).

The three-week trip Elaine and Christian took included visits to Los Angeles, Mexico City, New Orleans, and Jacksonville, Florida.

The Unlimited Mileage Fare, at today's prices, would have cost them $425 apiece on Eastern. I called Eastern's ticket office and, explaining my purpose, asked the agent if she would figure the regular coach fare for their itinerary in the least expensive (most direct) way. Disregarding carrier she calculated that the same trip, on regular coach, would have cost $945 each at today's prices. Unlimited Mileage Fare saved them nearly 60%.

Compensation
$ $ $ $

Airlines can no longer "bump" passengers with confirmed reservations without paying compensation. They must first ask for volunteers willing to take a later flight in exchange for monetary compensation of the airline's choice. If no volunteers come forward, involuntarily bumped passengers must be rebooked on flights which will reach their destination within two hours of the originally scheduled time on domestic flights (four hours on international flights) *plus paid compensation* equal to the full value of a one-way ticket to a maximum of $200. If they cannot get you there within the specified time, they must double the compensation, up to $400. Be sure to ask for such compensation.

Edward: "On one flight to California from New York it worked like this: The agent asked for volunteers who would agree to rebooking and a bonus of $25. Three passengers accepted. (The agent needed nine seats, a fact he had not yet revealed.) Next, he again asked for volunteers, but this time offered $50. Four people raised their hands. No one responded to an offer of $100 and so the last two seats were taken from passengers in exchange for the one-way fare compensation.

"I know some people who purposely book their trip for peak travel hours and check in as late as possible in hopes of collecting the compensation."

Delayed Flights
$

If your flight is expected to be delayed more than four hours, most airlines will pay for a telephone call or telegram to your

213

destination to let people there know your flight will be late; arrange and pay for a hotel room if you are stranded away from home overnight and pay cab fare to and from; provide a meal voucher for the airport restaurant. They may not, however, volunteer any of these things—so ask.

Edward: "If you are making a connection and have booked and paid for the through trip and a late arrival of the first leg requires an overnight layover, these rules also apply. If the agent won't oblige, ask to speak to his supervisor. Airlines are obliged to do these things, and so if necessary tell them you are going to register a complaint with the FAA. Be sure to keep receipts and records to substantiate your claim if you are unable to settle this on the spot."

Direct Flights
%%

I discovered, unfortunately too late, that flights which are not direct cost more (even though the added inconvenience ought to mean lowered, not raised, prices), so I always ask whether the flight I have been booked on is direct; if not, I ask about the availability of direct flights which might come close to fitting my needs. I have saved as much as 15% since that first mistake by doing this.

Fare Deductions
$$$$$

To try to ferret out any tips I might not have come across in my research or been sent by contributors, I stopped by the nearest airline ticket office and discovered that a former neighbor, Bob, was one of the agents. I was delighted, as I knew he had been working for the airline for many years and would be able to provide the information I was after, if it existed.

"Here's one you may not know about," he said. "When your reservation agent indicates that you must change airlines en route to your destination ask if the fare you are being quoted is a *published joint fare*. If unpublished, the agent must deduct $25 from her point-to-point calculation. For example, you begin at point A, change planes (and airlines) at point B, and eventually arrive at point C. If there is no published joint fare for this combination, the agent will add together the fares for A to B and B to C and must deduct $25 from the total; adding another plane change with an unpublished joint fare (to point D) requires another $25 deduction—total $50. Agents sometimes forget, ignore, or don't know about this rule, so always ask."

Fare Discounts
%%%%

With planning and flexibility, you can save up to 50% on most plane travel. Most major airlines have now instituted promotional fares (called "super-savers," "night flights," and the like) which involve variations on the theme of making reservations and paying for your tickets early—often as little as a week ahead, flying at certain times or on certain days, spending specific nights between departure and return.

Before you need them, call all the airlines serving your area and ask to be sent their "Promotional Fare Guide" booklets; or pick them up next time you're in an airport or passing a travel agency. That way the information will be right in front of you when you call to make your reservations and you will have a better idea about which discount plans might suit your travel requirements.

It is a smart idea to make your reservations as early as possible (you can always cancel later) if you hope to take advantage of these discounts, since only a small percentage of seats can be sold for any flight at these rates. Also, airlines make frequent changes, so periodically update your guide collection.

"If you travel by air frequently," says Edward (who does), "it pays to read the travel section of a major newspaper such as the Sunday New York *Times*, especially the ads. On heavily traveled routes the airlines compete for your business with a wide array of special prices. The ads, being prepared by the marketing department of the airline, will be more revealing than an agent sitting at a computer in some faraway reservation booking terminal."

Bob: "When you are making a reservation without benefit of having a 'Promotional Fare Guide' in front of you, keep in mind that if you ask for coach, some reservation agents will simply give

215

you coach without telling you that there may be discount fares available which could save you as much as 50% over coach.

"This is not laziness on the part of the agent—she is simply complying with your request. Instead, ask for the least expensive fare (she has a computer in front of her to help locate these) and, importantly, if your plans permit wide flexibility, tell her that also—i.e., she will ask what time you want to depart or arrive and if you say early afternoon she won't check night flights (late-evening departures which might save 20% or so). If you say, 'anytime day or night as long as I get there before ——' you will stand a better chance of obtaining one discount fare or another."

Lost Baggage

Current airline liability for lost baggage is a maximum of $750 (extra coverage, purchased at check-in, costs only 10¢ per $100). Airlines recover about 98% of missing luggage, but if loss does occur, reimbursement may take six weeks to three months and will be paid at depreciated rather than replacement costs.

If your baggage is delayed, airlines will pay for emergency expenses and rentals within reasonable limits (be sure to save receipts): sports equipment rental; half the cost of necessary clothing (or, if you insist, full cost—but in this case the airlines will ask that you turn in such purchases after your baggage is returned); toiletries. If your baggage doesn't meet you at your destination, be sure to file your claim before you leave the airport; usually it will be delivered to you within a few hours (be sure to clearly label your luggage with name and address both inside and outside).

Using Credit
%

If you pay for your tickets with a credit card and subsequently cancel and rebook, ask the airline to apply the original charge to your new ticket rather than crediting and recharging: Otherwise you may end up paying interest on the original tickets never used.

Edward: "By their self-admission, one airline processes the billing on the same day but takes sixty days to clear a credit."

216

WATER

Bathrooms

The bathroom accounts for 75% of residential water use, 45% for flushing alone. Here are some ways to cut down on that use:

- Take short showers. Showerheads allow five to eight gallons of water to flow per minute. In five minutes at eight gallons, a tub will be full. Time yourself and cut back or install shower restricters.
- Don't leave the water constantly running while you brush your teeth and shave.
- To cut into the high cost of flushing—the average person flushes 29 gallons per day—you can cut down from the six gallons per flush which most toilets consume to the three or four gallons they actually require by displacing the water in the tank with plastic milk-type jugs weighted with pebbles. You can cut them to precisely the shape you need to attain most efficient water-saving flushing. *Don't* use bricks to displace the water, as many people do, because they could damage your tank, according to our water company spokesman.

Heating
%%

Straight from the U.S. Department of Energy's mouth: "Most water heaters are set at 140° or higher, but you may not need water that hot unless you have a dishwasher. A setting of 120° can provide adequate hot water for most families. If you reduce the temperature from 140° to 120°, you could save over 18 percent of the energy used at the higher setting. Even reducing the setting 10 degrees will save more than 6 percent in water heating energy."

If your water heater just says high, medium, low (or just says nothing) test the water with a thermometer and make adjustments till you get it right.

Gas versus Electric
%%%%%%

If you have a choice, choose to heat your water with gas. Electrically heated water costs more than two and one-half times more!

Kitchen

Dishwashers require fifteen gallons per run, full or empty. Be sure they're full.

If you do dishes by hand, get in the habit of turning off the water between rinses or rinse in a sinkful of clear water rather than in a running stream.

Leaks

Let me quote from our local water company literature. It will encourage you to get that running toilet fixed.

"If your faucet has a pinhole leak, 1/32 of an inch in diameter, or just this size (•), over 13 gallons of water will flow down the drain in an hour. In a month, that'll cost you $17.67. If your leak is 1/8 of an inch wide—210 gallons, $214.43; ½ inch, 3,650 gallons, $2,202.98."

Outdoors

Use a bucket rather than a constantly running hose to wash the car or you could be costing yourself immense amounts in wasted water. (See WATER—Leaks)

WILD FOOD
%%%%%%%%%

Cinda: "Collecting wild edible plants is fun and free. It's not a bad idea to know what's out there in the wild you can put in your mouth and not get dead from. This is not for the casual penny-pincher or Sunday stroller though: It takes considerable study to learn what is edible, what is poisonous. Euell Gibbons's books are the wild-plant collector's bibles—*Stalking the Wild Asparagus, Stalking the Healthful Herbs, Stalking the Blue-Eyed Scallop,* and *Beachcombers Handbook,* published by David McKay, New York."

WOODSTOVES

More and more people are returning to use of wood-burning stoves as a home-heating source, either to replace more modern and costlier methods, or to supplement the latter (and thus reduce the cost).

There are quite a number of woodstove designs and sizes available and the cost range is also wide ($300 to $1,200), so to find out how to go about making a choice I called my friend Genevieve, who owns one. She and her husband built their house (I mean with their own hands) and so know its dimensions and crannies better than most homeowners might. She suggested beginning with a careful measuring of your house. This is the knowledge you must have in order to decide upon the woodstove which will best suit your needs.

To familiarize yourself with terms and types, the books most often recommended by owners and dealers alike are:

The Woodburners Encyclopedia
Jay Shelton
Vermont Crossroads Press, 1976
$6.95

which is as comprehensive as the title suggests. Dr. Shelton is considered *the* authority on woodstoves and his book includes a great deal of scientifically technical material *re* the hows and whys as well as descriptions of designs and options.

A book with more "down-home" flavor, which digresses now and then to tell you about soapmaking and the like, but which covers the main things you will want to know before you begin shopping, is

Wood Heat
John Vivian
Rodale Press, Emmaus, Pennsylvania, 1978
$7.95

The next step would be to visit a number of dealers. You should at this juncture be well-informed enough to judge which ones are knowledgeable and honest enough to advise you on how to fill your needs without exceeding them.

(See also WOODSTOVE SAFETY.)

WOODSTOVE SAFETY

You are not going to save anything if you burn down your house due to an improperly installed woodstove. And the incidence of home fires caused by wood-burning stoves is rising rapidly as ownership rises. It's true that years ago *everyone* heated with wood, but in the words of one local fire chief in New England, "Yes, and in those days every village firehouse could also field a full marching band."

New Hampshire insurance companies estimate that in 1979 15% of fires causing over $5,000 in damages were caused by woodstoves. Oregon reported 1,300 major woodstove-related fires in 1979. In Maine, in 1978, there were no deaths attributed to improperly installed or maintained woodstoves; in 1979 there were fifty-three.

Heating with wood is simply more dangerous than more modern methods unless precautions are undertaken—proper installation, correct maintenance, and knowledgeably safe operation are musts. Wise owners will ask their local fire marshal or building inspector to check and approve their system. Insurance agents should also be notified when a woodstove has been installed.

You can get free information from the government *re* all of the above safety factors. Request a free reprint of "Fire Safety Tips for Wood Burning Appliances: Proper Installation, Operation and Maintenance" from:

National Bureau of Standards
Administration Building, Room A617
Washington, D. C. 20234

or call, toll-free—800-638-8326 (the U.S. Consumer Product Safety Commission) and ask for: "Product Safety Fact Sheet No. 92."

Dr. Jay Shelton's newest book, appropriately titled *Wood Heat Safety*, was called by one dealer I spoke to "the best in the world regarding the safety aspects of heating with wood" (published in 1979 by Garden Way Press, Charlotte, Vermont 05445, it sells for $8.95). If your library doesn't have a copy, most woodstove dealers will.

YARN
%%%%%%%%%

Anyone who knits probably knows that most yarn shops will accept in return and refund the purchase price of unused leftover skeins. But what do you do with all those *half*-used skeins left over at each project's completion? You do what my friend Natalie does—make a patchwork blanket. She knits or crochets her squares into being as soon as each original project is complete so that the task never seems monumental. When her box of squares of various sizes is full, she arranges them in a pleasant pattern and whip-stitches them together. The resulting blanket serves as a remembrance of the vest she made for her son's bar mitzvah and the sweater she made for her daughter's first day of school, long after the clothing itself has been outgrown and passed on.

YEAST
$
%%%%%%%

Yeast is the best example I know of the rule that individually packaged things usually cost more per measure.

When your recipe calls for "1 package active dry yeast" it is actually calling for 1 scant tablespoon (to be precise—2¾ teaspoons). If you buy it at the supermarket or grocery store in the well-known 3-pack for 45¢, you will be paying 15¢ for each of those scant tablespoons.

If you buy it in bulk (health-food stores and many grocery stores will have it that way), it will cost you 3¢ for each scant tablespoon ($2.09 per pound; one pound = 64 scant tablespoons).

Even if you don't bake bread often (see BREAD, though, to find out how much money home baking can save), yeast bought in bulk will keep practically forever in a tightly closed jar in the refrigerator. I really mean it; I have some I've been storing that way for five years and it still does the job perfectly.

YOGURT
%%%%%%

Commercially made yogurt costs between $4 and $8 per gallon, depending on where and in what quantity you buy it. Homemade yogurt will cost you the price of whatever milk and starter you use—89¢ to $2.10 (about), per gallon.

Cinda and Ruth and Joan (Edward's wife) contributed directions for making yogurt at home without a machine. The method below incorporates their suggestions:

1. Heat a quart of whole or low-fat milk to the brink of a boil, remove from heat, allow to cool to about 100° to 110° F. (Instead of fresh, you can use *non-instant* dry milk powder, reconstituted according to the instructions in the *Inflation-Wise* MILK entry, except: use water which you have heated to a boil and cooled to about 110°, and, instead of ¾ cup milk powder, use a generous cup.)

2. Now plop in a couple of generous tablespoons of "starter"—which can be any plain (unflavored) brand *without preservatives* or yogurt from a previous homemade batch—and *mix well*.

3. Pour the mixture into individual containers or a large stainless-steel or glass or crockery bowl (don't use

222

aluminum), set it in a warm place and don't move it till it's set.

Yogurt cultures most quickly if kept at a constant temperature of about 100° to 110°F (according to *Laurel's Kitchen*, the active range is 95° to 120°). Ruth puts hers on a towel-covered heating pad set at low (which will add approximately 1¢ per batch to the cost), covers the pot with another tea towel to keep it cozy, and tells me that the usual time it takes to set is about 4 hours. Cinda puts hers in the oven (turned on to warm a bit on cool days—but keep in mind that the culture will be killed at temperatures above 120°); it takes 10 to 12 hours to set (8 on warm days). Joan recommends the top of a radiator and says hers sets in 12 to 36 hours.

Once set, the yogurt should be refrigerated. If you use quite a lot of it, you may want to make it by the gallon (using a couple of extra tablespoons of starter).

The longer it's kept, the tarter the yogurt will become; and yogurt made with tart starter will be tart, so if yours gets too tart for your taste, start your next batch with commercial plain.

Getting Out
Of Debt

In the spring of 1980, President Carter's inflation-control announcements prompted several well-known department-store chains to declare a doubling of their minimum monthly-payment requirements. We had accounts at some of those stores, but I reacted with a ho-hum.

Six months earlier I would have experienced an anxiety attack. Six months earlier my family had been on the brink of financial disaster and it would not have taken much more than just such a nudge to push us over the edge.

Thanks, primarily, to the impetus of insights gained during the researching of *Inflation-Wise,* we have now inched ourselves back to a position of relative safety. It will be many, many months before we are on absolutely sure ground, but we *have* moved out of the danger zone, and it feels *wonderful!* Which is not to say that the process has not been painful; at times it has been. Early on it included a Christmas essentially bereft of gift-giving—*extremely* difficult for us. But looking back, I can now say that it was worth every *un*borrowed penny, every moment spent analyzing our buying habits.

And because I was convinced that our situation was not unique, I decided that *Inflation-Wise* would be incomplete without a cautionary parable concerning the use of real and imaginary money. The tale I will tell is my family's own: what we discovered regarding our attitudes about money and our spending patterns; the techniques we learned and employed to circumvent a near plunge into bankruptcy; and why we can be sure we will never wander anywhere near the edge again.

To those of you who find the story more than vaguely familiar, I mean those for whom it is painfully, personally familiar, I urge this: Keep reading. Even my husband, John, read the first draft with teeth clenched against the pain. But he (and'I) discovered, as you will, that the story can (and in our case did) have a happy ending.

The Revelation

I began to notice, early in the questionnaire returns, that the contributors from my mother's generation quite often wrote: "We have a written budget and we stick to it. Furthermore, credit-card balances are paid in full every month because we refuse to pay interest charges." Many even said that they avoided the use of credit cards entirely, some that they totally avoided the use of credit. When I mentioned this finding to a friend of my own age, she laughed and said, "Really! Do people actually live like that?"

My corresponding laughter was weak, nervous, and owing more to hysteria than amusement, because my own family was at a point where, more and more often, we were reaching midpay period already nearly broke and relying on our ever-dwindling credit limits to get us through to the next paycheck. I was beginning to wonder if perhaps these budget-makers had something important to teach me.

John and I had always just muddled along where money was concerned. We said that money was unimportant. Like others of our generation, we disdained valuing material possessions and approved of valuing people and ideas. We made career choices primarily to suit our philosophical ideals, never based (more than minimally) on salary considerations.

All of which is perfectly all right, except that short of home-steading on your parents' property (and I mean free), it takes money to live in this world. And *particularly* if income is going to be a minor player in life choices, it needs to be carefully handled. Somehow along the way we had equated careful handling with overvaluing; we had equated budgeting with a consumption ethic which made us uncomfortable—ergo, the idea of paying attention to where the money was going made us uncomfortable.

What a mistake. What a *big* mistake. And it was compounded by the fact that, by placing little value on real money, we of course placed even less value on credit's imaginary money. We treated our credit limits as if they were savings, as if what we were in fact borrowing we had earned. And to compound *that* mistake even further, we saved virtually nothing. But I'm getting ahead of my story.

In the Beginning

Our slow but steady escalation into out-of-control debt began shortly after we were married, twelve years ago. John was in graduate school receiving a small stipend; I worked at a series of office jobs—for high-ideal/low-pay organizations. Our furniture, kitchen equipment, and such was handed down from relatives and friends, and rather than feeling deprived we liked the idea of heritage in our house (we still do). Neither we nor our workplaces nor our friends cared whether or not our clothes were new, so we hardly ever bought any. We had no plan, no budget, but we managed quite easily to pay the rent and utility bills and to eat (rather well, and out rather often, as I recall). We owed nobody, required nothing else.

But our debt-free and requirement-free status didn't last long. We lived some distance from the city where we studied/worked which meant daily commuting, and when our old rusty car began to gasp its last, we decided it was time for a new one. And so we walked (waltzed is more like it) into a showroom, picked out the car of our dreams, filled out a few forms, and were handed the keys. The dealer had arranged a loan even though I was between jobs at the time and without any specific prospects. I was soon back among the ranks of the employed, however, and I suspect we surprised that dealer by making every one of those thirty-six payments precisely on time. It was rather easy—both getting the credit and repaying the loan. We just ate out a little less often.

The experience made us a bit heady, I think, and soon we had wallets full of credit cards. We still had given no thought to a budget. Yet somewhere in the recesses of our minds we must have known we were heading into dangerous territory for we stipulated use of these credit cards for emergencies only. But the definition of emergency widened as our salaries increased and came to include many a half-price towel we felt we couldn't afford to pass up, many a gift we couldn't bear not giving, many a restaurant meal we were sure we deserved as a reward for having worked so hard all week. Each indulgence required only that we hand over a small plastic card and a signature. The getting was easier than ever; the repaying, though not quite as easy as it had been at the beginning, continued to be manageable.

And then along came two things which threw a wrench into the budgetless works. First, there was sweet baby James, after whose birth I decided to switch jobs (from administrative assisting to mothering)—the former had paid little; the latter paid nothing (though in joy a great deal). And following close on James's heels came runaway inflation, which meant in essence another salary cut.

The trouble was that since we had no idea how the money (real or imaginary) was actually being spent, our spending habits changed little. Meeting monthly obligations was becoming more and more difficult. And *still* we made no budget.

The Crisis

By the time I began research for *Inflation-Wise,* the danger-signals-to-the-overextended had begun to manifest themselves:

- Nearly every month we were dipping into our checking account's instant-loan option in order to purchase month's-end groceries.
- We were paying (at best) the minimum amounts due on an increasing number of credit accounts with increasing balances and fast-approaching limits.
- We had begun to receive an occasional "second notice" asking for a missed payment.
- Our *only* savings was the minimum (a minimal minimum) our bank required in exchange for free checking.

According to credit counselors, an ordinarily manageable percentage of monthly take-home pay devoted to installment debt and other loan repayments (excluding mortgage, which is considered more of an investment) is 15 percent; ours exceeded 35 percent.

But that wasn't the worst of it. Counselors also suggest that total outstanding debt (again excluding mortgage) should prudently be no more than 15 percent of *annual* take-home pay. I knew ours was higher than that, but when I actually sat down and totalled it, I discovered that the figure was *staggering*. We owed a half-year's wages to creditors!

It was at that postsummation, panic-stricken moment that I knew no amount of penny-pinching alone would save us, that drastic measures were in order. Terror loves company; good financial management in a family absolutely requires it. I called John into the room. "My dear," I said, "you had better sit down."

The Solution

That very evening, duly shaken, we together resolved:

- To discontinue *all* credit purchasing until we had rendered ourselves debt-free *and* had formulated a plan for wise use of credit in the future.
- To make a budget with priorities, including regular savings deposits, to stick to it, and to review it monthly.

Later, following the making of that budget, when we discovered that large sums of cash were also being unaccountably spent out-of-pocket each month, we agreed:

- To each keep a precise daily account of any and all outgoing money (with the exception of our small personal allowances) and review those accounts at our monthly budget meeting.

Still later, having learned still more, we determined to adopt the following rules *re* all possible (distant) future use of credit:

- To discuss *all* credit purchases beforehand (thereby eliminating impulsive credit buying of incidentals).
- To keep the *cost* of credit (i.e., the interest) foremost in our minds rather than lost in the recesses, and always to shop for the lowest-possible annual percentage rate.
- To borrow the very least we required for the shortest possible period rather than the most we were allowed for the longest.
- To record all credit purchases (in our cash-expenditures notebooks) as soon as they were made, reviewing monthly.

Our new-found fiscal responsibility has proved, as I've mentioned, enormously satisfying. However, even for those who are not overextended or for whom there is absolutely no danger of that happening, a written budget will make Section 1 of this book

231

much more useful. It will highlight spending patterns in a way which will permit deliberate rather than haphazard implementation of the *Inflation-Wise* cost-cutters.

The following pages, therefore, describe the budget-making process itself—from the preliminary fact-finding to the final projection and follow-up. (I've discovered that there *are,* in fact, budget-makers among my own contemporaries, but many seem less willing to shout it out than my mother's generation. I hope that will change; it *is,* I have discovered after all, an undertaking of great value.)

THE BUDGET-MAKING PROCESS

I was unable to find, in my research, a description of budget-making techniques which completely suited my purposes, so the system which follows is my own concoction. However it was critiqued by a friend, a budget analyst.

Table A (Debt Calculation) and Table B (Credit Purchases) are optional—not required for the budget-making process itself, but intended primarily as a starting place for those who use credit. They will be particularly useful for those who may be concerned about becoming overextended. The figures from these first two tables will be transferable to later tables, however.

The remaining tables are budget-making essentials. Table C (Income) and Table D (Cash Expenditures) will show where your money has come from and where it has gone during the previous year. Table E (Priorities) and Table F (Projected Budget) allow you to plan for the upcoming year.

When you are unable to locate exact figures, estimate; but be realistic rather than wishful. Expect the initial process to be time-consuming, but know that the more intimate you become with your financial lives, the smoother and quicker the undertaking will be in the following months and years. The first four tables may be completed by whichever family member most enjoys working with figures, but the last two must involve everyone.

Begin by gathering together as much of the following material as you are able, from the previous twelve months: credit-card statements and invoices, bank statements, check stubs, paycheck receipt stubs, tax-form copies, and any other records you think might be helpful in gleaning income and expense figures.

You will also need pencils and lots of paper. A calculator, if you have one, will speed up the task. It's my intention that this section of *Inflation-Wise* be used in workbook fashion, but you may find it necessary to add or substitute pages as your circumstances warrant.

Table A

Table A's figures should be gleaned from credit-card statements and installment-loan records from the month just preceding. Immediately following the table are the formulas I used for calculating percentage of income being spent on debt repayment and percentage of income owed to creditors. If you find that either of these percentages is greater than 15%, consider it a danger signal, but *don't panic*. Wipe your brow, take a deep breath, and continue on. What follows becomes even more essentially important for you.

Table A—DEBT CALCULATION (Optional)

Creditor	Portion of Payment which is Interest	Minimum Monthly Payment Currently Due (Including Interest)	Outstanding Balance
Auto loan:			
Personal loan:			
Consumer Goods loan:			
"Instant" checking account loan:			
Home Improvement:			
School:			
Department Stores:			
Major Credit Cards:			
Oil Companies:			
Doctors:			
Dentists:			
Other:			
TOTALS:			

To find the percentage of monthly income being applied to repayment of loans and other installment debts:

$$\frac{\text{Total of Minimum Monthly Payments}}{\text{Monthly Take-home Pay}} \times 100 = \underline{\hspace{1cm}}\%$$

To find the percentage of annual income represented by total debt:

$$\frac{\text{Total of Outstanding Balances}}{\text{Annual Take-home Pay}} \times 100 = \underline{\hspace{1cm}}\%$$

Table B

Table B was designed to show credit-spending patterns specifically—credit only; (*cash* expenditures are covered in Table D). It will highlight areas of waste due to impulsive use of credit. For instance, I found (by comparing the figures on Table B with those on Table D) that when I visited our local specialty shop to buy coffee, I bought *only* coffee when I paid by check, but *doubled* my expenditure (by buying "just a few" other things) when I paid with a plastic card.

In other words, Table B will be especially useful in combination with Table D in showing just how much, totally, you may be exceeding your income and will assist you in honing and projecting the upcoming year's budget (in Tables E and F).

Glean the figures for Table B from the previous twelve-months' credit-card statements and/or invoices, loan statements, and savings records. Remember, include *only* items you charged—i.e., if you made a cash down payment on a car, that will go on Table D; Table B should include any amount borrowed to cover the remaining cost of that car. The monthly cash repayment of the loan will also appear on Table D.

Note that savings withdrawals appear on this table (since you are borrowing from yourself). Be sure to include in "Other" any cash borrowed but unaccounted for in another category. If the last months of the year's receipts are not easily findable, use three months' totals multiplied by four to give annual approximations.

Table C

I have arbitrarily chosen, in this entire system, to work with actual spendable cash, to assume that tax and other non-discretionary fixed deductions have already been made by your employer, so

Table B—CREDIT PURCHASES (Optional)

Category	Last Month Month 1	Month Before Month 2	Month Before Month 3	Etc. to Month 12
Automobiles				
Food (to be eaten at home)				
Food eaten out				
Sundries*				
Drugs				
Clothing**				
Gasoline and Oil				
Auto repairs				
Tires				
Haircuts				
Toiletries				
Tobacco products				
Liquor				
Furniture				
Appliances				
Linens and such				
Home-related repair or improvement				
Gifts				
Books				
Concerts or other such entertainment				
Hobbies				
Vacations				
Savings withdrawals				
Other (including cash borrowed but unaccounted for)				
Monthly Totals:				

Annual Total: $_____ (4 times the 3-month totals if you go back only that far)

*Sundries can include various consumables such as paper products, animal food, film, cosmetics, and such, but if any one of these constitutes a large expenditure—because it represents hobby supplies, for instance—separate it out, move it to the appropriate category or to "other," annotated.

**You may want to break clothing expenditures down for each family member.

that any refund at tax time becomes income. If you are self-employed or for some other reason *owe* and pay undeducted taxes, these become an expense (for Table D).

Paycheck stubs, checkbook stubs or bank statements, and your copies of tax forms will be helpful in gleaning figures for the following table.

Table C—INCOME

	Last Month Month 1	Month Before Month 2	Month Before Month 3	Etc. to Month 12
Wages (after taxes and other deductions)				
Other regular income				
Sporadic income				
Interest on savings				
Tax refund				
Monthly Totals:				

Annual Total Income: $

Table D

In completing this table, you may need to refer to nearly all the material you have gathered, but bank statements and/or check stubs primarily. You should include *only and all cash* expenditures, whether by check or out-of-pocket, including *payments* on credit accounts and loans. Credit purchases, remember, should be on Table B. Tables B and D, in combination, will provide a complete picture of your spending habits.

You may want to itemize these repayment figures, noting the specific creditor, under the categories of "loan repayments" and "credit-card repayments" (I've left space for that), but the point is that this is a *cash*-expenditures table, and in order to compare it with Table C (Income) it must be limited to cash only.

For example: if you paid cash for gasoline, the amount should be shown in the "Gasoline and Oil" category on this table (D), but if you bought gas with a credit card, the amount should appear on Table B in that category; the monthly *payment* to the oil company, however, should appear here on Table D, in the "credit-card payments" category, annotated if you like (from Table A, if you've done it).

Payments made once annually should be recorded under the month actually paid. Be sure to add any categories applicable to your particular family which I may have inadvertently left out.

To reiterate: IMPORTANT—where guessing is necessary (as in out-of-pocket expenditures, for instance) be realistic. If you have no earthly idea where that $20 written to "cash" in your checkbook went, record it in the "spent but unaccountable" category along with any money you know you received but never deposited; that category's total may be exceedingly telling.

Table D—CASH EXPENDITURES

Category:	Last Month Month 1	Month Before Month 2	Month Before Month 3	Etc. to Month 12
Mortgage/rent				
Property taxes				
Electricity				
Natural Gas				
Heating Oil				
Water				
Garbage				
Telephone				
Food eaten at home				
Lunch eaten out				
Dinner eaten out				
Sundries* (see first note under Table B)				
Health insurance				
Homeowners insurance				
Auto insurance				
Life insurance				
Doctor				
Dentist				
Drugs				
Clothing				
Dry cleaning				

Table D—CASH EXPENDITURES

Category:	Last Month Month 1	Month Before Month 2	Month Before Month 3	Etc. to Month 12
Gasoline and oil				
Auto repairs				
Tires				
Public transportation and tolls				
Personal allowances				
Haircuts				
Toiletries				
Tobacco products				
Liquor				
Furniture				
Appliances				
Linens and such				
Home-related repair				
Tuition				
Alimony/child support				
Child care/babysitters				
Contributions/charity				
Dues				
Undeducted income taxes				
Undeducted social security taxes				
Stamps and stationery				
Gifts				
Books				
Magazines				
Movies/concerts				
Other entertainment				
Sports				
Hobbies				
Vacations				

Table D—CASH EXPENDITURES

Category:	Last Month Month 1	Month Before Month 2	Month Before Month 3	Etc. to Month 12
Savings deposits				
Spent but unaccountable				
Credit-card payments				
Installment-loan payments				
Monthly totals:				

Annual Total: $

Congratulations! That was a tough job, I know. Here now, is what you can learn from the information you have so painstakingly gathered and posted:

1. Are you spending more than you are earning? To find out, subtract Cash Expenditures (Table D) from Income (Table C). You might want to do this for each month as well as the year; the year may balance, but holiday months such as November or December or vacation months might not—it's worth knowing. The optimal balances should, of course, be zero or a positive number. If you come up with a negative balance (i.e., if cash expenditures exceed income), the remedy: complete Tables E and F, using the previous tables to help you decide where to cut down.

2. Are you *buying* more than you are earning? To find out, subtract Credit Purchases (Table B) from the balances you found in number 1 above. If *this* then gives you a negative balance, the remedy is the same as in number 1 above.

3. Are you having any difficulty meeting those payments on bills which come due annually? Look to see if you tend (as we did) to borrow cash in those same months (Tables B and D). If so, the remedy: total all the once-annual entries from Table D (and B, if appropriate), divide the total by 12, and deposit the result monthly in a passbook savings account specifically opened and earmarked for the purpose. And, complete Tables E and F.

4. Do Tables B and/or D include large sums of "unaccountable" spending? If so, the remedy: purchase a small notebook for

each spending family member and ask each to carry it (everywhere) and record every penny spent. It might help you develop the habit if you think of these recordings as you would check stubs, remembering how much difficulty a missing entry can cause. The result will assist you during monthly reviews and updating Tables E and F.

The one important exception is personal allowances. At your family budgeting conference, decide what these should cover for each family member (e.g., restaurant lunches? tobacco? hobbies?) and figure the necessary amount for each. The recipient should be given her or his total allowance once each month and should not be held accountable for how it is spent; although coming back for more before month's end, of course, is nixed. Even young family members, if given small allowances (beginning at about age six), will soon see the increased purchasing power gained by saving.

5. How much are you paying (and I don't mean just in anxiety) for the use of credit? Table A may show graphically how often monthly payments are one step forward, two back, how large a percentage of the payment may actually be the finance charge. Remedy: shop for and use credit wisely (see BORROWING in Section 1 and *The Solution* in Section 2).

Now it's time for completing the last two tables, a process in which all family members should be involved. Arbitrary priority choices by a single family member are unlikely to work even if nominally accepted.

Table E
The purpose of Table E is to identify and settle on family priorities. Each family member old enough to write should independently complete a Table E, ranking the items under each heading, and including everything wanted and needed. At the family budget meeting, then, the lists can be compared and discussed and choices can be mutually agreed upon for inclusion in Table F.

Table E — PRIORITIES

High	Medium	Low

Table F

The following table will be your projected budget for the upcoming year. Use the information in *all* of the previous tables to make your projections and be sure all family members agree on the choices. Schedule a regular monthly meeting to go over the previous month's actual expenditures and make any necessary adjustments, based on this, in the following month's projections.

You will note that this table is an almost exact duplicate of Table D, with a few important exceptions.

One difference is that savings, both the "future annual bills" account previously explained, and regular savings, are placed in a priority status position. Five percent of take-home is the minimum figure most often recommended for regular savings. If you are heavily in debt, however, you may wish to reduce the percentage temporarily and apply the difference to repayment of your debts; but it's important to develop the saving habit, so don't forgo this deposit entirely.

Another difference is that the "unaccounted-for" category has been eliminated.

Table F—PROJECTED BUDGET

Category:	Month 1	Month 2	Month 3	Month 4	Etc. to Month 12
Savings ("future annual bills" account)					
Savings (regular account)					
Mortgage/rent					
Property taxes					
Electricity					
Natural gas					
Heating oil					
Water					
Garbage					
Telephone					
Food eaten at home					
Lunch eaten out					
Dinner eaten out					
Sundries* (see first note under Table B)					
Health insurance					
Homeowners insurance					
Auto insurance					
Life insurance					
Doctor					
Dentist					
Drugs					
Clothing					
Dry cleaning					
Gasoline and oil					
Auto repairs					
Tires					
Public transportation and tolls					
Personal allowances					
Haircuts					
Toiletries					
Tobacco products					
Liquor					
Furniture					
Appliances					
Linens and such					
Home-related repair					

Table F—PROJECTED BUDGET

Category:	Month 1	Month 2	Month 3	Month 4	Etc. to Month 12
Tuition					
Alimony/child support					
Child care/babysitters					
Contributions/charity					
Dues					
Undeducted income taxes					
Undeducted Social Security taxes					
Stamps and stationery					
Gifts					
Books					
Magazines					
Movies/concerts					
Other entertainment					
Sports					
Hobbies					
Vacations					
Credit-card payments					
Installment-loan payments					
Projected Totals:					
Actual Totals:					

The budgeting process has rendered us slightly (happily) obsessive about paying close attention to our expenditures. Enough so, in fact, that we have invariably found ourselves able to trim a dollar here and there from every month's projected budget. On discovering the amount of remainder at each month's budget review, we halve that remaining balance. One-half is immediately deposited in savings as a hedge against misprojections in future months; the other half is deemed "mad money" and spent madly as our reward for good financial behavior.

I hope the months and years ahead provide you with "mad money" as well, and in great measure.

(See BORROWING—Professional Help for the Overextended, in Section 1, if you are already in deeper trouble than we were and in need of more help than *Inflation-Wise*, Section 2 can provide.)